Oedipus Anne

Oedipus Anne
The Poetry of Anne Sexton

Diana Hume George

University of Illinois Press
Urbana and Chicago

Publication of this work was supported in part by a grant
from The Pennsylvania State University, Behrend College

Portions of this book appeared in different form in "Beyond
the Pleasure Principle: Anne Sexton's 'The Death Baby,' "
Hartford Studies in Literature; "Anne Sexton's Suicide Poems,"
Journal of Popular Culture; and "How We Danced: Anne
Sexton on Fathers and Daughters," *Women's Studies.*

This book is printed on acid-free paper.

LIBRARY OF CONGRESS CATALOGING-IN-PUBLICATION DATA

George, Diana Hume, 1948-
    Oedipus Anne: the poetry of Anne Sexton.

    Bibliography: p.
    Includes index.
    1. Sexton, Anne—Criticism and interpretation.
I. Title.
PS3537.E915Z68   1987   811'.54   85-29019
ISBN 0-252-01298-4

I dedicate this book to the memory of

Myron Kinney Hume (1904–54)
Harvey Albert (1937–84)
Marisa Cullen (1955–84)

and to the presence of

Mac Nelson
Bernie George
Janice Ruth Hume

Contents

Acknowledgments

Completion of this book was supported by a grant from the American Council of Learned Societies. The Pennsylvania State University/Behrend College has been generous not only with financial support but with flexible arrangements that allowed me periods of study and research, for which I thank Provost John Lilley. Ann Lowry Weir, senior editor at the University of Illinois Press, has encouraged me steadily over a period of years to complete this study, and I thank her for her continued support. Aaron Appelstein made the copyediting process both fruitful and painless. Kim Krynock compiled the index skillfully and with finely tuned attention to detail. Norma Hartner typed and retyped and retyped the entire manuscript and has been a personal as well as technical friend in this endeavor.

Among Anne Sexton's family and friends, I have benefited from the continued support of Linda Gray Sexton and Maxine Kumin, both of whom have given me their time and their support at various stages of my work. Houghton Mifflin and the Sterling Lord Agency generously made special arrangements for permissions to quote from Anne Sexton's poetry.

Colleagues, friends, or family members who offered criticism and affectionate support include Richard Lehnert, Kristine Luce, Kim Carpenter, Karen Mills-Courts, and Robert Cullen. Diane Christian's influence endures after years of absence; this book really began in one of her seminars at the State University of New York at Buffalo. For places to work where I could find silence and peace, I thank Virgil and Sophie Peterson for special haven on Martha's Vineyard, and Ruth Nelson and Helen Dietrich for sanctuary in California.

Bernie George has perfected an imitation of me at the typewriter and the terminal, turned toward work with fierce concentration; thank you, Bernie, for being my son and for making sure that I don't take myself too seriously. Mac Nelson, helpmate and collaborator on everything in my life, listened to all my ideas, read every word, helped me change not a few, and got excited or somber with me when I needed either response or both. And my mother, Janice Ruth Hume, has more to do with this work than she could imagine. As Anne Sexton wrote to Mary Harvey, "I love you. I don't write for you, but know that one of the reasons I do write is that you are my mother."

Introduction

Anne Sexton's poetry tells stories that are immensely significant to mid-twentieth-century artistic and psychic life. Sexton understood her culture's malaise through her own, and her skill enabled her to deploy metaphorical structures at once synthetic and analytic. In other words, she assimilated the superficially opposing but deeply similar ways of thinking represented by poetry and psychoanalysis. Sexton explored the myths by and through which our culture lives and dies: the archetypal relationships among mothers and daughters, fathers and daughters, mothers and sons, gods and humans, men and women. She perceived, and consistently patterned in the images of her art, the paradoxes deeply rooted in human behavior and motivation. Her poetry presents multiplicity and simplicity, duality and unity, the sacred and the profane, in ways that insist on their similarities—even, at times, their identity. In less abstract terms, Sexton made explicit the intimacy of forces persistently treated as opposites by the society she lived in.

I appreciate the intention of statements made since her death that caution readers against becoming enamored of Sexton's illness and that encourage concentration on the celebratory aspects of her poetry. But another cautionary note is perhaps in order: that readers not ignore the expression of poetic and personal anguish for which the celebration is counterpart and foil. "The soul is, I think, a human being who speaks with the pressure of death at his head," Sexton wrote in a 1963 letter. Her poems articulate some of the deepest dilemmas of her contemporaries about their—our—most basic fears and wishes. Although Sexton's canon reaches for the unities of human experience, she did not abandon duality, even dichotomy. Poets must transcend us in some ways to be counted great of mind, but they must also be *of* us. Her poems vibrate in that energetic, passionate area between everlasting certainty and everlasting doubt. When she perceived the sameness of everything, it was against the background of the difference; when she perceived the difference, it was in reference to the sameness—just as metaphor, the imaging of connectedness, always implies a prior discontinuity.

Sexton flashed a sparkling, multiple light on human faces from the beginning of her writing career until the month of her death. For seventeen years she spoke in a direct, intimate way of people she loved. Her concentration on human relationships produced sharp, masterful portraits of people who were worth keeping alive, or worth resurrecting. That they were often "all her pretty ones" creates part of her poetry's poignancy. Her personal relationship to many of those who people the world of her poems amplifies the resounding creation of whole, complicated characters whose compelling presence is perhaps more deeply artful for having been lived. If many of Sexton's people had not so lived, her skill and art would have been solely responsible for breathing the life into them. As it was, she most often worked from the life and perhaps must share her credit with those who died before her and those who have outlived her: her mother, her father, her daughters, her husband, her lovers, her aunt, her grandfather, and her remarkable friends. I am glad there was or is an Eleanor Boylan, whatever name she bears.

When Sexton tells her dead father that she will bend down her strange face to his and forgive him, she is speaking of what we all need to do: to bend down our faces to our fathers, living or dead, and forgive them. When she calls her mother her mocking mirror, her overthrown love, her first image, she speaks for all of us of woman born and first nurtured against "her plump and fruity skin." When she becomes the child of "elbows, knees, dreams, goodnight," she is the child in all of us, recapturing those moments when "love grew rings around me." When she says to her daughter, "Everything in your body that is new is telling the truth," she may be transcribing what she said to her daughter; she is also expressing for the collective mothers of her readership what we all want to be saying to our daughters, what we sometimes have not the courage or the attentiveness to say. The mother of "life is not in my hands" tells a terrible truth, but she is also the mother of "Darling, stand still at your door, sure of yourself, a white stone, a good stone. . . . " This is a mother who tells the truth, one who gives you "the images I know."

In her lively, lonely telling of her truth, in her giving of the images she knew, Sexton looked for "uncomplicated hymns/but love has none." So the daughter who has loved and watched her mother closely enough to see "that blaze within the pilgrim woman" will also confess that this most important death does not equip her with grief. The friend who watches Eleanor Boylan talking with God, "as close as the ceiling," will warn her to speak quickly, "before death uses you up." The great aunt who climbed Mount San Salvatore, that "yankee girl, the iron interior of her sweet body," will one day careen into the streets and stop passersby "to mumble your guilty love while your ears die."

In "Her Kind" and "The Black Art," Sexton characterizes the poet as one who feels too much, thinks too much, and lives in an atmosphere of "weird abundance." In a 1966 letter she writes about the abundance that "runs wild with love as cancer." Sexton did, in some respects, connect the sources of poetic inspiration with death. Certainly the connections between extremist art and suicide as a form of poetic destiny have been destructively romanticized. My intention in raising the point is not to confirm it but to suggest something that it indicates. The limited extent to which Sexton connected art and self-destruction may have been symptomatic of her illness. I think she would have agreed: "Suicide is the opposite of the poem." That she *might* have felt called upon to fulfill a poetic as well as personal destiny by suicide— and I do not necessarily think she did—is better viewed as symptomatic of the cultural conditions she so clearly perceived and lived with.

Poets are among the few whom our culture still invests with a ritual function. We ask them to speak the unspeakable for us, and when they do, we are capable of effecting a violently negative transference. Critical response to Sexton's poetry seems to me to bear this out. Particularly if the poet has exposed our pain, seen into our darkest selves, we need to purge ourselves of the violating member, to punish the one who has broken boundaries and violated taboos. That Christianity depends for salvation on a sacrificial lamb whose death permits us to abrogate responsibility for the human failings we call "sin" speaks of our need to transfer guilt. Sexton's identifications with the crucified Christ sometimes have the ring of a self-aggrandizing and self-appointed martyrdom. But to whatever extent she may have been martyred, it was at the invitation, if not the insistence, of an exceptionally hungry audience.

Yet we are angry with Anne Sexton for killing herself, partly because she is the same poet who wrote with such commitment and intensity of the delight of being alive. If Sylvia Plath was always removed from her readership by the consistency of her "dead hands, dead stringencies," if she was always somehow beyond the merely human, always "the arrow, the dew that flies/Suicidal, at one with the drive," Sexton was not always so. Before and after she was sometimes that, she was also the mother of "Little Girl," the lover of "Us," the daughter of "Oysters," the child of "Young." She spoke to us of celebration of the sun, that "excitable gift," of all the wicked, pure, lovely fun of being alive. Perhaps we could not tolerate knowing that this was the same woman who saw "rats in the toilet." If she was more clearly one of us, then her defection was more serious. It endangered us more deeply. She was an anomaly, a fish with wings.

Many of the qualities of Sexton's poetry so often seen as inconsistent I see as part of the vitalizing struggle to make of her art a salvation both spiritual and bodily. Much like the early Blake, Anne Sexton moved between contraries with equal force, equal conviction, and equal doubt. One can experience disappointment or frustration in the presence of such vacillation and label it a failure of nerve or will or imagination—or one can experience it, as I do, as one's own truth. To make it more concrete: if you think linearly about the building of a body of truth, then you must think only in terms of progress and regress. Anne Sexton comes to happy resolutions repeatedly in her work, from poem to poem, volume to volume. *Live or Die* is structured in just such a pleasing, simple shape: after a struggle with destruction, it ends with the affirmation of life. Yet in subsequent volumes she backslides continuously, seeming to erase her previous truths, to compromise them, or to give them up. In the early *All My Pretty Ones*, Sexton first forgives her father. In later works she sometimes appears to renege on that forgiveness and to exhume the old ghost she had, we thought, laid to rest. In a literary and moral tradition presided over by *Paradise Lost* followed by *Paradise Regained*, and a theological one structured by the external resurrection of a crucified god, the linear progression of truth is denied by the return of the ghost from eternal rest.

The wish that art may carve into permanent perfection either our hope or our despair is understandable but too limiting. There is ample room in my own notion of poetry for the repeated reflections of that imperfectibility that separates humans from the gods they create. The repetition of a set of emotional and mental acts is central to Anne Sexton's poetry and represents a striving after personal and poetic catharsis that is never quite achieved, even when it is claimed. Her poetry enacts the repetition compulsion that may justly be called thanatopic from one perspective. From another, the movement that seems repetitive represents an intricate tension between contraries that is at the core of all creative process.

Another intricate tension between contraries is central to this study:

that between feminism and psychoanalysis. I have written elsewhere that mainline American feminism makes excellent use of sociological, historical, and especially political inquiry; but as theory, as ideology, and as political movement, American feminism has until recently lacked a coherent depth psychology. Unlike our European (and especially French) counterparts, American feminism's elevation of *consciousness* to a code term indicates the psychological geography of our inquiries. For a theory and a human rights movement whose claim is that "knowledge is power," the implications of evading psychic depths are crucial. Consciousness emerges in large part from continuous interactions with unconscious mental processes established in infancy and early childhood; such processes are documented in painstaking (and often painful) detail in Anne Sexton's poetry. American feminism has something to learn from this poet, for we are prematurely convinced that we have dealt with psychic complexities that continue to evade our halfhearted gaze. One measure of mainline feminism's evasions is its attitude toward psychoanalytic theory. Although objections to Freud are often styled as (quite proper) rejections of his patriarchal biases, I believe that a denial of the shaping power, if not the very existence, of unconscious mental processes is often central to our difficulties with psychoanalytic theory. Anne Sexton's poetry is a powerful reminder of the necessity of understanding and dealing with the psychic underworld. Feminism has sometimes appropriated Sexton by fragmenting her vision and halving her truths. It is my hope that Sexton's poetic enactment of psychic processes can continue recent efforts to represent the uses of psychoanalytic theory for feminism. In this respect, I intend *Oedipus Anne* (as I intended *Blake and Freud* in 1980) to be a literary contribution to American "psychoanalytic feminism," represented by Dorothy Dinnerstein's *The Mermaid and the Minotaur,* Nancy Chodorow's *The Reproduction of Mothering,* Jane Gallop's *The Daughter's Seduction,* Luise Eichenbaum's and Susie Orbach's *Understanding Women,* and *The (M)other Tongue: Essays in Feminist Psychoanalytic Interpretation,* edited by Shirley Garner et al. The English mother of most of these studies is Juliet Mitchell's *Psychoanalysis and Feminism;* the recent French maternal texts are Luce Irigaray's *Speculum of the Other Woman* and *The Sex That Is Not One.*

I have divided *Oedipus Anne* into four parts that represent the major emphases of this study. Part I, "Mother, Father, I'm Made Of," concentrates on the achievements of Sexton's poetry in psychoanalytic terms. Here, as in the "Death Baby" section of Part III, I follow the method of my earlier *Blake and Freud:* I treat the poet not as case history or as patient on the analytic or theoretical couch but as poetic analyst of her culture through poetry. "Oedipus Anne" identifies Sexton as a contemporary Oedipus—in Bruno Bettelheim's terms, a truth-seeker; a subsequent chapter on fathers and daughters extends Sexton's connections with psychoanalysis as interpretive exemplar rather than clinical example. While this entire study might be said to be about the poetry of relationship, Part I is specifically familial. Conspicuous by its absence is a single chapter devoted to mothers and daughters; by the time I might have written such a chapter, projected as central from the inception of this book, I found that almost every page was already suffused with the luminosity of that primary relationship. Part II, "That Dear Body," explores Sexton's attitudes toward the dualities of the physical and the spiritual and examines the relationships among feeding, feces, and creativity in Sexton's canon.

Part III, "Person, Persona, Prophecy," treats Sexton's poetry in both traditional and feminist terms by discussing the functions of her first-person speakers. I use Maxine Kumin's designations in "Many Kinds of *I*" to differentiate among lyrical, ideational, autobiographical, and persona forms of the first person in Sexton's canon. "The Prophetic *I* (Eye)" extends the work of such critics as Ostriker, Lauter, Juhasz, and Middlebrook on Sexton's archetypal and mythic transformations of the *I*, which I believe participate in the tradition of prophetic poetry associated with Blake and Whitman. Extending the analogy with Blake, "The Girl-Child and the Middle-Aged Witch" deals with Sexton's songs of innocence and experience.

I have devoted three lengthy chapters to Part IV, "Wanting to Die," which takes its title from the poem of that name in *Live or Die.* In "Beyond the Pleasure Principle," I discuss Sexton's contribution to analytic theory on the death instinct, encoded in "The Death Baby" sequence from *The Death Notebooks.* "Wanting to Die" examines the suicide poetry Sexton produced from the beginning to the end of her poetic career, and "Leaves That Talk" advances my own hypotheses for some of the more obscure reasons she chose to die. More than the other sections of this book, Part IV implicitly criticizes common cultural assumptions. The reader will suspect I have an ax to grind here, and the reader will be right. If, as Sexton felt, poetry should serve as the ax for the frozen sea within us, perhaps the critic can help the poet sharpen it.

I have benefited greatly during the final stages of this study from the contributions of three writers: Maxine Kumin, who has been gener-

ous with her time and her comments; Alicia Ostriker, whose perceptions on Sexton in published and spoken form have continually
germinated my own; and Diane Middlebrook, Sexton's biographer, who
has shared her innovative insights with me during the last year. This
declaration belongs in an introduction rather than buried in an acknowl-
edgments page, because the process of exchange has been crucial, if not
to the writing of this book, then certainly to the form it has taken.

Part I

Mother, Father, I'm Made Of

1
Oedipus Anne

What the story of the Sphinx seems to emphasize is that the answer to the riddle of life is not just man, but each person himself. . . . In contemplating Sophocles' *Oedipus* as Freud did, one realizes that the entire play is essentially Oedipus' struggle to get at the hidden truth. It is a battle for knowledge in which Oedipus has to overcome tremendous inner resistance against recognizing the truth about himself, because he fears so much what he might discover. . . . What forms the essence of our humanity—and of the play—is not our being victims of fate, but our struggle to discover the truth about ourselves.

—Bruno Bettelheim, *Freud and Man's Soul*

Not that it was beautiful,
but that I found some order there.
There ought to be something special
for someone
in this kind of hope.
This is something I would never find
in a lovelier place, my dear,
although your fear is anyone's fear,
like an invisible veil between us all . . .
and sometimes in private,
my kitchen, your kitchen,
my face, your face.

—Anne Sexton, "For John, Who Begs Me Not to Enquire Further"
(*To Bedlam and Part Way Back*)

Oedipus, Sophocles, Freud: this is preeminently a man's story, told by men to and for men, about a tragically fated hero who unknowingly slays his father and marries his mother. Despite Freud's attribution of the Oedipus complex to women as well as to men—the feminine version in psychoanalytic theory required a revision to work out those troublesome sequential glitches—the story of Oedipus has also remained essentially masculine in the popular imagination. That imagination, sensing perhaps the culturally masculine tenor not only of the myth but

3

of its symbolic meanings, has even tried (with a brief assist from psychoanalysis) to provide a womanly equivalent: the Elektra complex. But Freud stuck stubbornly to his assertion that the story of Oedipus was that of all humankind, and revisionist theorists and practitioners have attempted to explain why. Among the most convincing retellings is still Juliet Mitchell's in *Psychoanalysis and Feminism,* in which she urges us to construe the Oedipus complex as more than a term for normal childhood sexual conflicts revolving around intense attachments to the parents, by which measure the significance attributed to it by psychoanalysis may indeed seem inflated. According to Mitchell the Oedipus complex designates a set of internal and external acts through which every person is initiated into the cultural order; it is not only "a metaphor for the psychic structure of the bourgeois nuclear family under Viennese capitalism" but "a law that describes the way in which all [Western] culture is acquired by each individual."[1]

Bettelheim's Oedipus

Beginning with her first teacher, John Holmes, Sexton was accused throughout her writing life of childishness and of infantile preoccupations with her relationship to her mother and father. She insisted that these relationships were at the heart of the matter—and not only her matter but, by implication, everyone's. "Grow up," said the decorous world of poetry to her throughout her career; "stop playing in the crib and the sandbox—and especially stop sniveling about your childhood losses." Her poetic reply asserted again and again that grown woman though she might be, successful artist though she might be, the process of working out her relationship to her parents and her childhood was a life's work. Nor did she permit us to suppose it was only *her* life's work. If we acknowledged it as hers, and as the legitimate domain of poetry, then we would have to come to terms with the possibility that it might represent our own lifelong process as well; perhaps, if she was more than a garish freak, such work is never quite completed. Blind as Teiresias, she revealed to all of us the truth about Laius's murder. As Bruno Bettelheim writes in *Freud and Man's Soul,* "We encounter in Teiresias the idea that having one's sight turned away from the external world and directed inward—toward the inner nature of things—gives true knowledge and permits understanding of what is hidden and needs to be known."[2] Like anyone before us, we do not necessarily want to understand the hidden, nor to know what needs to be known. "Little children do not like it," remarked Freud acidly about the public's resistance to psychoanalysis.

But it is not Teiresias, finally, with whom I wish to identify Anne Sexton. Rather, it is Oedipus, and specifically the Oedipus of *Freud and Man's Soul*. Bettelheim attempts yet another rereading of Freud's Oedipus, and I find it the most moving and accessible that contemporary psychoanalysis has offered to an audience larger than its own members. Freud's Oedipus, through Bettelheim, takes on the luminosity of the prophet and becomes not merely a tragic victim but an embattled seer. According to Bettelheim the suggestiveness and referential richness of the Oedipal story only *includes* the implication that little boys want to kill the man they know is their father and marry the woman they know is their mother. This common simplification ignores the fact that Oedipus did not know what he was doing when he killed Laius and married Jocasta, and that "his greatest desire was to make it *impossible* for himself to harm those he thought were his parents." This crucial detail expands the story's mythic power to include the child's guilt for having patricidal and incestuous wishes and the consequences of acting on such wishes.[3]

As Bettelheim reads both the Sophocles play and Freud's adaptation of it, the central issues are Oedipus's guilt and his discovery of the truth. Oedipus's lack of initial awareness about what he has done is reflected in psychoanalysis's version of the story by the repression in adulthood of both the murderous feelings toward the parent of the same sex and the incestuous feelings toward the parent of the opposite sex. Oedipus behaved as he did as a consequence of his real parents having rejected him in the most brutal and literal way possible; he loved the parents he thought were his. "It is only our love for our parents and our conscious wish to protect them that leads us to repress our negative and sexual feelings for them."[4]

Bettelheim also emphasizes another portion of the story often glossed over by theory and by practice: when he fled Corinth, Oedipus did not fully heed the temple inscription, "Know thyself," which implicitly warned against misunderstandings of the oracle's prophecies. He was not sufficiently self-aware in his flight and later acted out his metaphorical blindness by literally blinding himself. So Oedipus, truth-seeker, sought the complex truths too late; or, translated into psychic parlance, self-knowledge requires an understanding of the normally unconscious aspects of ourselves. It is Bettelheim's conviction and that of psychoanalysis—and here I part company with him and it regretfully—

that knowledge really is power, that to know the unconscious is to be able to control it, more or less completely. "This is a crucial part of the myth," writes Bettelheim: "As soon as the unknown is made known . . . the pernicious consequences of the Oedipal deeds disappear." That is indeed the most hopeful reading of the cease of pestilence in Thebes, but not the only one. No one, after all, can restore Oedipus's sight to him, and his wanderings toward ultimate peace in Colonus are still torturous and tragic. Not until he awaits death does he find his peace. Bettelheim sees the Oedipus in us all as able to be "free" from our own "destructive powers" and their ability to "harm us." This is, of course, the expression of psychoanalysis's own profound wish that it might provide cure, a wish that Freud himself became suspicious of near the end of his life. I prefer a more realistic phrasing of what the search for self-knowledge might hope to accomplish: a lessening of the destructive hold of unconscious material over people's lives and a diminished likelihood that one might single-handedly cause a pestilence in the city.

This important quibble aside, I find Bettelheim's reading of Oedipus convincing and important stuff, if not entirely new: Oedipus is a hero who is fated to feel guilty for something he has done but did not know he was doing and did not mean to do; and, more important, he is a quester after truth against tremendous inner and external odds, determined to recognize that truth when he finds it, no matter how painful it may be for him and for other people he loves. That truth is peculiarly his own—Bettelheim points out, through DeQuincey, that the Sphinx posed different problems for different people, so that the answer to the riddle is not merely man in general but Oedipus in particular. But it is also universal. "The answer to the riddle of life is not just man, but each person himself."[5]

In the Oedipus story it is the woman/mother/wife, Jocasta, who says that she does not want to know the truth and who cannot cope with it when it is revealed. She kills herself because she possesses unwanted knowledge—not, as Bettelheim points out, the knowledge that she has committed incest but the repressed knowledge that she helped to abandon her son to death years earlier. Perhaps it is ironic that I should see Anne Sexton as Oedipus and not as Jocasta. Anne Sexton killed herself. Yet despite that final irony, the essential characteristics of Anne Sexton's poetry identify her not with the overwhelmed and helpless victim/victimizer, Jocasta, but with the hero, Oedipus, whose struggle for the truth was determined and tragic. Her failure to save herself was heroic rather than pathetic, courageous rather than cowardly. Unlike Jocasta, who is immediately defeated by the revelation of the truth, Sexton grappled with her truth again and again, in a deadly hand-to-hand combat she might be said, on some terms, to have won.

Anne's Oedipus

Anne Sexton identified herself with Oedipus only once, in the epigraph for her first collection, *To Bedlam and Part Way Back.* The epigraph is from a letter of Schopenhauer to Goethe in 1815:

> It is the courage to make a clean breast of it in face of every question that makes the philosopher. He must be like Sophocles's Oedipus, who, seeking enlightenment concerning his terrible fate, pursues his indefatigable enquiry, even when he divines that appalling horror awaits him in the answer. But most of us carry in our heart the Jocasta who begs Oedipus for God's sake not to inquire further. . . .

Although she never repeated the allusion, its prefatory placement in her premiere volume of poetry constitutes an announcement of intention, a declaration of independence, a bill of poetic rights. It is here that she both defines and defends her kind of poetry for the first time. Anne Sexton made good on her promise to herself and to American poetry to seek enlightenment concerning her, concerning our, fate.

While her contemporaries, encountering her work poem by poem in journals and volume by volume from Houghton Mifflin, might soon forget this initial identification with the truth-seeking Oedipus, *The Complete Poems* published after her death inevitably showcases the epigraph at the front of over 600 pages of poetry, reminding us of the startling chutzpah Sexton demonstrated from the beginning of her career. A reading of the canon shows that the epigraph remained appropriate to every subsequent volume in one sense or another, to the distress of those who do not find worth in such an "indefatigable inquiry."

Modest though this one reference to Oedipus might seem, Anne Sexton made through its use a claim on the territory of the tragic hero, and she made it on behalf of a gender as well as a poetic subject. Although her private struggles caused her to recognize, even capitulate to, the cultural patterns that demanded the ritual sacrifice of "all beautiful women," she appropriated for her (and their) poetry a fiercely defended autonomy. Right at the start of her writing life, she took on (in both senses) masculine authority in the Western world, from the Greek hero through Schopenhauer, from Goethe to Freud.[6]

An early workshop encounter led to the epigraph and to the poem that opens part 2 of *Bedlam*, which contains the most intensely confessional material in the collection. As part of her therapy following her first mental breakdown, Sexton enrolled in John Holmes's workshop at the Boston Adult Education Center. A later spin-off workshop convened in 1958 and continued until Holmes's death in 1962. With other workshop members Holmes was personally warm and professionally helpful. But Holmes grew to dislike Sexton intensely and conducted what can only be called a campaign against her poetry and her person to other workshop members. He warned Maxine Kumin against Sexton's poetic and personal influence and solicited censure of her from other poets. A traditional and decorously formal poet himself, he found her subjects distasteful, selfish, childish, and even dangerous. He was the first authority figure in the world of American poetry with whom she had had direct contact and under whom she had received tutelage. A few short years after her tentative and daughterly relationship with this important first teacher began, she was forced to make a choice that would in some senses determine the rest of her poetic life. She could capitulate to his authority and abandon her subject matter, or she could confront him and appropriate that authority for herself.

"For John, Who Begs Me Not to Enquire Further" became Sexton's ultimate poetic reply to Holmes's challenge to her "very source and subject."[7] The father figure who warned her against writing about her neuroses and about her experiences as a mental patient was cast, by this title, in the role of the symbolically weak woman, the Jocasta of the Schopenhauer epigraph. Although Sexton could not have known it at the time, Holmes was to be only the first of a series of Jocastas whom Sexton would have to confront in the many years of productivity ahead of her. Her argument in this thematically central poem is indeed that of the truth-seeker Oedipus:

> Not that it was beautiful,
> but that, in the end, there was
> a certain sense of order there;
> something worth learning
> in that narrow diary of my mind,
> in the commonplaces of the asylum. . . .

Like Oedipus, Sexton does not pretend to be a seeker after beauty here, although she will seek beauty as well later in her poetic life; she seeks, rather, "a certain sense of order," if knowing the truth about oneself, however awful, can yield a pattern, a structure, that will teach one "something worth learning" about how one's mystery can be unwoven. The "narrow diary of my mind" elicits images of the private person confiding confidences to a small and secret book, and she is aware that in employing this image she addresses everyone's reservations about the divulgence of such confidences. Straightforward as this image is, Sexton certainly intended some irony, for the "narrow diary" alludes to Holmes's use of the term against her. She had been angry during the process that led up to this finally loving, forgiving, giving poem addressed to a father figure, teacher, and friend who was, as she later said, "in the long run, ashamed of me where you might be proud of me."[8] The "common-places of the asylum" include the "cracked mirror," in which the beholder must acknowledge the fragmented pieces of the self, held up to the scrutiny of whatever wholeness that perceiver can manage. It also pre-figures the next and central image of the poem, which Diane Middlebrook finds central not only to this poem but to Sexton's entire poetics:

> I tapped my own head;
> it was glass, an inverted bowl.
> It is a small thing
> to rage in your own bowl.
> At first it was private.
> Then it was more than myself;
> it was you, or your house
> or your kitchen.

Like that other star-crossed poet, Plath, Sexton is trapped in her bell jar, "an inverted bowl." But by the act of tapping it, she tentatively releases powers that reveal to her that her pain is more than private, that she shares with other isolated beings this "small thing" enlarged by sympathy and empathy.

The scene of this coming into connection with others trapped in their inverted bowls is, significantly, the "house," and more particularly the kitchen, locale of so many of Sexton's scenes of recognition, as it was of Plath's. It is not only, I think, that the kitchen is such a female place but that here the ritual of preparing and eating food takes place; here all modern people are most literally nourished. This is the room in which her world, suburban America, finds itself most at home. The domesticity suggested by the kitchen implies that here, in this most ordinary and yet formally ritualized room, the most extraordinary human truths will emerge, in the midst of simple converse about the everyday matters of commonplace lives. In this respect, the kitchen and the asylum are perhaps closely related. Neither is Thebes or Corinth, but either may be the crossroads at which one kills one's father or the ceremonial place in which one marries one's mother.

> And if you turn away
> because there is no lesson here
> I will hold my awkward bowl,
> with all its cracked stars shining
> like a complicated lie,
> and fasten a new skin around it
> as if I were dressing an orange
> or a strange sun.

It is on this passage that Middlebrook bases her contention that tapping the head "produces 'stars,' signs radiant with significance, uniting sufferer and beholder despite the 'glass bowl' that shuts them off from other forms of contact."[9] I would add that the cracked stars resulting from tapping the bowl are yet another reflection of the cracked mirror in the asylum, that we all, in kitchens or madhouses, aim toward the same general human truths that shine differently in different lives. The speaker, under the critical scrutiny of the one who has "turned away," must hold her bowl awkwardly, partially disarmed by the withdrawal of an invited commonality. The cracked stars shine "like a complicated lie," Sexton's acknowledgment that we each create our own story, are trapped within private perspectives in which we style and shape a truth that has as much of the necessary lie as of authenticity; the lie is "complicated" by our complicity in the egotistical desire to make ourselves, perhaps, the heroes of our stories. There is also a suggestion here, muted from reprimand into plea, that the stars will more likely constitute that "complicated lie," that partial denial of the sought truth, if the invited other rejects the partnership by which a complicated *truth* might emerge: "And if you turn away. . . ." When the fellow sufferer changes to the detached or disdainful observer, the speaker must "fasten a new skin" around the bowl, an action that defensively separates her from him; yet the stars shine underneath, a luminous invitation toward truth.

This is something I would never find
in a lovelier place, my dear,
although your fear is anyone's fear,
like an invisible veil between us all . . .
and sometimes in private,
my kitchen, your kitchen,
my face, your face.

Whatever truth the speaker seeks, it will not be available in "lovelier places" than the private mind speaking its halting language to another private mind, trying to make contact. What separates them, she knows, is the hearer's fear, "anyone's fear," not only of the sick or mad or sordid; "your fear" is also the subject of the inquiry itself. Although the grammatical construction of the last lines is ambiguous, I read them to mean secondarily that the fear pulls down the veil between them in their kitchens and on their faces, and primarily that this "something," this "special sort of hope," takes place in the kitchen and is revealed, through the mutually cracked glass bowls, on their distorted, human, striving faces.

The two lengthy poems that follow this preface to part 2 of *Bedlam* reveal the "source and subject" of the cracked stars that John/Jocasta does not want to hear. "The Double Image" and "The Division of Parts" show us this other "cracked mirror" of the mother, image of fragmentation and wholeness for the speaker:

my mocking mirror, my overthrown
love, my first image. She eyes me from that face,
that stony head of death
I had outgrown.

Addressed to her daughter, "The Double Image" tells the story of a thirty-year-old mother who goes to live with her own mother after the speaker's suicide attempt. An "outgrown child," she inhabits her mother's house as an unwelcome guest who must submit to her mother's resentment for her suicide attempt and who must sit for a portrait of herself to be hung on a wall opposite her mother's portrait, freezing in time her dependence on her mother, herself as reflection of that "mocking mirror," and her stubborn refusal to become that bitter woman. The mother contracts cancer (blaming her daughter), the daughter is institutionalized again, and the mother begins her slow dying. The speaker, estranged from her own daughter by her inability to mother her, tells herself one of those complicated lies and then unravels it:

> And you came each
> weekend. But I lie.
> You seldom came. I just pretended
> you. . . .

The lesson she learns she must pass on to her daughter—this complicated truth made up of so many self-serving lies that must be exploded—is
"why I would rather/die than love." And this has much to do, she
knows, with her relationship to that "overthrown love" and the speaker's
need to turn away from her:

> The artist caught us at the turning;
> we smiled in our canvas home
> before we chose our foreknown separate ways.
>
> . . . .
>
> And this was the cave of the mirror,
> that double woman who stares
> at herself, as if she were petrified
> in time. . . .

If she is to survive, she will have to acknowledge that she is unwillfully
guilty of her own mother's sin, passed now to another generation:

> And this was my worst guilt; you could not cure
> nor soothe it. I made you to find me.

In telling her young daughter this truth, she is giving that child a
chance to escape the prison of poisonous identifications handed from
mother to daughter to mother to daughter. Mary Gray, Sexton's mother,
could not admit or acknowledge this human truth inherent in the
reproductive urge; it is Sexton's hope that, in admitting her own complicity in this complicated lie, she will provide her child with a way to
escape its implications or, if not to escape them entirely, then to know
that the trap lies baited for her.

But I have called Anne Sexton Oedipus, and Oedipus wanted to
marry his mother, not to harm her. Sexton's Oedipus/Anne knows that
the mother is the "first overthrown love" for both sexes and that the
differentiation of desire in males and females occurs later. It is my
contention that Oedipus/Anne does "slay" her mother and "marry" her
father, just as Oedipus slew his father and married his mother. In
chapter 2 I will discuss in detail the marriage to the father, as well as the
possibility of an unconscious guilt connected with the father's death.
Here I will represent her perception of the deadly Oedipal configuration

through three poems from the early, middle, and late periods of her writing life: "The Double Image" (*Bedlam*), "Those Times . . ." (*Live or Die*), and "Divorce, Thy Name Is Woman" (*45 Mercy Street*). In "Double Image" the speaker is accused of her mother's death; in "Those Times . . ." she acknowledges this unintentional sin; and in "Divorce, Thy Name Is Woman," she speaks of her lifetime "marriage" to her father. This is what Oedipus must discover himself guilty of: the murder of the parent of the same sex and forbidden incest with the parent of the opposite sex.

"The Double Image" includes one of the most startling and frightening of Sexton's stanzas, made more so by the clever facility and unexpectedness of the rhyme:

> They hung my portrait in the chill
> north light, matching
> me to keep me well.
> Only my mother grew ill.
> She turned from me, as if death were catching,
> as if death transferred,
> as if my dying had eaten inside of her.
> That August you were two, but I timed my days with doubt.
> On the first of September she looked at me
> and said I gave her cancer.
> They carved her sweet hills out
> and still I couldn't answer.

The speaker of this poem is the same woman who knows that "all my need took/you down like a meal" and who, although she does not know it as a child, will utterly defeat her mother in "Those Times . . .":

> I did not know that my life, in the end,
> would run over my mother's like a truck
> and all that would remain
> from the year I was six
> was a small hole in my heart, a deaf spot,
> so that I might hear
> the unsaid more clearly.

The "hole in the heart," that "deaf spot," becomes the poet's source of the knowledge of absence; blocked by childhood indignities from hearing the ordinary music of daily life, she takes on the special sensual acuity of the handicapped: what she will hear is the unsaid, just as blind Oedipus will "see" with the sight of the blind visionary.

And like Oedipus, Sexton did not want to run over her mother's life like a truck, to give her cancer, to defeat her, or to slay her; she intended, rather, like Oedipus, the opposite: to protect that beloved if rejecting parent. Oedipus is utterly rejected by his biological parents, who wish to murder him that he might not murder his father; his other parents, unknowingly adoptive, are those he flees Corinth to protect when he hears the Oracle. In so fleeing he fulfills the prophecy. In the Oedipus myth, then, the parental figures are split into the actual and rejecting parents and the adoptive and loving ones, who might after all be called the "real" parents. In the normative infant and childhood psyche, these roles of rejecting and loving parents are united, so that reality and imago emerge from the same identities and bodies; it is the real parents we love and wish to protect, their imagos we wish to murder and marry. Seeking this complex truth, Sexton knows that she must make reparation for the split inside her that duplicates the split in the psyches of her parents, who both rejected *and* loved her, just as she rejects and loves them.

Having "murdered" her mother in the psychic sense, she processed such guilt as if fated to do so. It matters little whether or not Mary Gray actually told Anne Sexton that Sexton "gave her cancer," and it matters equally little whether the mother's trauma over her daughter's suicide attempt actually contributed to the development of her disease. Like Oedipus, Sexton has sought and found her psychic truth: she slew her mother, *and* she dearly loved the mother that she slew. That hard truth is Anne Sexton's; it is also mine and may be any woman's, for daughters both love and symbolically slay their mothers.

In Sexton's case, the symbolically lethal relationship of daughter to mother includes details she never alludes to in her poetry, wholly exposed as that poetry appears to be.[10] Mary Gray was herself the daughter of a writer, newspaper editor Arthur Gray Staples, and, according to Diane Middlebrook, Gray and her father formed the "literary cohort" of the family. Rivalry between Sexton and her mother was punctuated by several episodes of accusation, confrontation, and rejection, beginning with Mary Gray's assertion that Sexton had plagiarized Sara Teasdale in high school—a notion later confirmed wrong. After Sexton's first suicide attempt in 1956, she wanted to go to college, but her mother refused to help pay for her ailing daughter's education. Mary Gray also found it necessary to inform Sexton, at the same time that she withheld her support, that she herself had gotten the highest marks ever recorded on IQ tests at Wellesley. Mary Gray composed letters, verses, and elaborate invitations and expressed her writerly aspirations only in these acceptable and conventional ways, with the exception of a few (interestingly good) poems about her daughter's breakdown; and of these Sexton was contemptuous. There is ample indication that Mary Gray feared and resented her daughter's intellectual ability, especially as that ability might manifest itself in poetry. There is also slight indication that she was proud of the daughter of whom she was clearly jealous, and generous indication that she loved Anne deeply and enduringly and identified with her when she was not alienated from her.

Sexton's awareness of these patterns is clear from letters and from transcripts of therapy sessions. She craved Mary Gray's approval and yet did not need it in order to be a poet—in fact, it was as a poet that Sexton would surpass this powerful mother, by fulfilling her own literary aspirations. "I don't write for you, but know that one of the reasons I do write is that you are my mother."[11] Either or both of them, mother and/or daughter, could choose to see this emerging fulfillment of a gratification long deferred for the women of the family as a gift from daughter to mother, and perhaps both sometimes did; but the overwhelming sense of competitive rejection that marked their relationship made Sexton's writing a kind of threat to her mother. One final detail confirms this in at least the psychoanalytic sense. Mary Gray died in March 1959; a few weeks later, in May, Houghton Mifflin accepted the manuscript for Sexton's first book, *To Bedlam and Part Way Back*. If, in the talon law of the psyche, the daughter's suicide attempt could cause her mother's cancer, then the daughter's birth into the world of professional letters at almost the same time as her mother's death might have "caused" that death.

Oedipus/Anne acknowledges the paternal part of her sin in dozens of father poems distributed throughout the canon. Because I devote the next chapter to a discussion of this lifelong romance, I will rely here on the late poem, probably composed almost fifteen years after "The Double Image," in which she most explicitly acknowledges her marriage to the father. Part of the sequence in *45 Mercy Street* called "Eating the Leftovers," "Divorce, Thy Name Is Woman" begins in the aftermath of that lifelong marriage:

> I am divorcing daddy—Dybbuk! Dybbuk!
> I have been doing it daily all my life. . . .

The speaker remembers the father's "long midnight visit/in a dream that is not a dream" and knows that even though both parents are long dead, "I am still divorcing him." The poem concludes with the speaker

> waiting, waiting for Daddy to come home
> and stuff me so full of our infected child
> that I turn invisible, but married,
> at last.

To divorce her husband (which Anne Sexton was in the process of doing when she wrote this poem) is to divorce her father, because she knows that the men she has sought throughout her life, in particular the husband of her long marriage, are stand-ins for that first heterosexual romance with the father. The poem's central irony is that while she can divorce her husband, she cannot, ultimately, divorce her dead father; the speaker is left eternally awaiting the culmination of their marriage in the form of their "infected child."

Oedipus Iscariot

Sexton transformed her story, and Oedipus's own, into a religious parable in *Live or Die*'s "The Legend of the One-Eyed Man," which begins:

> Like Oedipus I am losing my sight.
> Like Judas I have done my wrong.

Sexton does not name the source of the "legend" of her speaker, the title's one-eyed man, nor does she mention Oedipus again;[12] the remainder of the poem is the one-eyed man's telling of his crimes, which "dropped upon me/as from a high building," through the story of Judas:

> The story of his life
> is the story of mine.
> I have one glass eye.
> My nerves push against its painted surface
> but the other one
> waiting for judgment
> continues to see. . . .

What the single oracular eye left to him "sees" is "much/about Judas . . . that you overlooked." In a series of reflections about the nature of the New Testament and the construction of the cross, the narrator seems to deflect the focus from Judas's real crimes; but in this he is deliberately duplicating what he sees as the "mistake" we have all made about Judas. Instead of being bought off and disappearing, Judas should have owned his crime directly by placing Christ on the cross with his own hands. Judas did not know this, for he was only "avaricious and dishonest," not "inspired." But there were other "forbidden crimes":

> Judas had a mother.
> His mother had a dream.
> Because of this dream
> he was altogether managed by fate
> and thus he raped her.
> As a crime we hear little of this.
> Also he sold his God.

This must be the most heavily freighted and heretical noncoordinating conjunction—that harrowing and dismissive "also"—in American poetry. The betrayal of his Lord becomes ironically incidental to this other "forbidden" and undeliberate crime, the rape of the mother, which the narrator says was "expressly foretold," just as was Judas's betrayal of Christ.

But in what sense was this "crime" foretold? Sexton's narrator, clearly intended to be more than a bit demented as well as inspired by his blindness, gives us no explanation of his strange charge against Judas—and, it is crucial to remember, against himself:

> Judas had a mother
> just as I had a mother.
> Oh! Honor and relish the facts!
> Do not think of the intense sensation
> I have as I tell you this
> but think only. . . .

The "confessional" feeling experienced by the speaker is beside the point; it lends us only a momentary frisson. As I read it, this extraordinarily complex poem, almost entirely ignored by critics perhaps because of its obscurity and its problematic connection to Sexton's confessional poetry, exemplifies Sexton's early appropriation of the prophetic voice— archetypal, mythic, and collective rather than "merely" personal. (See Part III, "Person, Persona, Prophecy.") Among her most analytic as well as prophetic works, it offers an intricately sketched outline of psychic and cultural malaise; among her most heretical religious statements, it provides a revisionary reading of Christianity she would develop in depth in later works, including "The Jesus Papers" and "O Ye Tongues." It also belongs to and with Sexton's psychosexual poetry and is closely related to the voice I am here calling Oedipus/Anne.

"Like Oedipus I am losing my sight." Although the one-eyed man will not again mention Oedipus and will nearly abandon even his own story in his ramblings about Judas and about Christianity's central tragedy of betrayal and crucifixion, the forbidden and foretold crime with which the one-eyed man charges Judas is the sexual violation of the mother. The other portion of his crime, the one our culture has *not* "overlooked" and "forgotten"—the one now completely identified with Judas's name—is betrayal of the "father," resulting directly in the father's death. He might as well have murdered Christ himself, says the one-eyed man: "He should have tried to lift him up there!" At least then, the narrator implies, we could accuse him cleanly and clearly of that murder for which his guilt has been only implied and indirect; at least then he could own that guilt, "that dead weight that would have been his fault." Instead, like all men, he inherits only a bastard guilt, and we remember him as merely avaricious, dishonest, and cowardly; such are the "degrading details" that the narrator declines to tell us of his own life, hinting only that "the story of his life/is the story of mine."

Because Christianity represses the feminine and debars femininity from direct participation in godhead, it forgets this other forbidden crime, the rape of the mother, "foretold" as surely as Christ said to the disciples, "One of you will betray me." For the betrayal of the father, Christianity offers us this specific prophecy; the other prophecy, which comes in the form of a woman/mother's "dream," remains repressed. The one-eyed man's prophecy as he becomes blind in one eye, while the other one, "waiting for judgment/continues to see," is the vision of this wholesale repression of the feminine in Christianity, the same quality that will later cause the God of "The Author of the Jesus Papers Speaks" to declare: "We must all eat beautiful women." This is the other "sacrifice" of Christianity, corresponding to Christ's sacrifice on behalf of humanity in the person of his male body. Christ, who in Sexton's "gospels" rejects the sexual and the feminine in the person of his mother, first institutionalized this denial. We know, we "remember," that Judas had a "father"; we "forget" that he had a mother and that her sexual violation and sacrifice are among the conditions of this peculiar form of redemption that proceeds only by fulfilling the prophecy of betrayal and murder.

"Judas had a mother," and she "had a dream"; and because of this dream, "he was altogether managed by fate." The mother's dream is not specified, but we may guess its nature by reference not only to the configuration of this poem but to the "dreams" of Sexton's other mothers. At one level the mother's dream is the prophecy that her son will rape her, just as the "father's" dream is that the son will murder him. But because this poem and the poetics from which it emerges are psycho-analytic, we may surmise that the mother's dream might also take the form of a projected hope that her son will be a great man, as she by definition cannot be, and a projected rage against him, against all sons and all fathers, for her own suppression of possibility, her own sacrifice as embodied in maternity. If dreams embody both wish and fear, and if they are in the unconscious identified with one another, as Sexton clearly believed, the condensations and displacements I have suggested are more mandated than merely possible: this dream managed his fate, and "thus he raped her."

Lest this seem to excuse Judas and his counterpart in the narrator and in Oedipus, and displace the guilt onto the mother who dreamed, we are again told that this was indeed a "crime," although we hear "little of this." Whether or not crimes "dropped upon me/as from a high building"—i.e., whether or not one is managed by fate—one's crimes are one's own. The assumptions of this situation and its rhetoric are peculiarly biblical and are concerned with patterns of lineage through "begetting." (Judas was the son of, who was the son of, who was the son of....) We always identify biblical personages through the paternal lineage, forgetting the mother and her fate, which is the fate of the feminine in Christianity. Even God's "only begotten Son" had a mother who, despite centuries of Maryolatry, is relegated to the maternal/sacrificial and is denied by her son—in Sexton's revision in "The Jesus Papers," he violates her body and sacrifices her, that he may learn to sacrifice himself. But he gets the credit.

I have thus far omitted discussion of one important section of "The Legend of the One-Eyed Man," which enlarges upon the theme of Christianity's violation of the feminine. Near the beginning of the poem, just after the one-eyed man has told us that his good eye "continues to see," he comments in a misleadingly offhand way about the entire New Testament:

> Of course
> the New Testament is very small.
> Its mouth opens four times—
>
> . . . .
>
> It gouges out the Judaic ground,
> taking its own backyard
> like a virgin daughter.

In this reversal upon the usual relative positions of the Old and New Testaments on the issue of patriarchy, the narrator gives us a New

Testament that is a "prehistoric monster" gouging out the Judaic ground as the "stone jaw of a back-hoe" might plow a backyard. If the simple talon law of the Old Testament is plowed over by a gospel of love and forgiveness that seems more compassionate and, perhaps, even more friendly to the feminine, the narrator invites us to look at it in another, a "one-eyed," way: the New Testament institutionalizes sacrifice, unaware that it is the sacrifice of the woman on which that archetypal god-act is founded. This is certainly another distortion of truth, but one, says this poem throughout, whose partial validity we have "forgotten" or "overlooked." The "taking" of the virgin daughter of Judaism is the poem's first and largest rape. This exaggeration is styled deliberately to resurrect the repressed, to give it its due, just as is that final "Also he sold his God."

In a series of such ironic reversals, the speaker trivializes that crime we have regarded as most heinous—the betrayal of God—in favor of the ones against the feminine that our culture has itself trivialized. The narrator uses against an entire culture its own strategies of dismissal, claiming centrality for the most literally marginal (i.e., almost completely nontextual) act. The version of the story of Judas that is canonized (with canon equivalent to law, rule, and textual truth sanctioned by the father) is put aside by Sexton in a movement that brings into play the other meaning of sanction, here a coercive measure practiced by scripture against apocrypha; in this case the apocryphal (hidden, obscure, unauthenticated) "text" is repressed until the female poet claims it on behalf of the mother of our most celebrated criminal son.

"Like Oedipus I am losing my sight." This is the story of Oedipus's other eye; one is already blinded for the crime of patricide, but the one that still sees waits for "judgment" for this other crime of sexually violating the mother. I have called the voice of this narrator archetypal or mythic or collective—terms I will expand upon in "The Prophetic *I* (Eye)"—because in this poem Anne Sexton expanded her own story, already that of Anyone, to include a specifically male perspective as well as a cultural and religious analysis implied in the earlier and more nakedly confessional work. "The Legend of the One-Eyed Man" looks backward to "For John" and forward to the mythopoesis that will begin with *Transformations.* Among the special achievements of this poem are the dual attempts to embody and understand the male perspective, to take on the identity of the son, the actual Oedipus/ Judas, and to rescue for us the feminine tragedy encoded in that son's transgressions.

While both Sexton and her narrators take on magical and fated guilt, she was also superbly accomplished at "mercy for the greedy," whether the greedy one was herself or any other needy human being, any other "rat" who will be redeemed on "no evil star." "For John" was written as an answer to bitter, vitriolic, frightened contempt on the part of someone she cared for deeply; her response was not in kind, entirely lacking the biting retort of which she was certainly capable. Nor did she tug her poetic forelock, however much she might sometimes have made such gestures in her personal life. Instead, "For John" is a graceful, affectionate, compassionate response that retains its humane eloquence even as it establishes its own credentials beyond any reasonable dispute. The tone is one of graceful restraint, without the shadow of any spectrally girlish curtsy in the voice.

"The Legend of the One-Eyed Man" continues to embody this largeness of both mind and heart, at the cultural rather than the personal level. While Sexton may, sadly, have accepted on behalf of all "beautiful women" the sacrificial role, as Alicia Ostriker has commented, she was capable of a clear-eyed and intricate anger that borders sometimes, as in "Legend," on prophetic wrath. That she disarmed her wrath with muted irony leagues her—ironically again—*with* rather than against the mainline and male poetic tradition; but there is no mistaking the biting reprimand of "Legend" and of many of her later religious poems against the spiritual blindness and complacencies of Christianity. She is angry at the entrenched patterns that "manage" the "fate" of both men and women. Yet the obvious gap between poet and speaker—based, if on nothing else, on gender—suggests her sympathy for *this man,* this human managed by his fate as she was by hers; she identifies with him rather than distancing herself from him. While I understand the dangers of this compromise, of bedding down with one who might be in his cultural form the enemy, I celebrate it more than mourn it. This method of finding commonalities and of trying to build upon them together as men and women may not ultimately have saved Anne Sexton's life, as we might wish it had. But Sexton was right to think that this is the way for us—Oedipuses all—to proceed together toward "some special kind of hope."

Far from being done with the horrors he discovers in his pursuit of truth when he does indeed uncover it and blind himself, Oedipus does not find peace until he awaits death at Colonus, in the wake of years of blind wandering. The Jocastas in Anne Sexton's life begged her not to inquire further; when she did, psychoanalysis held out to her the hope of which Bettelheim speaks on behalf of psychoanalysis: that knowledge of the truth will set one free. Her truth, tougher by far than either the willed ignorance of Jocasta that cannot endure revelation or the mandated liberty of analytic cure, is more like that of the original Oedipus: complex, tragic, and visionary. Sexton did not, like Jocasta, find the sought truth and simply die of it; in the many years between her first exploration of personal and poetic truth in *Bedlam* and her death in 1974, she triumphed over her guilt and her ghosts again and again. The "strange goddess face" of the slain mother whom the infant ate—"all my need took/you down like a meal"—is redeemed in a dream of reparation and mutual forgiveness in "Dreaming the Breasts":

> The breasts I knew at midnight
> beat like the sea in me now.
> . . . .
> In the end they cut off your breasts
> and milk poured from them
> into the surgeon's hand
> and he embraced them.
> I took them from him
> and planted them.

The planting of the mother's severed breasts enables "those dear white ponies" to "go galloping, galloping,/wherever you are"; and the daughter, for the moment of this poem, is renewed into her own life, free of guilt and pain. In "All My Pretty Ones," the daughter who discovers her deceased father's flaws in reading her mother's diary is able, by coming to terms with them and with their duplications in her own life, to reach some kind of catharsis of pity and fear:

> Only in this hoarded span will love persevere.
> Whether you are pretty or not, I outlive you,
> bend down my strange face to yours and forgive you.

If this act of mutual forgiveness with mother and father must be repeated more than once, this is a sign not of weakness of resolve and will but of their strengths and determination. No resolution is ever quite so permanent as humans might wish. Anne Sexton could not be utterly and finally freed of her ghosts and her guilt in this life, and her poetry thus reveals these other "complicated lies": of poetry as celebration only, of knowledge as ultimate freedom. "What forms the essence of our humanity—and of [*Oedipus Rex*]—is not our being victims of fate, but our struggle to discover the truth about ourselves."[13] What forms the essence of Anne Sexton's poetic achievement is not her status as victim but her struggle to discover the truth about herself, to turn her blindness into insight. And unless we "turn away," like Jocasta, like John Holmes, there ought indeed to be something special in this kind of hope, perhaps in private,

> my kitchen, your kitchen,
> my face, your face.

2
How We Danced:
Fathers and Daughters

Within modern society, woman's "dependent" and "incestuous"
personality probably stems from not being experienced as "divine"
by the mother (and father). Most women are glassed into infancy,
and perhaps into some forms of madness, by an unmet need for
maternal nurturance. Thus, female children turn to their fathers for
physical affection, nurturance, or pleasurable emotional intensity—a
turning that is experienced as "sexual" by the adult male, precisely
because it is predicated on the female's (his daughter's) innocence,
helplessness, youthfulness, and monogamous idolatry. This essentially satyric and incestuous model of sexuality is almost universal.
... Patriarchal marriage, prostitution, and mass "romantic" love
are psychologically predicated on sexual union between Daughter
and Father figures.

—Phyllis Chesler, *Women and Madness*

"Love Grew Rings around Me": With Father in *Bedlam*

In *To Bedlam and Part Way Back,* Anne Sexton began composing the
mythopoeic music of the father-daughter dance, which echoes now as a
swan song for her poetic and personal lives. "We bent together/like two
lonely swans," she later wrote in "How We Danced," a central poem in
the "Death of the Fathers" sequence in *The Book of Folly.* The father-
daughter motif is equaled in resonance and poignancy in Sexton's
canon only by the mother-daughter relationship, and for similar reasons:
Sexton saw the nuclear family as the microcosmic analogue of the social
and psychic structure of her culture.

   The clearest shift from personal to "transpersonal" or "cultural" in
Sexton's work takes place in her fourth volume, *Transformations.* But
while in this middle-period volume such a shift is mythically embodied and newly garbed, there is within the "narrow diary" of even the
early poems a structural outline for the psychic biography of a gender,
and particularly for what Phyllis Chesler calls woman's dependent and

incestuous personality in relation to her father[1] — a pattern long known to and exploited by psychoanalysis, to the degree that therapeutic method colludes with patriarchy. If Anne Sexton learned about her own incestuous dependencies from Freud and his proxies during the early stages of her life as a career mental patient, hers was still the first contemporary voice outside of the psychoanalytic world to describe the normative relationship between father and daughter from the daughter's perspective.[2] Sexton's early poetry both represents and dissects the subtle and pervasive psychosocial pattern that Phyllis Chesler would later discuss, and damn, in *Women and Madness* and that now, in the wake of feminist inquiry, seems almost obvious: "romantic" love in the Western world is "psychologically predicated on the sexual union between Daughter and Father figures."[3]

The "normal" woman in Western society, whether or not she is a poet, and whether or not she is fully aware of the psychic dynamics, falls in love with her father, who delights her, despises her, seduces her, betrays her, and dies. The father who dies in 1959 in the poet's personal life undergoes a series of resurrections as man and imago—husband, doctor, lover, and priest—and is finally reborn as the deity of *The Awful Rowing toward God.* Burial and resurrection of the fathers becomes a central theme in Sexton's poetry, as it is in the personal lives of her contemporaries and the collective life of her culture. In all of his incarnations in Sexton's poetry, the father finally fails himself and his daughter, for he is a god not sufficiently omnipotent, a man not sufficiently humane, a male principle not sufficiently able to accommodate feminine powers and desires. But this ultimate failure is never judged harshly in Sexton's poetry, never evoked without empathetic insight, for the shortcomings of the father-god in a patriarchy are nearly definitive of the failures of the human enterprise, one in which all men and all women engage. This is not to say that Sexton's poetry lacks anger, or what Blake called "prophetic wrath"; that is quite another matter. In the world of Sexton's poetry, the men born into their myths are often as helpless and hapless as the women born into theirs, and Sexton was inclined to portray the sad worthiness of all human effort, however doomed. Although she saw, relentlessly, the relentless "gender of things," her poetic eye was androgynously kind.

To Bedlam and Part Way Back lays the foundation for Sexton's version, or inversion, of Freud's *Totem and Taboo,* in which the father in the family evolves into the defiled and then worshipped God. Five poems in *Bedlam* establish the father figure as god, doctor, and cultural myth, as well as biological parent and great-grandparent. The collection opens with "You, Doctor Martin," which immediately establishes the therapist as modern mediator between the religious and the familial. He is the confessor who is "the god of our block," the father of all the "large . . . foxy children" who inhabit Bedlam.

"You, Doctor Martin, walk/from breakfast to madness." The speaker, a patient in a mental institution, narrates from both within and without her own madness. Mad enough to be among the "moving dead," mad enough to be "queen of this summer hotel," mad enough to "make moccasins all morning," she is sane enough to look at the anatomy of her relationship to her confessor with insightful equanimity: "Of course, I love you." That calm awareness of psychic process (specifically, of the clinical phenomenon of transference) does not stop her from being "mad," nor does the madness inhibit her clear-sighted analytic knowledge. The speaker knows that the patient always "loves" the doctor, the sinner always loves the confessor, the daughter always loves the father. Speaking out of her own awareness of individual pain and comfort, the narrator is nevertheless detached enough to see exactly how that individual situation is an enactment of a paradigmatic drama, in which she plays her inevitable role of the crazy daughter in a scenario with the grown-up father-doctor whose very business is the eminently sane management of madness. He is the "god of our block, prince of all the foxes":

> Your third eye
> moves among us and lights the separate boxes
> where we sleep or cry.
>
> What large children we are
> here. All over I grow most tall
> in the best ward. Your business is people,
> you call at the madhouse, an oracular
> eye in our nest. Out in the hall
> the intercom pages you. You twist in the pull
> of the foxy children who fall
>
> like floods of life in frost.

Although the speaker talks of the doctor's third eye, she gazes from her own third eye, painfully and sanely aware of the psychic dynamics she and her fellow inmates play out. She ironically and consciously regards the doctor as both god and father, herself as queen and daughter. His "third eye" is "oracular," prophetic, and all-knowing, for it has, godlike, known all the separate sins of his patients. With his third eye he is able to "light" their separateness, illumine their pain, and comfort merely by his presence. But he is also only human, a man attending to his "business": treating sick people. He is not, after all, one of them, for he only "call[s] at the madhouse" after his breakfast. With her own third eye the speaker sees that they have all become his children, whom he can leave only by extricating himself from their desperate and clever grasps. The third eye is the doctor's blessing, his ability to see and to cope, but it is also his curse; the speaker-poet's own third eye is her blessing and curse as well, for when the father-god has gone, the patients become "magic talking to itself,/noisy and alone." When the magic of therapy departs, leaving only the magic of madness, the speaker turns her third eye toward what we might call "vision," toward the magic of the poem.

"You, Doctor Martin" serves as frontispiece not only for the theme of madness but for the further explorations of the father-daughter relationship in this first volume, one that ends with an extended discussion of the other and feminine source of the self—what Sexton will later call, in "Old Dwarf Heart," the "mother, father, I'm made of." During the transference process of psychoanalysis, the therapist *becomes* in his person a condensation of all the imagos of the mind; although, ideally, he will "become" mother as well as father, his gender and the patriarchal nature of the process identify him most clearly with the gods and fathers, rather than the goddesses and mothers, of one's memory. The tightly condensed father-god figure of "You, Doctor Martin" fragments into his component parts in subsequent poems of *Bedlam*, becoming father, great-grandfather, Apollo, and, in a transcultural and quasi-mythic incarnation, a dead Arabian father buried with his daughter.

Personal memory is the stuff of myths both individual and collective. Evoking a not too distant past in America and in her personal life, the speaker of "The Bells" laments a circus poster scabbing off a wall. "Father, do you remember?" Memories of a childhood circus come back to her, especially the bells that "trembled for the flying man." The child might have been afraid, but "you held my hand," while "love love/love grew rings around me." While the flying man who performs in the circus dwells in a "ring of danger," the daughter, "laughing,/lifted to your high shoulder," is safe in the ring of love, inhabited only by herself and her father. Grown up now, she can inhabit that ring of love once again through the memory of the bells:

> I remember the color of music
> and how forever
> all the trembling bells of you
> were mine.

By an act of associative substitution, the father himself becomes the flying man for whom the bells tremble. In the mind of a young child, the father is always a "flying man," a courageous performer in life who can brave anything, ring all dangers round with love, and protect both himself and his child from harm.

But the music of remembrance that the speaker hears in "The Bells" comes back strange and out of tune in other poems here. In "Music Swims Back to Me," the music "sees more than I./I mean it remembers better." When the speaker is first left in the mental hospital, "music pours over the sense," and she dances in "a circle/and [is] not afraid." But the man she speaks to here—"Wait Mister. Which way is home?"—is not her father. He cannot help her or protect her, as the final and one word plea indicates: "Mister?" The father-daughter music diminishes into its final and minor key in *Bedlam* in a cruel parody of the "trembling bells" of childhood, in "Ringing the Bells," wherein the "bell-lady" comes each Tuesday morning to the asylum to conduct the patients in musical therapy:

> And this is always my bell responding
> to my hand that responds to the lady
> who points at me, E flat;
> and although we are no better for it,
> they tell you to go. And you do.

The process of diminution the speaker experiences in her relationship to personal fathers is traced back to her great-grandfather, the New England patriarch who "begat eight/genius children" and "bought twelve almost new/grand pianos" in "Funnel." "Back from that great-grandfather I have come/to tidy a country graveyard for his sake." Visiting his grave, she finds,

> I like best to think of that Bunyan man
> slapping his thighs and trading the yankee sale
> for one dozen grand pianos. It fit his plan
> of culture to do it big. . . .

But the passing of generations from Bunyan man to suburban woman is a process of growing increasingly cramped. That almost mythic great-grandfather is dead and buried under the stone she "puzzles," and she cannot replace him or live up to his size. She comes to "question this diminishing and feed a minimum/of children their careful slice of suburban cake." Sexton speaks here not only of her own heritage but of the diminishing resonance of the American myth itself, one created by (and for) fathers. No more thirty-six pines, giant steps, eight children, and twelve pianos to make that music in "seven arking houses." Two children now, one saltbox house, the "careful" slice of cake. The speaker's position here is ambiguous, for she is both the perpetrator and the victim of this diminishing. She lives at the mouth of the funnel.

In the purely mythic "The Moss of His Skin," Sexton employs Arabian anthropological data reported in a psychoanalytic journal as an epigraph: "Young girls in old Arabia were often buried alive next to their dead fathers."[4] In Sexton's poem father and daughter share a single grave. Her speaker is the buried-alive child herself rather than the father, an observer, or an omniscient narrator. Speaking from the grave where she beds with her father, the daughter lies down

> to rest awhile,
> to be folded up together
> as if we were silk,
> to sink from the eyes of mother
> and not to talk.

In a deadly parody of the scenario of "The Bells," the child is lulled to a feeling of safety and comfort in her father's arms. "I held my breath/and daddy was there." The mother is both betrayed by and betrayer of the daughter, participating helplessly in her death and yet excluded from the final embrace in that "black room." The daughter falls "out of myself" in the special oneness with the father, while the "moss/of his skin . . . grew strange" in death. We are presented here with a young girl willingly buried alive with her father, holding his body in a final embrace while it decomposes beside hers, with hers; that embrace is both familial and sexual, one that the child hides not only from the jealous "eyes of mother," and her sisters, but from God himself; she pretends

> that Allah will not see
> how I hold my daddy
> like an old stone tree.

Perhaps Anne Sexton meant this as a parable for her own life and her own time and place: daughters, dependent upon their fathers for a sense of their own womanhood, initiated into it by means of seducing and being seduced by their fathers, lie down to die with their fathers. Withdrawing from the gaze of the mother, the daughter embraces her father eternally, her life and death extensions of his.

"Where I Live in This Honorable House of the Laurel Tree" is a mythopoeic exploration of classical sources closer to our own culture's enactment of the relationship between man and woman. Ostensibly about lovers, "Where I Live" is just as clearly about fathers and daughters. Now the tree is the daughter-lover who lives "in my wooden legs and O/my green green hands." Apollo, sun god and patriarch of reason, victimizes Daphne's honor with his "untimely lust," which has "tossed/ flesh at the wind forever." Whereas the "stone tree" of "Moss" is the dead father, a cold phallus embraced by the hapless and deceived daughter, the green tree of "Where I Live" is the living daughter trapped "out of time" by the power and lust of the male god who is also her father. She, unlike the stone tree, lives perpetually, blood moving in her "bark bound veins," her only consolation the honor with which she "builds the air." Even that leftover, useless honor is the gift of the careless god, who passes on unthinking and unknowing. When he is gone, when he does not care,

> There is no one left who understands
> how I wait
> here in my wooden legs and O
> my green green hands.

"Mother, Father, I'm Made Of": *All My Pretty Ones* and *Live or Die*

The title of Sexton's second book, *All My Pretty Ones*, comes from the *Macbeth* epigraph spoken in Macduff's voice. "All my pretty ones?/Did you say all? O hell-kite! All?" The allusion in the poet's life is to the deaths of her family members, especially the mother and father who both died the same year, within three months of each other. The poems take place in an ever-present past, in the "deep museum" of entombed memory carved with words into a monument of the living dead. Here, perhaps more deliberately than in any other volume of Sexton's poetry, the ambiguity of inheritance is the single strongest issue. The "frozen sea within us," Sexton knew, is always iced by consciousness, which keeps us from the depths of both pain and pleasure that arise from breaking the surface and plunging into the past that creates the present. The poems are not restricted to the speaker's personal losses but range instead into poignant portraits of unknown people, unknown lives ("Doors, Doors, Doors"), lives that never were ("The Abortion"); and they reach from the sacred to the profane with the ease that will more and more characterize Sexton's religious quest. The "mother, father, I'm made of" is the mother and father we are all made of, in whom the concept of deity resides. So profoundly did Anne Sexton believe that family relationships are the foundation of all tragedy, all joy, that even God's plight is best understood through his son.

In the title poem, "All My Pretty Ones," the dead father is now mothered by the daughter, who at last discovers his flaws as man and as father. His grown survivor, she finds his picture in a family album, where "a small boy/waits in a ruffled dress for someone to come. . . . " Waiting herself for something unnamed, the speaker realizes that "My father, time, meanwhile/has made it unimportant who you are looking for./I'll never know what these faces are all about." The living can never adequately understand the dead, whose secrets finally die with them. Picking through the remains of lost lives captured for moments in photographs, the speaker must finally "fold you down, my drunkard, my navigator,/my first lost keeper, to love or look at later." The puzzle of inheritance holds the poet in her own photograph, where she feels compelled to live out the mythology of family albums, which represent inheritance:

> My God, father, each Christmas Day
> with your blood, will I drink down your glass
> of wine? The diary of your hurly-burly years
> goes to my shelf to wait for my age to pass.
> Only in this hoarded span will love persevere.
> Whether you are pretty or not, I outlive you,
> bend down my strange face to yours and forgive you.

One's father is at least half of one's God, one's "first lost keeper," and the longing for God is the longing for that lost father, whose reincarnation in a son or a daughter is the ritual enacted in Christianity. (I read "My God, father," as an appositive construction, as well as an interjection.) To celebrate Christmas is, in Sexton's poem, to celebrate the blood ties of family, which are symbolized by wine, and through which we celebrate the rebirth of the father through the son—or, in this case, the daughter. The child outlives the parent in the natural order of things, and only the love lasts, reborn again through memory. As the child-inheritor matures, he or she must learn the parental flaws here represented by "your alcoholic tendency," which may be inherited by psychological if not physiological predisposition. "Forgiveness" of such sins is necessary once the flaws of betrayal are discovered by the inheritor. The imperfections of human body and spirit must be forgiven by those to whom such expiation belongs: the next generation. The daughter-speaker outlives her father, and in order to continue living, she must forgive, just as Christ, whose birth Christmas celebrates, is forgiveness embodied.

Forgiven or not, the father continues to exert his influence over the daughter in "Old Dwarf Heart." The heart learned too much when the speaker's parents died, and it cannot forget, even if it has forgiven:

> When I lie down to love,
> old dwarf heart shakes her head.
> Like an imbecile she was born old.
> Her eyes wobble as thirty-one thick folds
> of skin open to glare at me on my flickering bed.
> She knows the decay we're made of.

The heart "knows" such things not only through the agency of death; rather, it is *in her nature* to know: she was "born old," because she is essentially a reincarnation rather than a new being:

> . . . Old ornament, old naked fist,
> even if I put on seventy coats I could not cover you . . .
> mother, father, I'm made of.

Deterministic? Yes. True enough of the human heart? Probably.

The second section of *All My Pretty Ones* is preceded by a Guardini epigraph: "I want no pallid humanitarianism—If Christ be not God, I want none of him; I will hack my way through existence alone." Here Sexton explores this other and related betrayal: that God is, after all, only the mortal father whose child inherits his weakness, which ends in her own death. The grandfather enters as mediator of this process in the final poem of the volume, "Letter Written during a January Northeaster," in which the speaker is alone, awaiting letters from a lover that never come. The poem begins on a Monday, with snow falling upon "the small faces of the dead," in particular the mother and father. Divided into six days, the poem is an elaborate pretense: "I have invented a lie./There is no other day but Monday." By this narrative device the poet emphasizes the repetition enacted in time, the stasis underlying movement. The letters do not come:

> Dearest,
> where are your letters?
> The mailman is an impostor.
> He is actually my grandfather.
> He floats far off in the storm
> with his nicotine mustache and a bagful of nickels.

Tenderly evoking the grandfather to whom Sexton dedicates the last section of poems in this volume, the speaker reveals the identity not only of the mailman but of the letter, the word, as mediator between the present beloved (who is absent) and the past beloveds (who are dead). "Now he is gone/as you are gone." The grandfather, too, is dead; the lover is absent and in his absence as good as dead; and the mailman who should have brought the lovers together through the efficacy of words has proved an impostor. But he, grandfather-mailman, "belongs to me like lost baggage." The simile is especially appropriate, for it suggests the mobility not only of the lover but of the speaker, who has traveled through a week in which time has artificially stood still because of the storm that makes her environment appear identical from day to day. Constructing the fiction that time has stood still, she is free to find her comfort in another kind of travel, in her memory of a grandfather who always came with a bagful of nickels. As the mailman recedes into the storm, so does the figure of that grandfather; unlike the mailman, and like the lover, he belongs to her in the same way that lost baggage still belongs to its owner. "Letter Written" establishes the virtual identifications of its imagined components: of one day with the next, of the present lost lover with the dead grandfather.

The identification of a woman's husband with her father remains implicit in the first two volumes, where it is hinted at, leapt beyond, or discussed at one remove through mythology, anthropology, or the buffer of an extra generation. In *Live or Die,* Sexton's third volume, that identification is made explicit for the first time. The speaker's father was "a born salesman" who sold wool and a born talker "in love with maps," who "died on the road." Her husband also sells wool, also travels on the road:

> And when you drive off, my darling,
> Yes, sir! Yes, sir! It's one for my dame,
> your sample cases branded with my father's name,

> your itinerary open,
> its tolls ticking and greedy,
> its highways built up like new loves, raw and speedy.

This is a world where women stand and wait—"I sit at my desk/each night with no place to go"—while men explore and conquer, "greedy" for the open road and all it represents: freedom, independence, possession, the familiarly "raw and speedy" litany. The salesman father and husband of Sexton's real life symbolize a cultural axiom she would later explore in *Transformations,* where the fairy-tale world is one of masculine and feminine principles meeting and conflicting. The man brings home "one for his dame," who sits and waits while he conquers a world in which the highway inflicted on the countryside is the equivalent of the penis entering the body of nature—always a woman's body. The "new loves" allude to the infidelity inherent not only literally in the salesman's life but figuratively in the desertion of the wife or daughter for that new love, the road that is always open, offering adventure.

In "Mother and Jack and the Rain," a child speaker becomes the daughter figure of "One for My Dame," in which the woman was both wife and daughter. The speaker

> went to bed like a horse to its stall,
>
> . . . .
>
> and heard father kiss me through the wall
> and heard mother's heart pump like the tides.
> The fog horn flattened the sea into leather.
> I made no voyages, I owned no passport.
> I was the daughter. Whiskey fortified
> my father in the next room. He outlasted the weather,
> counted his booty and brought
> his ship into port.

Rain is here the replacement for the snow in "Letter Written." (The sexual encounters of Sexton's fathers and daughters take place in a medium of fluid or fire or music or flight.) Sexton continues the mercantile motif of "One for My Dame," this time in a portrayal of an unseen, but vicariously felt, primal scene. Identifying with the mother, the daughter feels the father's kiss and inhabits the mother's heart that pumps "like the tides," the final destiny of rain. Once again, woman is the medium for man's journeying, the water buoying his ship. The wry metaphor of shipping brings an unlikely note of humor to the scene of parental intercourse, in which the sailor's booty is the mother's body.

The sexual act is one of conquering and possession, as "raw and speedy" as the highways of "One for My Dame."

In the third stanza the speaker is a ripe sixteen, and the father has been replaced by a boy named Jack, with whom she remains as technically virginal as she was in the vicariously imagined intercourse with her father. Again it is raining, and again woman is water, now a "blind lake" instead of the sea that was her mother. "All that sweet night we rode out/the storm back to back." In the final stanza the speaker is restored to her womanhood, her mother is dead, and Jack has become a priest. "Mother and Jack fill up heaven; they endorse/my womanhood." Jack, potential lover, has become a father-priest, safely desexualized, a stand-in for the father whom she will also never win as lover, yet in whose imagined arms she fantasizes herself in memory.

The Father of "Cripples and Other Stories" emerges as doctor once again, taking up where he left off in *Bedlam*. Responding to his laughter at a "silly rhyme" she wrote for him ("Each time I give lectures/or gather in the grants/you send me off to boarding school/in training pants"), she insists in sing-song rhyme that he and she both look at the facts:

> God damn it, father-doctor.
> I'm really thirty-six.
> I see dead rats in the toilet.
> I'm one of the lunatics.

The poem moves through childhood rituals that revolve around the speaker's mother and father. The child puts her hand through the wringer-washer. "I put it in the Easy Wringer./It came out nice and flat." The indignities of childhood are remembered with a humor both gentle and bitter. In response to the washing-machine accident, "My father took the crowbar/and broke that wringer's heart." Yet even if he was her champion here, he is usually indifferent, "fat on scotch," which "leaked from every orifice," or a "perfect man,/clean and rich and fat," intent only on making money and smoking cigars. The doctor is the father's surrogate, but, unlike the father who "didn't know me," he responds on her behalf with tenderness instead of rage: "How strange that you're so tender!" At the end she drops the "doctor" of the original address:

> Father, I'm thirty-six,
> yet I lie here in your crib.
> I'm getting born again, Adam,
> as you prod me with your rib.

The same process, that of rebirth through psychoanalytic therapy, of starting over and getting this time around a father who holds and kisses and is loving to her in her "fever," might be merely sentimental or silly if it were not for Sexton's choice of rhyme and meter. In carefully wrought tetrameter and trimeter lines, Sexton both exemplifies and parodies the process of therapy, through which the analysand becomes again a child responding to her parents. The process, and the poem, are thus tinged with a gentle, wry irony. Can it really work, this process? Phyllis Chesler asks the same question in *Women and Madness,* as part of her discussion of the infantilization of women in the therapeutic process: "Can a technique based on transference, or on the resolution of an Oedipal conflict—i.e., on a romanticization of a rape-incest-procreative model of sexuality—wean women away from this very sexual model?"[5]

The poet does not answer such polemical questions—that is not her role as she perceives it—but the tonal complexities of this "nursery rhyme" suggest her knowledge of the difficulties as well as of the dynamics involved. Although I think we are meant to see the doctor's tenderness (he kisses and holds her in the poem) as properly humane rather than prurient in intent, there is something comically prurient in the very process Sexton describes: a grown woman first put in training pants by her doctor, then kept in a crib, and finally, in the regressive evolution of both the method and the poem, being reborn—all in the cadences of "This Little Piggy." And while I think Sexton's poem vindicates rather than damns the doctor's motivations, there is also no escaping the sexual overtones of the final line, in which the doctor, a new Adam, "prods" her with his "rib," corresponding neatly with Chesler's rape-incest-procreative description of psycho-analysis's modus operandi. This is particularly so since we are left with the image of a passive infant female being sexually assaulted (with whatever ostensibly benign motivation or effect) by an adult male doctor's prodding rib—or, in the illuminating vernacular, his pushy cock.

Sexton neither endorses nor damns the method here but merely subjects it to an interested and insightful scrutiny. The tone of the poem suggests that she is benefiting from this process of rebirth in which she reenacts a traumatic childhood "in your crib" and receives the love from the doctor that she was denied by his prototype, the father. The doctor may be able to bring to life the primal and potentially strong woman of the speaker's unconscious depths, and she accords him and his method this accession; but she is also suspicious, ironic, detached, and a bit alarmed both at herself and at the method that seems to deny that she is "really thirty-six." Yet, thirty-six or not, if she sees "dead rats in the toilet," she needs help. And if her father is one of those dead rats, beyond either saving or damning her himself, then perhaps, she seems to say, she needs this second chance. She needs the mediation of the doctor as Father and Adam and God, in her effort to get the rats out of the toilet.

"What Voyage This, Little Girl?": *The Transformations of Daddy*

While the father of *Love Poems* is almost entirely subsumed by the lover's transmutation into the carpenter-god (see chapter 3, "The Zeal of Her House"), he returns in *Transformations* in differently transmuted form. It was indeed at this point in her career that Sexton first and most deliberately broke free of the confines of autobiography in order to explore cultural myth, yet I see *Transformations* at least as much in terms of continuity as of departure. The old themes are all here, even if in new guise: the dynamics of relationships between men and women, mothers and daughters, fathers and daughters, "gods" and mortals, madness and sanity, conscious and unconscious—these are the subjects of *Transformations,* as they were of previous volumes. If Sexton had "one story and one story only," as Robert Graves says of his own in "To Juan at the Winter Solstice," then Sexton's was spacious enough to accommodate many metamorphoses, many "transformations."

The part of that story in which fathers and daughters figure is here, no less and no more clearly than it was in *Bedlam,* than it would be in *Words for Dr. Y.* The hearts of the passive princesses and daughters of *Transformations* are bonded as surely to the "mother, father, I'm made of" as are Sexton's early speakers. In "Snow White," "Cinderella," "Red Riding Hood," "The Maiden without Hands," "The Twelve Dancing Princesses," and "Briar Rose," fathers and mothers save or thwart or damn or damage or love or devour their mythic offspring in both literal and surrogate capacities. Most of the tales begin at home, with the heroes and heroines in domestic peril or at domestic peace; similarly, most of the tales end with either restoration or transformation of that domesticity. The lovers who marry the girls and women of most of the tales I mention above are barely disguised protector figures who take their new wives home to live together in infinitely protracted patriarchal bliss. Because it most directly and sardonically addresses the subject, I will deal here with "Briar Rose."

In the prologue Sexton introduces us to a "little doll child":

> Come here to Papa.
> Sit on my knee.
> I have kisses for the back of your neck.
> A penny for your thoughts, Princess.
> I will hunt them like an emerald.
> Come be my snooky
> and I will give you a root.

The tale Sexton has transformed here tells us only that the king dearly loved his child and that, because of this love and the fairy's curse, he overprotected her—a circumstance that, with or without a fairy's curse, is common enough to be normative in our culture. In her version of "Briar Rose," Sexton plays out the effects of such smothering and overprotective love on the part of fathers for the "purity" and "safety" of their daughters—effects also sufficiently common to be normative. Briar Rose manages to get in trouble despite her father's obsessive restrictions on her activities; in due course she pricks her finger on the spinning wheel and falls asleep. The prince who finally gets through the briars to wake her up gets a greeting not included in Grimm:

> He kissed Briar Rose
> and she woke up crying:
> Daddy! Daddy!

Since "Daddy" is the only man she has ever been permitted to know, the single source of love and safety, the prince is her daddy for life. The only hitch is that she has become an insomniac because of her fear of sleep—her long sleep was initiated, it is probably important to remember, by her father's omission of the proprieties; he did not propitiate the proper female deities by recognizing the thirteenth fairy. When Briar Rose sleeps, she returns to a kind of death-in-life. "You could lay her in a grave, . . . and she'd never call back: Hello there!" Only the kiss can wake her when she gets this way, so the prince is forced to wake her always in a repetition of that initial awakening:

> But if you kissed her on the mouth
> her eyes would spring open
> and she'd call out: Daddy! Daddy!

Presto!
She's out of prison.

Permanently infantilized by her earlier relationship to an idolatrously
loving father and a long and symbolic sleep in which no other men could
come near her, she is never quite a woman, always a daughter and a child.

In a rhetorical move uncharacteristic of the other "transformations"
here, which have only prologues, Sexton appends an epilogue to the tale
of Briar Rose. The identity of the speaker is ambiguous; because of an
abrupt tone shift and a sudden change from third to first person, we
cannot be sure if the "I" of the epilogue is Briar Rose or "Dame Sexton."
The speaker tells us that "there was a theft," and "I was abandoned" and
"forced backward." The closing of the poem also constitutes the end of
the book:

> Each night I am nailed into place
> and I forget who I am.
> Daddy?
> That's another kind of prison.
> It's not the prince at all,
> but my father
> drunkenly bent over my bed,
> circling the abyss like a shark,
> my father thick upon me
> like some sleeping jellyfish.
> What voyage this, little girl?
> This coming out of prison?
> God help—
> this life after death?

The tone change is remarkably abrupt and complete. Throughout the
tale Sexton has maintained that tongue-in-cheek tone so characteristic
of *Transformations,* in which deadly serious matter is relieved by casual
and sardonic wit. The seductive father of the prologue—"Come be my
snooky/and I will give you a root"—is both doting daddy and dirty old
man, and for him we are invited to feel an affectionately dismissive
contempt. But the father of the prologue is a daylight daddy, a bringer of
lollipops as well as that vaguely threatening "root." At only one moment
does he appear truly sinister: "A penny for your thoughts, Princess./I
will hunt them like an emerald." But the father of the epilogue comes to
the daughter at night, "circling the abyss like a shark." This is the flip
side of the daddy who bounces her on the knee, just as this new

perspective is the flip side of the daughter's irresistible seduction when she awakes: "Daddy!" If the body of the tale gives us the way in which the incestuous romance of father and daughter is carried *by the daughter* to her husband's bed, the epilogue is a sinister echo of the genesis of that behavior in the prologue. While Sexton is not afraid to acknowledge the daughter's part in the sexual drama of father and daughter, neither is she reticent to insist that the father be held responsible for its most exploitive and darkest form in the actual seduction or rape of daughters by their fathers.

We know from other sources that Anne Sexton was an insomniac and that her intensely ambivalent relationship to her father, Ralph Harvey, may have included such a "midnight visit," as she calls it elsewhere. (Middlebrook's biography will undoubtedly clarify the ambiguity, if not entirely resolve it.) In view of these circumstances and the internal evidence of the poem, I think it safe to say that the speaker of the final words in *Transformations* is a conflation of the mythical Briar Rose and the poet Anne Sexton. If the speaker of "Mother and Jack and the Rain" is also Sexton, we have both sides of a story Anne Sexton knew to be not only her own but that of countless American women: fantasized seduction in which the daughter not only participates, but that she initiates in the close private recesses of her own bed and her own body, accompanied by actual seduction that becomes the source of lifelong trauma for the daughter. Certainly the normal female child might dream of romantic love with her father, of bearing him a baby, of replacing her mother; and just as certainly, when the father makes that dream come true, the daughter is betrayed. As Chesler says, in patriarchal society the father-daughter incest taboo is "*psychologically* obeyed by men and disobeyed by women."[6] Although Chesler does not expand on this, I take her to mean something such as this: a female child, because of the stages of her psychosocial development, is nearly compelled to desire the father, while the male is not compelled to desire the daughter by that same process; rather, he will desire, and possibly find, the mother. But the *actual* disobedience of the taboo is usually initiated by the father, who is not only older, more powerful, and in a position of authority, but who is also—and this is probably crucial—a male member of a patriarchy. (The incidence of mother-son seduction is comparatively minor.) "What voyage this, little girl?" After the shark circles her in the dark, after the jellyfish is thick upon her, she will always awake crying, in more ways than one, "Daddy!"

"The Lost Signalman" and "The Train That Comes No More": The Death of the Fathers

Nothing for it but to put the father to death, and that is what Sexton does, mournfully and lovingly, in the sequence titled "The Death of the Fathers" in *The Book of Folly*. The death of the fathers marks the passage from innocence to experience for the daughter. The sea is always feminine in Sexton's poetry, but I have said that father-daughter rituals, especially those tinged with sexuality, take place in mediums usually fluid, although sometimes also in music, fire, or flight. In this sequence we find all of these motifs, echoed from earlier poems such as "The Bells" and "Mother and Jack and the Rain." In "Oysters" a simple seafood meal between father and daughter becomes her rite of passage into womanhood.

Through eating oysters for the first time—which, despite or because of their source in the sea, the speaker calls "father-food"—the speaker incorporates and conquers the sea in herself:

> Oysters we ate,
> sweet blue babies,
>
> . . . .
>
> It was a soft medicine
> that came from the sea into my mouth,
> moist and plump.
> I swallowed.

While the daughter makes her first attempts to get them down, her father laughs at her fear and drinks his martini, "clear as tears." This laughter, fatherly and benign, is tinged with friendly ridicule of her fear; but the clear tears of his martini reflect, perhaps, his own disguised sorrow at the ritual into which he knows he initiates his daughter. The challenge to her to eat something soft, moist, plump, and alien, which she must swallow in order to pass a test, hovers on the border between sensuality and sexuality; this might as easily be a description of fellatio as of eating oysters.

> Then I laughed and then we laughed
> and let me take note—
> there was a death,
> the death of childhood
> there at the Union Oyster House
> for I was fifteen
> and eating oysters

and the child was defeated.
The woman won.

The woman becomes she who devours and incorporates the sea creature, the alien thing that is herself. It is particularly significant that the father, alone and without the mother, escorts the speaker through this ritual while he drinks his martini, surely another father-food, surely another sexual signal. The laughter between them is canny; alone together, sans mother or siblings, father and daughter have their sweet and slightly wicked tête-à-tête. The unspoken understanding between them, one the poem itself articulates, is that the father has introduced his daughter not only to adulthood but to the sexual ripeness of womanhood.

Yet this celebration of sexuality with the father, this triumph he shares with her, is also a defeat for him: "Oysters" marks one of his "deaths." By initiating her into womanhood, the father relinquishes his exclusive hold on her affections; and relinquishing the daughter-child status by which she has belonged only to him, she comes into her own. The event they celebrate together is his demise as the only lover in her life. Through this mediation from the sea, he hands her to her woman-hood, and thereby to other men who will take his place.

But not entirely. In "How We Danced" the dramatic situation is a family wedding. The speaker was nineteen, dancing with her father as man and woman rather than as father and daughter. They danced "like two birds on fire," and "we were dear,/very dear."

> Mother was a belle and danced with twenty men.
> You danced with me never saying a word.
> Instead the serpent spoke as you held me close.
> The serpent, that mocker, woke up and pressed against me
> like a great god and we bent together
> like two lonely swans.

The mother in this Oedipal scenario is conveniently out of the way, dancing with other men as her husband and daughter perform a wedding dance that is both reflection and parody of the actual wedding. The father's penis "speaks" what he does not, disregarding propriety and taboo, mocking both a cultural and a personal contract. His penis is godlike because in the mythic world invoked here, incest is the paradigm, not the deviation. Irrevocably joined in their unspoken and by now implicitly mutual sin, father and daughter do not acknowledge the silent speech between them. Again, something dies; "How We Danced" is the swan song of a fiction of sexless familial love, a demise that by the end of the poem compels the daughter's complicity. His "death" is his diminishment as "father," accompanied by his phoenixlike rebirth as the lover that he has always been, even if secretly, to his daughter. But the serpent is indeed a mocker, for the involuntary physical sign of his sexual desire constitutes a betrayal of his daughter *as daughter*, a betrayal of himself *as father*.

We are back to the sea in "The Boat," in which mother, father, and child are riding too fast in a speedboat on a rough sea. They go "Under. Under. Under." The father cries, "Give me a sign," and "the sky breaks over us." The three of them are left "dividing our deaths" and "closing out/the cold wing." The father is supposed to be responsible, almost to the point of infallibility; so we characterize him in our culture, and so he characterizes himself. But here he proves careless and foolhardy, risking himself and his family for a thrill of speed much like the one he risks on the highway through his surrogate, the husband, in "One for My Dame." The infallible father of childhood is helpless in the angry sea, the paradigmatically feminine force he tries to control but is here controlled by. He must ask for a sign, beg for mercy, because the sea-mother has told him he "has no business here." His actions constitute yet another betrayal, and not only that of carelessness or risk; the possibility of untimely death foreshadows his later, actual death, the one that cannot be bargained back and that constitutes the final desertion of his daughter.

In "Santa" the speaker remembers father dressing up as Santa Claus, another all-giving father, in the yearly Christmas scenario. "The year I ceased to believe in you/is the year you were drunk." That ends the family's ritual temporarily, until the father once again dons his ridiculous suit to play Santa for grandchildren. When the speaker was a child, the mother "would kiss you/for she was that tall." When the father plays grandfather, he and his daughter again become

> conspirators,
> secret actors,
> and I kissed you
> because I was tall enough.

Playing Santa is another in the series of kindly lies that separate children from adults and make mythology of family, and sanity of familial madness. "But that is over." The daughter has replaced the mother, and now father-Santa is dead:

> And you, you fade out of sight
> like a lost signalman
> wagging his lantern
> for the train that comes no more.

The father joins dead hands with the grandfather-mailman of "Letter Written" in *All My Pretty Ones*. The mailman with his "bagful of nickels" and the train signalman are both representatives of a life that is past, that passes even as it is lived.

In "Friends" and "Begat" the speaker addresses a universal fear of all children about fatherhood. These paired poems dramatize the fear that one's father is not, after all, one's father, that we shall all be declared "illegitimate at last," freeing us of inherited fear and robbing us of inherited right. "Oh Father, Father,/who was that stranger/who knew Mother too well?" The stranger declares, "I am your real father." Addressing the voice that cannot answer, and could not know the truth if he were alive, the speaker pleads, "Oh God,/he was a stranger,/was he not?" The speaker rejects this new father and turns back to the "old dead thing" who "is my history." Father and mother are evoked in familial embrace once again:

> And they kissed until I turned away.
> Sometimes even I came into the royal ring
> and those times he ate my heart in half
>
> . . . .
>
> Red. Red. Father, you are blood red.
> Father,
> we are two birds on fire.

In "Old Dwarf Heart" (*All My Pretty Ones*), the heart of the poet is the "mother, father, I'm made of"; here the father's love incorporates half of the heart, and through that incorporation the self is both wounded and made to live. To lose one's father is to lose half of one's self—"to take the *you* out of *me*"—and to be devoured by the father is also both to lose and find oneself. Blood is the final tie, the medium of inheritance and disinheritance. Father and daughter reunited in the lament for his death and displacement in her life become a union of fire and blood, in which the two are once again the fiery birds of "How We Danced." In the very process of reclamation of his seed in her, the speaker kills the father once again, for his death is reenacted in the question of her legitimacy.

"The Death of the Fathers" marks a series of broken taboos through which the poet rejects, reclaims, is rejected by, and reclaimed by the fathers of her life. The deaths are plural because there are many small deaths before the large and literal one represented in the poet's life by Ralph Harvey's death; and the fathers are many because, as Sexton knew, her speaker claimed and rejected that paternal presence in many guises: father, grandfather, doctor, priest, God. I think Sexton also intended a double plurality of deaths and fathers to signify the culturally representative nature of her own biography; just as Ralph Harvey was not her only father, and just as he and his surrogates were to undergo many symbolic deaths in her life, there are many Annes among her readership, each with her own several fathers and multiple deaths.

"Divorcing Daddy: Dybbuk! Dybbuk!": *45 Mercy Street*

The final father poems in Sexton's canon are more than presentationally or chronologically final, for they unite the father-husband motif in the severance of the marriage contract. The culmination of woman's marriage to her father is also the ultimate divorce: the divorce of oneself from childhood, the end of the Oedipal struggle. In *45 Mercy Street* the dance of "two birds on fire" from *The Book of Folly* echoes sadly in the speaker's solitary "Wedding Ring Dance," in which she pulls off the engagement and wedding ring of her marriage to the husband of twenty-five years. Performing "the undoing dance," she knows she is

> letting my history rip itself off me
> and stepping into
> something unknown
> and transparent. . . .

Directly after " 'Daddy' Warbucks," a eulogy "In Memoriam" to that comic strip character spoken in the voice of her surrogate, orphan Annie, Sexton says her final published words on the father in the poem I mentioned briefly in chapter 1, "Divorce, Thy Name Is Woman." The speaker tries to break that archaic and infantile tie at last, by acknowledging the marriage bond with and the divorce from her husband:

> I am divorcing daddy—Dybbuk! Dybbuk!
> I have been doing it daily all my life
> since his sperm left him. . . .

The speaker is all women who enact the paradigmatic relationship Sexton first explored in mythic terms in *To Bedlam and Part Way Back*. The dybbuk becomes a concretion of the mythic and the personal. The dybbuk, in medieval Jewish legend, may be either the spirit of a dead person who lives and speaks through a living human or a demon that possesses the living; here it is both. The spirit of the father is that of the dear dead, whom the speaker always remembers as Macduff remembers his slain wife and children; but he is also the demon who possesses the living in order to dispossess her of herself. We turn to the dead, to memory, as individuals and as a culture, for identity and meaning. It is clear that Sexton thought we have no choice in this matter, that we piece together a sense of self out of the inheritance of family, enlarged into an inheritance of culture.

But while the legacy of the dead provides us with a raison d'être and represents our own urge to propel ourselves into the future through the immortality of generations, it also represents the death wish, the urge to annihilate oneself, to follow the dead to what Sexton called their stone boats. In a woman the paradox is apparent in the relationship to the father, who may be succeeded by a reincarnation of himself in the husband. A woman can spend her life, in effect, divorcing and marrying her father. She appears to have little choice in this, for she normally tends to search out her father to marry and will likely reenact not only the positive aspects of that legacy but the negative ones as well. In this poem Sexton constructs a kind of allegory for woman in Western culture. The marriage of daughter to father is literal.

> Later,
> when blood and eggs and breasts
> dropped onto me,
> Daddy and his whiskey breath
> made a long midnight visit
> in a dream that is not a dream
> and then called his lawyer quickly.
> Daddy divorcing me.

The "dream that is not a dream" is a psychic fact, a fact of mental life, something that "actually happens" in the netherland of unconscious primary process. The father seduces the daughter, then rejects her, disowning his own passion and hers. "I have been divorcing him ever since" in the interior world of psychic realities, where Mother is her witness in the courtroom. The daughter keeps on divorcing him, "adding up the crimes/of how he came to me,/how he left me." Sexton's speaker takes on the voice of any woman working out her childhood love for her father, any woman still "waiting for Daddy to come home/and stuff me so full of our infected child/that I turn invisible, but married,/at last."

To be born a woman in a patriarchy is often to be compelled to live out precisely this ritual. The maternal urge becomes a parody of its first manifestation in the desire to present the father with a child. This, in the tortured psychic world of the poem, is the only true marriage; all others are only pale and inadequate reflections of this primal union. To marry one's father is, indeed, to "turn invisible," for it means that the daughter becomes not herself, not her mother, but an inverted parody of herself *and* her mother, of wife *and* daughter. Acknowledging the incestuous foundations of romantic love on which not only the family but all Western culture is based, Sexton exposes the underbelly of the myth—that we are all the infected child of incest, that we all become invisible, effaced, in the need to "marry." Marriage is the sanctification of incest, the sacred profanity whose nature we expend our sublimated energies denying. We are all possessed by the dybbuks of our personal and cultural pasts. What Sexton speaks of here is as narrow as the room of each womb we come from, and as broad as our dedication to classical culture. We are all implicated, fathers and daughters alike, all dwelling in a shadow world in which the realities we perceive are shadows of original forms—and of original desires. We stay in the cave willingly, perceiving reflected forms, because we cannot look upon those forms directly without becoming "invisible." Yet we seek that original form, that original desire, never quite content with its substitute.

While Sexton breaks this ultimate taboo, thereby acknowledging her self-effacement, her speaker also wants to affirm the divorce. The "solution" of the poem is a continual process of divorce, an unending courtroom scene, but one that always returns from courtroom to bedroom, where the woman is "opening and shutting the windows./Making the bed and pulling it apart." Before and after the divorce of man and wife is this continuous marriage to and divorce from the father, a permanent oscillation between two conflicting desires: to divorce and be done with and to "marry, at last."

"The Island of God": *The Death Notebooks, The Awful Rowing*

Although the father is entirely absent from *The Awful Rowing toward God* as a literal and familial presence, this entire collection has been accurately described as a monument to Anne Sexton's need for a God who is the embodiment of paternal authority, absolutism, and absolution; a God who will punish the "gnawing, pestilential rat" inside of her and then "take it with his two hands/and embrace it" ("Rowing"); a God who will finally guarantee her that immortality will be the replication, eternal and writ large, of a perfected and idealized family circle in which she will at last win the love and acceptance and protection and approval denied her by her parents. This heavenly family will be presided over by a benevolent but exacting Papa who will consume manna instead of whiskey, punish her justly instead of capriciously, and love her unconditionally instead of sporadically. Maxine Kumin calls this God of Sexton's deepest desires "a sure thing, an Old Testament avenger admonishing his Chosen People, an authoritarian yet forgiving Father decked out in sacrament and ceremony."[7] To Alicia Ostriker, the poet's attempt to "give imaginative birth to an adequate Godhead" becomes a "heroic failure," because the "decisive intelligence which dismantles religious myth is no match for the child-woman's ferocious need for cosmic love."[8] Estella Lauter finds that the "essential drama of her work in these years (1970–1974) lies in her repeated discoveries of the Father-God's inadequacy coupled with her inability to give him up."[9]

Before I regret the pathetic end of Anne Sexton's quest for the Father, I must remind myself of two equally important facts, one about Anne Sexton, one about the culture of which she is both member and visionary. First, and most humbling, is that Sexton's search for the traditional Father-God in dozens of poems that may be failures in the feminist sense is an eloquent representation of an entire culture's quest for that same God. The loving and admonishing Father for whom she searches is the Father for whom we have all searched. We have all sought his blessing, tried to conjure up his presence in times of crisis if not of ease. Even those of us who have rejected him outright in favor of no gods at all—or of gods that offend our sensibilities less, match our politics or gender better, or seem to us truer, more imaginative—catch ourselves wishing, or fearing, that he might exist. Sexton's failing Father-God is, in short, our own; I cannot see how it could be otherwise in a patriarchy as old and enduring as ours. The idea of such a God is not original or rehabilitating or appealing, except to those instincts that are conservative, repetitive, and fearful. But to deny his vestigial hold on us is to declare pridefully that we are not, at whatever seemingly safe remove, influenced by the conservative, the repetitive, the fearful. Who has not been "in this country of black mud," longing for that God through whom one could be "born again/into something true?"

Second, and more important, the poet who needs to be beaten by God in that final poker game is the same one who dreams she can "piss in God's eye" ("Hurry Up Please It's Time," *The Death Notebooks*). She is, as Ostriker and Lauter explain, the poet who dismantles religious myth and reimagines Christianity in the most daring ways. She undertakes to rewrite Genesis, the Psalms, and, most radically, the gospels. She is among the most original and radical of religious poets in our literary and spiritual heritage.

With this reservation in mind, I participate in regretting the imaginatively small and fraudulent God Sexton asked herself and her readers to settle for at the end of *The Awful Rowing toward God*. In *The Death Notebooks* the God she searched out was still pluralistic, still appealingly heathen and varied. "Mrs. Sexton went out looking for the gods" in the first poem of *The Death Notebooks*, in lowercase plural. Even *The Awful Rowing* finds God in the "chapel of eggs" with "the absurdities of the dinner table," sometimes "dressed up like a whore" or an old man or a child. He "lives in shit" and beans and butter and milk, in the poet's typewriter, in "the private holiness of my hands." It is, I think, primarily the final poem in the collection that so disturbs readers and critics. It disturbs me in more than one way: I know why her God is a man. But why is he an island?

In "The Rowing Endeth" God has diminished back into the father of "Oysters," who laughs as he drinks his martini and presides over a ritual of defeat as well as triumph for the speaker-poet. While "Oysters" may seem an oddly minor poem in thematic concerns compared with "The Rowing Endeth"—after all, one is about eating oysters for the first time, and one is about rowing to the island of God for salvation—they are similar in situation, tone, even in language. Listen to the central scene in both: In "Oysters" the father is laughing at and with the daughter as she gags down her first oysters and he drinks his martini— "Then I laughed and we laughed." We leave them laughing, celebrating "the death of childhood" and the speaker's rebirth into womanhood. In "The Rowing Endeth" God wins the poker game, probably by cheating:

> He starts to laugh,
> the laughter rolling like a hoop out of His mouth
> and into mine
> and such laughter that He doubles right over me
> laughing a Rejoice-Chorus at our two triumphs.

In both cases the triumph for the daughter-poet—rebirth into womanhood, rebirth into salvation—is presided over by a father figure who has the edge over the speaker. He is bigger, older, wiser, and male. He enjoys his power over her, and she enjoys it with him. In "The Rowing Endeth," as in "Oysters," the speaker is initiated into mysteries, made privy to secrets, included, endorsed, approved of, and loved. Yet in both scenarios there is no question of who enjoys the power. Reading both poems, I feel the edge of sexual humiliation through seduction, the kind felt by a girl who is told a dirty joke by an older man; she laughs, uncomfortably and too loud, half understanding the joke, half knowing that it is directed at her. Here, as in "The Death Baby" (*The Death Notebooks*), such "love" is both erotic and deathly, both the symbol of woman's self-assurance and of her self-annihilation. Her passionate responses enact both her wish to live and her wish to die. "You have seen my father whip me./You have seen me stroke my father's whip."

Just such an unsavory seduction takes place in an untitled 1965 poem from the posthumously published sequence of poem-letters to her psychiatrist in *Words for Dr. Y.* An unnamed male the speaker calls "Comfort" reads to the speaker, during her childhood, from the Bible, "to prove I was sinful":

> *For in the night he was betrayed.*
> And then he let me give him a Judas-kiss,
> that red lock that held us in place,
> and then I gave him a drink from my cup
> and he whispered, "Rape, rape."
> and then I gave him my wrist
> and he sucked on the blood,
> hating himself for it,
> murmuring, "God will see. God will see."

In this extraordinarily ambiguous seduction, the girl-child appears to initiate the ritual of blood that is both sexual and religious. But the dynamics of power are unmistakably on the side of the older male, who ironically whispers "rape" when, if there is such a thing going on, we know very well who is the victim. While the male ostensibly worries that "God will see" what they are doing, it is clear that he is playing the part of God himself, "allowing" himself to be betrayed by this Judas-child. It might be illuminating to know the identity of this male in the poet's biography, and to find it I turn to *All My Pretty Ones*, to the grandfather of the "bagful of nickels" in "Letter Written during a January Northeaster," to whom the final sequence of poems in that volume is dedicated: "For Comfort, who was actually my grandfather."

This seduction scene between granddaughter and grandfather is repeated in reverse form in the posthumously published "Leaves That Talk" in *45 Mercy Street*. (See chapter 8, "Leaves That Talk.")

> I dream it's the fourth of July
> and I'm having a love affair
> with grandfather (his real birthday)
>   . . . .
> and in my dream
> grandfather touches my neck and breast
> and says, "Do not be afraid!
> It's only the leaves falling!"

Here the grandfather is the initiator of sexual contact, and the process he interferes with is the suicide's conversation with her voices, the "green girls"—leaves that call her to "come to us" and die. His role here as "comforter" is compromised by his seduction of his granddaughter; if his comfort were merely paternal, we could be glad of his saving presence, which calls her away from the voices that urge her to die. But the fact that he "touches her breast" lends this scene the sinister aura of the dirty old man, whose motivations in urging her away from the feminine-suicidal to the masculine-sacrificial are highly suspect.

Sexton's grandfather is a minor character in the family drama that unfolds in Sexton's poetry during the eighteen years and ten volumes of her writing career, overshadowed as he is by the poet's mother, father, daughters, and great-aunt, Nana. Yet it is he, finally, who most clearly connects the God of *The Awful Rowing* and the father figures of the poet's personal life. Perhaps his title as "grand" father makes this connection appropriate, for what is a God in a patriarchy but a Grand Father? That he is also the person the child called "Comfort" is acutely apropos, for comfort is what she seeks from God. In "Grandfather, Your Wound" (*The Death Notebooks*), the speaker sits in a house on an "island" belonging to him:

> you are a ceiling made of wood
> and the island you were the man of,
> is shaped like a squirrel and named thereof.
> On this island, Grandfather, made of your stuff. . . .

Sexton the writer stands "in your writing room" in this poem, surrounded by his belongings and mourning the absence of "Mr. Funnyman, Mr. Nativeman, . . . Mr. Lectureman, Mr. Editor." Arthur Gray Staples was indeed a lecturer and writer, editor-in-chief of the

Lewiston Evening Journal (one of Maine's largest newspapers) and author of several books of essays. Squirrel Island was the summer home of seven five-story houses described in "Funnel" (*All My Pretty Ones*). Staples's writing room, setting for "Grandfather, Your Wound," was a spacious room with an ocean view.[10]

When Sexton moors her rowboat at the dock of the "island called God" at the end of *The Awful Rowing*, she is, I believe, mooring herself again at her beloved Squirrel Island. And "the flesh of The Island"—the flesh of God—is none other than her grandfather, that "ceiling made of wood" in "Your Wound." "I wouldn't mind if God were wooden," she writes in a peculiar and otherwise inexplicable line in "Is It True?"

> Oh wood, my father, my shelter,
> bless you.

And in *The Death Notebooks*, to receive "God's Backside," the "dark negative" turned against her, is cold, "like Grandfather's icehouse" ("God's Backside"). If we need any further indication that Grandfather is God, we find it in the closing of "Your Wound," when dead "Comfort" comes back, resurrected with the same appositive/expletive construction that closes "All My Pretty Ones":

> My God, Grandfather,
> you are here,
> you are laughing,
> you hold me and rock me
> and we watch the lighthouse come on,
> blinking its dry wings over us all,
> over my wound
> and yours.

The sun has gone down, but when he comes back to her, "it comes bright again." The unspecified "wound" of which he died is the flaw that she inherits, that she, too, will die of; but his presence, a resurrection from the dead, is the assurance that he lives to be her "comfort" once again—to tell her that she is sinful, to sin with her, to love her. He, perhaps alone among all her other familial gods, endorses her as a writer. (Mary Harvey, who once wanted to be a writer, inaugurated Anne's efforts with rejections and an accusation of plagiarism, while her father and husband, whose business was wool, were not able or likely to make her feel that such activity really qualified as "work.") The God "my typewriter believes in" ("The Frenzy," *Awful Rowing*) is her grandfather as writer as well as father. Elsewhere in *Awful Rowing* the typewriter is her "church," her "altar of keys." In her introduction to *The Complete Poems*, Maxine Kumin writes:

> An elderly, sympathetic priest she called on — "accosted" might be a better word — patiently explained that he could not make her a Catholic by fiat, nor could he administer the sacrament (the last rites) she longed for. But in his native wisdom he said a saving thing to her, said the magic and simple words that kept her alive at least a year beyond her time and made *The Awful Rowing Toward God* a possibility. "God is in your typewriter," he told her.[11]

"Your Wound" ends with the chillingly familiar scene of laughter between the daughter-poet and the father-God, but here the laughter seems genuinely mutual, truly benevolent. We may regret that in his metamorphosis from human grandfather to cosmic Grand Father, the male figure represented in this discussion by Arthur Gray Staples became such a sinister and fraudulent deity. It is difficult to "applaud" this "dearest dealer," as Sexton asks herself and us to do in "The Rowing Endeth." Doubling "right over me" in laughter, he is at least as much the circling shark and the "father thick upon me" like some "jellyfish" of "Briar Rose" as he is the benevolent "bagful of nickels" of "Letter Written," holding and rocking her as the lighthouse flashes on to illuminate the darkness. Yet what we *can* applaud is that, as Kumin says, the search for the God in her typewriter kept her going, inspired by an old priest who may have been reminiscent of her grandfather — and who certainly offered her "comfort" through affirming her worth as poet.

I find it poignant to discover that the "island of God" may have been the island of childhood where she summered, and where, as her editors remind us in the *Letters*, "Anne's happy memories centered."[12] I also confess that I find it beautiful; I contemplate that simplicity, that perfect circle of sought-after comfort, one that brings the middle-aged poet back to the finest moments of a troubled and unhappy past. Perhaps anyone's idea of heaven is some such journey into the past. Did Anne Sexton know that the island of God was Squirrel Island? This most psychoanalytic, most autobiographical, most naked of all contemporary poets did not say that she knew this, either in her letters or explicitly in the poems. It seems a strange omission, from one who was so willing to be explicit. But she was capable of the subtlest kinds of elusiveness, as all good poets are—"tell all the truth but tell it slant," as Dickinson put it. Whether or not she knew, she left us a wake through the water as she rowed to the island.

It is important to search out the biographical details that led the poet to characterize God as an island. But the biographical data beg the questions of what a metaphor is and why one chooses that metaphor over other symbolic possibilities. If, as Donne wrote, no man is an island, it is equally true that in our literary tradition no God is so clearly an island as was Anne Sexton's. The closest literary analogue is probably the lighthouse island in Virginia Woolf's *To the Lighthouse*, but it is not a near neighbor to Sexton's island of God. If we cannot ultimately know why Sexton chose the island metaphor, we can feel the waves of its implications.

The "mother, father, I'm made of" occupy, even constitute, the core of Sexton's poetry, and of what I would call her poetics. The quest for the father-god often appears to overwhelm the matriarchal deity whom Sexton searched out with equal diligence but could not as clearly name. To underscore the obvious: an island is a piece of land entirely surrounded by water. Sexton's patriarchal God, whose flesh is an island, is surrounded by the feminine and maternal medium through which she travels toward him. The waters are potentially lethal to both the daughter and the father-god, as they are in "The Boat"; they may also form themselves into the body of "The Consecrating Mother," without whom the father is himself without body.

Part II
That Dear Body

3
The Zeal of Her House

This little town, this little country is real
and thus it is so of the post and the cup
and thus of the violent heart. The zeal
of my house doth eat me up.

—"The Break," *Love Poems*

"I talk of the life/death cycle of the body," said Anne Sexton in an early interview.[1] Western culture has always expressed its ambivalence about the body in the anguished diction of dichotomy: humanity is immortal soul or rational mind or essential self, trapped in a mortal, mindless, decaying body. Sexton recognized that mind/body, soul/body, or self/body dichotomies symbolized the psychic fragmentation of her cultural and spiritual heritage. As both poet and product of her milieu, she eloquently articulated the schismatic view of the human body. Out of the anguish it caused her, she wrested many good poems, and several great ones. She was as eloquent a spokesperson for the unification of self and body as for their alienation—although, inevitably, her vision of unification remained nostalgic or wistful, projected more often than achieved.

Throughout Sexton's canon the physical body is a nexus for meaning and meaninglessness, for nurture and deprivation, for wholeness and fragmentation. Sexton portrays the body from three points of view, or in three voices that speak in harmony or discord, sometimes one at a time, sometimes all at once. The first "voice" is the woman's. "Women tell time by the body," she said. "They are always fastened to the earth, listening for its small animal noises."[2] The second voice is the suicide's. "Suicides have already betrayed the body," she wrote in "Wanting to Die" (*Live or Die*). She counted herself among them, a "stillborn" waiting for death to "so delicately undo an old wound,/to empty my breath from its bad prison." The self-destructive suicidal voice is at least superficially the negation or opposite of the third voice, which I call the maker. The maker's voice seeks unity, speaks in metaphors and images of wholeness, and uses the body as a symbol for that wholeness. In the late poems the maker's voice anthropomorphizes the universe and its forces in a quest for the embodied God. Ironically and appropriately, Sexton's spiritual quest is for the resurrected body.

"Fact: death too is in the egg" ("The Operation," *All My Pretty Ones*). For a poet so openly obsessed with mortality, the physical body is bound to be a source of violent ambivalence. The body decays and dies, but if there is a special something—call it soul, psyche, essence, self— then it might also be housed in the physical body, or better, it might *be* body. Although people seldom touch, "touch is all," Sexton writes in "Rowing" (*The Awful Rowing*). Complete human touch is a matter of body *and* "soul." The right ritual will set everything free. Thus, although the poet has "already betrayed the body," she turns to the body—her own, those of her parents, her lovers, her daughters, her gods—for salvation. Her speakers often live on deathbeds, waiting to die, wanting to be resurrected. Although the suicidal speaker, or the self-destructive aspect of the whole person who speaks, wants death, it is the deaths of others, all her pretty ones, that most terrify her. Sexton returns again and again to all the deathbeds, trying to raise the bodies and reclaim them from mortality in order to verify herself. People may live through their inheritors, as Sexton knew, but disembodied spirit or psyche is a tenuous immortality, notoriously difficult to reconcile with bodily absence. In a 1964 letter, she called the inheritor "what keeps us alive. That living thing we leave behind. That['s] the flame. But that the body should be gone, a piece of furniture only . . . that dear body. . . . "[3]

For the woman, "that dear body" is most poignantly the mother's. As Dorothy Dinnerstein detailed in *The Mermaid and the Minotaur*, the female in a mother-reared culture must face a complex crisis of guilt and loss when she transfers passionate affection from mother to father, from woman to man. Added to the sense of pervasive loss felt by both sexes is the need to do penance or, in Melanie Klein's terminology, to make reparation.[4] Sexton also identified with the mother's body, especially when she became mother herself. She recognized these patterns both symptomatically and mythically and explored their implications throughout her canon, from poems such as "The Double Image" and "The Division of Parts" in *To Bedlam and Part Way Back* through "The Angel Food Dogs" in *45 Mercy Street*. "A woman *is* her mother./That's the main thing" ("Housewife," *All My Pretty Ones*). The speaker of the early poems lives and relives the death of the mother's body, the slow bloating of "cancer's baby."

Mother-daughter relationships in Sexton incorporate the richness of the feminine heritage as well as the pain. Regenerative possibility is usually associated with the new womanly body, the reborn self, the emerging genitality of adolescence in daughters, the healing of old wounds in a new generation. Sexton is never simplistically optimistic, however. "I cannot promise very much./I give you the images I know" ("The Fortress," *All My Pretty Ones*). She is aware of the dangers and knows they are inevitable. "I look for uncomplicated hymns/but love has none" ("A Little Uncomplicated Hymn," *Live or Die*). Still, she encourages the daughter to accept and love her blooming body, to "strike fire/that new thing." Everything new in the body "is telling the truth." Growing into womanhood is itself a resurrection, for "women are born twice" ("Little Girl, My String Bean, My Lovely Woman," *Live or Die*). Anne Sexton knew intimately that her generation of mothers and daughters tended to be caught in a cycle of guilt and mutual recrimination, often dictated by patterns of behavior largely beyond their control and frequently beyond their knowledge. Her continuous poetic and personal effort was to reverse the process for her own daughters, for all the daughters, all the mothers. The mother-daughter poems in which she is daughter are painfully ambivalent, but the ones in which she speaks as mother attempt to establish bodily integrity, wholeness, and dignity.[5]

While the mother is the primary symbol of feminine bodiliness in Sexton's poetry, the male body is centrally symbolized by Christ and by the father in the early and middle poetry, through and including *The Book of Folly*. Until the late and posthumously published work, Sexton seldom evoked God the Father directly, but instead invoked the embodied God, the fellow traveler and "ragged brother." She portrayed Christ's Passion with overwhelming attention to physicality: "How desperately he wanted to pull his arms in!" ("With Mercy for the Greedy," *All My Pretty Ones*). Christ and the poet's mother suffer endlessly in the early volumes, perpetually on the cross and in the deathbed. But the constant return to the body clearly indicates Sexton's conviction that the most hopeful form of salvation is also bodily.

Sexton's hope for herself and for her poetic and personal inheritors was that she, that we, might learn to love the frail body, to be at home in it, and to shed it sensibly at the end. The body is a vile vessel in Sexton's poems—a prison, a madhouse, a box of dog bones, rotten meat—but it is also holy. Sexton yoked the clean and unclean, the profane and sacred, *through* the body. She continually and deliberately violated the ritual taboos of our culture in order to break down comfortable and limiting categories. She accomplished this by exploiting the body's potential for sacrificial defilement and holiness. Sometimes the result was an anomalous physical metaphor, like the "death baby" of *The Death Notebooks*. Sometimes it was an imagined transgression committed against strong taboos, such as "I dream I can piss in God's eye" ("Hurry Up Please," *The Death Notebooks*).

The project of representing in poetry a richly whole self that is at once bodily and psychic is immense. Sexton did not sustain it consistently. She frequently employed deliberately dichotomous language to express the dilemma of the mind/body problem: "I break out of my body this way" ("The Ballad of the Lonely Masturbator," *Love Poems*). "Fact: the body is dumb, the body is meat" ("The Operation," *All My Pretty Ones*). And the meat, fresh or rotten, is to be eaten: "All my need took/you down like a meal," her speaker writes to her mother. The reference is often far more horrific:

> One-legged I became and then
> you dragged me off by your Nazi hook.
> I was the piece of bad meat they made you carry.

> ("Eighteen Days without You, December 2nd," *Love Poems*)

Even Christ is meat, "frozen to his bones like a chunk of beef" ("With Mercy for the Greedy," *All My Pretty Ones*). It is Christ as fellow sufferer, as man-god, who often expresses Sexton's central concern with soul/body configurations, and especially with the potentially adversarial relationship of "self" to body:

> Surely my body is done? Surely I died?
> And yet, I know, I'm here. What place is this?
> Cold and queer, I sting with life. I lied.
> Yes, I lied. Or else in some damned cowardice
> my body would not give me up. . . .

> ("In the Deep Museum," *All My Pretty Ones*)

In the same poem Christ is meat for a hungry rat, whose consumption of the body will "correct the flaws" of the crucifixion and "keep the miracle" of resurrection: "His teeth test me; he waits like a good cook,/knowing his own ground."

Sexton invested oral incorporation with all the mythic resonance of its ritual roots. The infant's hunger at the mother's breast, both physical and emotional, is the source of pleasure and pain for both. Milk-hunger is transformed into meat-hunger and becomes ritual cannibalism. (See chapter 4, "Is It True?") Eating the enemy or the friend means taking on the strengths of the consumed person, and Sexton extended the possibilities of that act by connecting it to spiritual quest. The "rat" who gnaws at Christ's body is also the doubting quester who needs literally to "test" him, and Sexton identified herself with the rat.[6] The rat wants to incorporate Christ in order to be saved; Christ dies that he and humanity may be resurrected. Sexton wrung all possible meaning from the traditionally paradoxical diction of Christian eschatology: one must lose oneself to find oneself, die to live. At their most radical, Sexton's metaphors of consuming the other are transformed into consuming the self as a purge that simultaneously destroys and creates. In "The Sickness unto Death" (*The Awful Rowing*), the answer is found by turning toward the self, not away: "So I ate myself,/bite by bite."

These attitudes toward the body, violently ambivalent and painstakingly ambiguous, suggest that the "suicide" and the "maker" are not always negations of each other but are often rather more like Blake's contraries. Both voices desire deliverance, wholeness, and rebirth. The essential difference is in each voice's stance toward the body. The suicide distrusts and despises the body. Its voice is that of the terrible mother beyond the grave, who commands the living woman to die as penance for being born, for depleting the mother's body, for giving her cancer ("The Double Image," *Bedlam*). The deprivation leaves the adult woman hungry—hungry for an affirmative sense of femininity, hungry for absolution, and hungry for death. (The extremity is aberrant, of course, but the basic emotional pattern describes more mother-daughter scenarios than anyone might like to think.) In this sense, the suicide is genuinely self-destructive, genuinely at odds with the maker.

But in several other respects, Sexton was the acute analyst of connections between life and death, between sex and death, more ancient than poetry itself. In "Wanting to Die," the speaker explains the passion to "thrust all that life under your tongue!" (*Live or Die*). She speaks of "possessing" and "eating" the enemy, an enemy that is both life and death. Dying becomes a power game. If the result is nothingness—and that is sometimes the gamble, sometimes the reward—then perhaps the suicide loses. If there is life after death, then perhaps there is also resurrection of "that dear body," of whole self, not merely disembodied spirit. In Sexton's late poems the quest becomes acute, as the poet turns again and again to the body, knowing that "it is all a matter of touch," that God must be found "in the private holiness of your hands." A central goal of the suicide, then, is resurrection of the body after death; a central goal of the maker is resurrection of the body in *this* life.

The unity of body and psyche that underlies their duality, and the duality that underlies their unity, are illuminated by Sexton's use of house metaphors. Houses in Sexton are feminine places where mothers live, where daughters become wives and mothers, into which men enter as into an alien land. Rooms within houses are consistently imaged as parts of the female body; and that body, far from being always alien to the essential self, is deeply symbolic of that self. The identification of house with body is so complete that it becomes reversible. In "KE 6-8018" (*Live or Die*) the speaker equates the "center" of a familiar house with the heart of a known body:

> There will have been a house—
> a house that I knew,
> the center of it,
> a tiny heart. . . .

Perfecting the reversal, the house in "Housewife" (*All My Pretty Ones*) is a body with "a heart,/a mouth, a liver and bowel movements." In other poems such as "Menstruation at Forty" (*Live or Die*), the "place of the blood" is a "warm room" where the door is "open on its hinges." In the posthumous collection *45 Mercy Street,* the woman who "learned her own skin" became a "home" ("The Break Away"). Sexton described the opposite feeling as well, saying in a 1964 letter that "I am not at home in myself. I am my own stranger."[7] Similarly, her speaker in "Those Times . . . " (*Live or Die*) remembers the alienation of self and body that she—perhaps like most people in modern Western culture—has experienced since childhood:

> At six
> I lived in a graveyard full of dolls,
> avoiding myself,
> my body, the suspect
> in its grotesque house.

Grammatical ambiguity allows for the identification *and* the alienation of "myself" and "my body." Whoever "the suspect" is, she cannot get out of her "house."

The most complex metaphorical pattern for house and body is established in "The Break," published in *Love Poems.* Of all of Sexton's collections, *Love Poems* concerns itself most with the physical and spiritual body. In it she builds a literal "love's body" out of parts of her own body transformed by the experience of love. Each body part becomes symbolic of the whole body and finally the whole psyche. Body is the vehicle, and the lover is the mediator, in a Christly sense. When Christ is the dying man, he is the poet's dark self, the wooden bird, the skinny man, forever hanging on the cross and chained to the tree. In a neat turn on the delayed resurrection promised by Christ's sacrifice, Sexton makes resurrection bodily *and* immanent here: Christ as lover redeems her and himself. On the cross he remains Sexton's surrogate self, but as carpenter before and redeemer after crucifixion, he is the beloved other. That Sexton could not identify with the risen Christ but only with the dying Christ, that she required a mediator both other and male, speaks more directly to the patriarchal nature of Christianity and of our sexual arrangements than to any failure of nerve or imagination on her part.[8] It is, after all, not the lover who builds the body of love in these poems but the voice of the poet investing the lover with that power; as poet, Sexton played Christ to others without being able, finally, to redeem herself.

Love Poems builds the body of love through hands, mouth, breasts, legs, uterus. The hand is the central metaphor of "The Touch":

> For months my hand had been sealed off
> in a tin box. . . .
>
>   . . . .
> It lay there like an unconscious woman
> fed by tubes she knew not of.

This synecdochic hand is "bruised," alone, a small "wooden pigeon." The unconscious woman is reminiscent of the poet's mother in "The Double Image" (*Bedlam*), who grew both old and fat with cancer, as does the hand sealed off in its box, or the poet herself, after suicide attempts or surgery. The hand, the woman, is "nothing but vulnerable." And the metaphor is just that: "all this is metaphor." She is really speaking of "an ordinary hand," longing for "something to touch/that touches back." Enter the lover as savior:

> Then all this became history.
> Your hand found mine.
> Life rushed to my fingers like a blood clot.

The lover's hand touching hers retrieves the speaker from a condition of absence and deprivation as close to death as a coma. Moving from blood

63

as loss to blood as life, the poem also transforms lifeless wood ("wooden pigeon") to created artifact; in the first of many metaphors of building, the lover is characterized as "my carpenter." Now that the hand is a living creation transformed by love, "not even death will stop it," for "this is the kingdom/and the kingdom come." Although the relationship of the lover to Christ has remained implicit until now, based primarily on the carpenter analogue, these final lines join spirit and body through the literal identification of eschatology and orgasm. The poem begins in the dark night of soul and body and ends in immanent and passionately bodily resurrection.

Hands remained synecdoches for self throughout Sexton's canon, both before and after *Love Poems*. In her first collection, *To Bedlam and Part Way Back,* Sexton's Daphne speaks to Apollo from "Where I Live in This Honorable House of the Laurel Tree," telling him "how I wait/here in my wooden legs and O/my green green hands." In the late collections this association of hand and house becomes even more explicit, until hands frequently reach toward the reader, like amputated limbs, from windows or doors or rooms. "The Fury of Abandonment," published in the "Furies" sequence of *The Death Notebooks,* both summarizes and epitomizes the conflation of hand and house:

> I know that it is all
> a matter of hands.
> Out of the mournful sweetness of touching
> comes love
> like breakfast.
> Out of the many houses come the hands. . . .

The first two lines might fairly stand as representative of Sexton's deepest personal and poetic convictions. She invests the meeting of hands, the touching of fingertips, with an almost Michelangelesque quality, a significance as inescapably concrete as that demanded by representational art coming to grips with the ineffable. But if the first lines of this excerpt remind me of God touching spirit into Adam, the last line suggests a surreal dreamscape by Dali or perhaps Hans Bellmer, with disembodied hands reaching out of abandoned rooms.

In "The Kiss" mouth displaces hand as metaphor for the body and, by implication, the "self." The speaker's mouth "blooms like a cut." Blood was both life force and harbinger of loss or death in "The Touch," and this juxtaposition is consistent in Sexton, often within a single poem. Frequently it is the mouth that bleeds; in "Love Song" (*Live or*

Die), the speaker characterizes herself in adolescence as a girl "with an old red hook in her mouth,"

> the mouth that kept bleeding
> into the terrible fields of her soul. . . .

Here the bleeding is internal, a kind of emotional hemorrhage, but in "The Kiss" the bleeding mouth is kissed by the lover. "Before today my body was useless." The effect of his mouth on hers is electric and immediate: "Zing! A resurrection!" In an analogue to the "wooden pigeon" of "The Touch," Sexton moves once again from blood to wood, describing the body before the lover's kiss as "a boat, quite wooden," no more than "a group of boards." The lover is again carpenter, savior, Christ:

> You did this.
> Pure genius at work. Darling, the composer has stepped
> into fire.

Although the shift of body locale is subtle, I read this as a displacement from mouth to genitals, parallel to the movement from hand to genitals in "The Touch." The displacement—and therefore the identification—that remains implicit here is explicit in many other poems, of which "Angel of Fire and Genitals" (*The Book of Folly*) is only the most obvious example: "Mother of fire, let me stand at your devouring gate." In "Little Girl, My String Bean, My Lovely Woman" (*Live or Die*), the speaker urges her daughter to accept her blooming body, to "stand still at your door," where "you will strike fire,/that new thing!" The door (which is again the entrance to the house of the bodily self) is "the place of the blood," the "warm room" of "Menstruation at Forty" (*Live or Die*). Fire is nearly always located at a gate or an entrance in Sexton, and one steps into it in passionate surrender to creativity and (usually sexual) energy. In "The Kiss" the lover steps into the fire of her sexuality and his own creativity; note that the fire has burned up the "wood," and the carpenter metaphor is subsumed, or perhaps consumed, by this conflagration. In the process the lover is promoted from craftsman to creative genius, from carpenter to composer.

In a polymorphous profusion of body parts, the sequence moves next to "The Breast," now seen as "the key to everything." Predictably, breasts are symbols of maternal nurture in Sexton; but, not so predictably, their presence (as well as their absence) can signify the withholding of nourishment. Inevitably, their most consistent connection is with the poet's mother, a victim of breast cancer; also inevitably, they are a permanent focus for symbolic and literal womanhood, and thereby for guilt and pain, celebration and pleasure. In "The Double Image" (*Bedlam*), as I noted in chapter 1, Sexton speaks of her mother's cancer in lines whose power to shock is as much a product of meter and rhyme as of subject matter:

> On the first of September she looked at me
> and said I gave her cancer.
> They carved her sweet hills out
> and still I couldn't answer.

The speaker, and probably the poet, internalized that accusation completely, whether or not it was actually made against Sexton by Mary Gray in such explicit terms. Years later, in *The Book of Folly*'s "Dreaming the Breasts," she would write:

> Mother, I put bees in my mouth
> to keep from eating
> yet it did you no good.
> In the end they cut off your breasts. . . .

Her mother's breasts are magically her own, so that her own can seldom be a source of pleasure. In "Christmas Eve" (*Live or Die*), she thinks of her mother "as one thinks of murder," and then she touches her own breast, and then the floor,

> and then my breast again as if,
> somehow, it were one of yours.

But in "The Breast" of *Love Poems,* those sad evocations are conspicuously absent. This poem celebrates the breast and the entire body brought to life through the lover's touch. "Your hands found me like an architect." She is "alive when your fingers are." The architectural image continues the "building" of love's body established in the first two poems, and the profusion of body parts is cumulative; hands and mouths are not abandoned in favor of breasts but are brought to fondle and suckle them. The lover's touch on her breast makes the speaker "mad the way young girls are mad,/with an offering, an offering. . . ." The offering is spiritual, maternal, sexual: a sacrifice to the personified god the lover is, a "jugful of milk" for the infant in him, and a passionate gift that burns "the way money burns," spent hot and quick.

Thus far in this sequence, each body part represents and then becomes the whole through the mediation of the lover. The body is that which makes the self whole, renewed aright, because "it is all a matter of hands"—or breasts or mouths. "In Celebration of My Uterus" strikes a significantly different note if only because the lover is absent in bodily form. A kind of fertility chant, "In Celebration of My Uterus" is a one-woman chorus of praise for the force of life:

> Sweet weight,
> in celebration of the woman I am
> and of the soul of the woman I am
> and of the central creature and its delight
> I sing for you. I dare to live.
> Hello, spirit. Hello, cup.

Whimsically ritualistic ("let me carry bowls for the offering," "Let me make certain tribal figures"), "In Celebration" is also an earnest evocation of that "central creature" who urges the speaker to "dare to live." It is a relief to find that central creature singing to her soul in the absence of a savior always male, always other, always externalized. Here the "others" are women, "many women . . . singing together of this," from Arizona to Russia, Egypt to Thailand. In other Sexton poems the uterus is often associated with the speaker's "hunt for death," that "night I want" which was "in the womb all along" ("Menstruation at Forty," *Live or Die*). She is elsewhere unabashed at the intimation of death in the egg, but here she speaks in the voice of "Little Girl, My String Bean, My Lovely Woman," in which "everything that is new is telling the truth." The lover's touch, which after all is one reason to celebrate the womb, remains pleasantly and unobtrusively in the background.

Like "In Celebration," "Barefoot" is a simple, naked poem. Now feet and legs are brought to life through human touch:

> Loving me with my shoes off
> means loving my long brown legs,
> sweet dears, as good as spoons;
> and my feet, those two children
> let out to play naked. Intricate nubs,
> my toes. No longer bound.

Taking off shoes means removing inhibitions, and the lovers do not confine themselves to footsie:

> Further up, my darling, the woman
> is calling her secrets, little houses,
> little tongues that tell you.

In the displacement from foot to genitals, the poem's tone changes from this little piggy to come hither. Finally the lover will "pierce me at my hunger mark." Beginning like "Knee Song," "Barefoot" ends like "Us," in a harvest of sexual fulfillment.

In the "December 11th" poem of the sequence "Eighteen Days without You," Sexton's speaker achieves complete unification of body and psyche through lovemaking. Speaker and lover "gnaw at the barrier because we are two." When he takes her "blood cup" and her "brine," then

> we swim in tandem and go up and up
> the river, the identical river called Mine
> and we enter together. No one's alone.

Man and woman are literally embodied in penis and vagina. They break down the barrier of two bodies by entering body completely. Sexuality is a way into literal body and self, the "central creature" of "In Celebration of My Uterus." If there is such a thing as salvation, these poems suggest it is found with other people, through relationships with lovers in particular. "No one's alone." She could not—and most of her contemporaries cannot—rely solely on self for meaning. The lover enables her to realize the potential for wholeness in her own body. (Psalm 23 is the spiritual analogue to the poet's sexual salvation. "Thou art with me, thy rod and thy staff they comfort me.") The female genitals are often the valley of death in Sexton's poems; but in "December 11th" entering orgasm, and/or the end of the vagina—the uterus or "central creature"—is the entry into the bodily promised land, the place of life, the house of the Lord. No one is alone when bodies are perfectly joined with souls, when the stranger is at home in her own body, when a lover enables her to worship the god in that body.

While "December 11th" celebrates the body's apotheosis in love, another poem from the same sequence anatomizes the fragmentation of that body. "December 2nd" is a collector's item of hardcore nightmare motifs, brought together in one single dream. It begins:

> I slept last night
> under a bird's shadow
> dreaming of nuthatches at the feeder,
> jailed to its spine, jailed right
> down to the toes, waiting for slow
> death in the hateful December snow.

The "bird's shadow" is reminiscent of the "wooden pigeon" of another speaker's hands and the wooden bird that is Christ on the cross. Here the speaker is "jailed" to the spine of the feeder, just as the birds are chained to the trees in "Those Times." After this first dream-state image, the speaker's mother slams the door in her face, followed by the appearance of the lover at another door, his face grown white. Whether the doors are to her own house or her mother's is unimportant, as one learns from other Sexton poems: "A woman *is* her mother." And as always, a woman's house is her body.

The lover in her dream is a "weird stone man" with a "caved-in waist" and no legs. The mouth that was open to kiss her in other poems is now "sewn like a seam." In his other and benevolent incarnations, the lover has been both soft and strong for her—the touch of his fingers infinitely soft, yet strong enough to guide her and to penetrate her. Here he is ironically still both soft and strong, but the strength is that of stone, and the softness is sewn up. His virility in the earlier poems is underscored by the symbolic castration he has somehow suffered here—he has no legs. Unable to deal with this situation, the speaker-dreamer tries to "rearrange" his body:

> I put you in six rooms to rearrange
> your doors and your thread popped and spoke,
> ripping out an uncovered scream
> from which I awoke.

It is not clear whether the scream is the lover's or the dreamer's; possibly it is both. Lover and dreamer are separated from each other, united only in the cry of pain that seems a parodic inversion of their cries of sexual and spiritual fulfillment in the other poems. The mutilation of the lover's body is ironically appropriate, since elsewhere it is always he who makes body whole or builds it anew.

The speaker wakes, then sleeps and dreams again:

> And I was a criminal in solitary,
> both cripple and crook
> who had picked ruby eyes from men.

In the image language of dreams, the self becomes a cripple when those upon whom she depends for strength, even for identity, are themselves mutilated. There is perhaps also an implication that she herself is responsible for the lover's mutilation, as she was "responsible" for her mother's cancer: she is criminal as well as cripple here, and her offense has been picking "ruby eyes from men." The displacement of body parts from genitals to legs has been doubled, this time from legs to eyes. Appropriately, the dreamer next loses one of her own limbs: "One-legged I became and then/you dragged me off by your Nazi hook." The moral universe of this poem is that of Jahweh's vengeance ethic—an eye for an eye, a leg for a leg. Her own mutilated body now represents the dreamer's emotional state. The lover turns antagonist, dragging her off by his Nazi hook, reminiscent of the "old red hook in her mouth" in *Live or Die*'s "Love Song," and of Plath's "Daddy." The poem's final image echoes the language we have seen elsewhere in Sexton's body metaphors: "I was the piece of bad meat they made you carry." The lovers are united again now, a mutilated stone man carrying a piece of bad meat on a hook. The reversal from "December 11th" is complete.

The last poem I will discuss from *Love Poems* is "The Break," which presents Sexton's most complex equation of house and body and gives the previously constructed body a heart and bones. But like "December 2nd," "The Break" is an ironic reversal of the building conceit on which so many of the poems in this collection depend. It has all been a matter of hands—or breasts or mouths or feet or wombs. Now it is a matter of the heart, whose "break" undoes the building of love's body. The mediator that has transformed and built the body—and the self that sometimes *is* the body and sometimes resides *in* the body—has always been the lover, as carpenter or Christ. But when there is no lover, or worse, when the lover becomes a helpless antagonist who fails and injures the speaker, and whom the speaker fails and injures, the physical cathexis of the body is broken. The "maker," unable to be the self-sufficient woman of "In Celebration," returns to the death-in-life condition of the suicide.

I find it an interesting omission that in the poems I have discussed thus far, all of which depend upon the conjunction of the physical and the spiritual, not one has used the heart as either metaphor or literal body organ. But Sexton does use "heart" in the conventional manner elsewhere, to signify the emotional core of body and psyche. She seldom employs the heart positively, however; instead, it is most often the wound, the mutant, the mortuary, the eyeless beetle. It is never redeemed, but it can always be damned. In "Old Dwarf Heart" (*All My Pretty Ones*), the heart has its own body, complete with arms, wrists, and fists, all finally identified with "mother, father, I'm made of." "The Break" concerns itself with a broken hip, but as the first line clarifies, "It was also my violent heart that broke." Bones become identified with the physical body, and heart with the "signature of myself." The alienation from the body is expressed by objectifying it: "The body is a damn hard thing to kill." The outer structure of bone will heal, but the heart will not, for it is a "cripple," and "that other corpse." While the bones heal, the heart "builds a death crèche."

> My heart had stammered and hungered at
> a marriage feast until the angel of hell
> turned me into the punisher, the acrobat.

The "angel of hell" is internal, analogous to Job's accuser. The angel punishes her for her joy and her guilt. Figures are placed at the "grave of my bones," but it is "the other death/they came for," that of the "child of myself," the heart dead long before, which cannot formally be mourned until the bones join it. The heart is old and decayed, and knows secrets, because it is made of the father and mother, both old, lethally wise, and dead. Together, "Old Dwarf Heart" and "The Break" anatomize the process by which parents displace their failed hopes and bitternesses onto their children, ensuring that their children will grow up guilty of disappointing the parents if they fail, guilty of transcending them if they succeed. In "Those Times . . . " (*Live or Die*), the six-year-old speaker's life will "run over my mother's like a truck." What remains from childhood is a "small hole in my heart, a deaf spot" that enables her, paradoxically, to hear "the unsaid more clearly."

The "unsaid" represents the dark underside of familial love, and its beauty and nurture as well. Ironically, the unsaid is an implicit source of poetic inspiration: it is in the poems that she *says* the unsaid and, judging from many responses to her poems, the unsayable. The magical punishment for hearing the unsaid, and then saying it, is death. One of the "unsaids" is the inexorability of death, a fact of life our culture pathologically avoids.[9] What kills the heart in "The Break" is the effort to defeat death with love: "The heart burst with love and lost its breath."

The poem ends with the stanza I employ as epigraph. The little town is the body, the post and cup the hip bone and its socket. The zeal of her house is the zeal of the body violently inhabited by the heart. The explicit biblical reference is to Psalm 69, and there may also be an allusion to Donne's *Holy Sonnets*, no. 5, which begins, "I am a little world made cunningly/Of Elements, and an Angelike spright. . . . " Whether or not Sexton knew the Donne sonnet, the thematic bond between the two poems attests to the metaphorical mainstream the body problem touches in poets who quest after wholeness. It is not, however, the zeal of the Lord's house that eats the speaker in Sexton's poem; it is her own. The biblical speaker has lost family and friends because of his passion for the Lord, whose deliverance he trusts. The zeal of Sexton's house has caused her to be outcast and alone as well. That zeal is the poet's passion and energy for life, the violent capacity to love, the violent need to be loved.

Sexton's posthumous volumes, in particular *The Awful Rowing toward God* and *45 Mercy Street*, continue the complex body metaphors of the early and middle periods, but with significant qualifications and one encouraging development. The ambivalence remains untouched. The body is still a prison and still the source of salvation. But we have seen that in *The Awful Rowing* Sexton turns substantially from the fellow sufferer that was Christ, the always-human being, to an image of God the Father that began to emerge in *The Death Notebooks,* an image projected outside the self, an absolute Other. He is no longer the ragged brother but the symbol of spiritual perfection. This is Sexton's clearest expression of the need for the omnipotent. But even as she turns more toward a source of omnipotence, she remains poised at the heart of the matter. This God, pure spirit, envies body, and the body is still the literal locale of his entrance into her. The men of God are God. The island of God has flesh. God's otherness, his spiritual purity, asserts itself perversely only as he plays that superhuman game of poker with her at the end.

The collection *45 Mercy Street* more clearly and convincingly develops motifs begun in *The Awful Rowing.* The poems often read like rough drafts, marred by imprecision and overwriting. Nevertheless, there are several fine poems here and some vintage Sexton imagery. The collection is utterly consumed by body images, many of them images of fragmentation and destruction. Fragmentation and division, especially through divorce, are the themes of fully half of the collection. As the series in *Love Poems* builds the body, "The Divorce Papers" section of *45 Mercy Street* systematically destroys it. Parts of the body lie all over the emotional battlefield of the book.

But the other major theme of the collection is unification and wholeness. *Mercy Street* contains a vision of bodily integrity different from those offered in the earlier work. Until this collection the redemptive and redeemed body was always associated with lovers or with the legacy left to daughters. It seemed unavailable to the lone woman who occupied the central narrative. Here, for the first and last time, the voices of the woman and the maker speak of the body in harmony. In fact, these very late poems embody the entire universe, moving toward a mythic framework. Sexton seems to have been operating under an anthropomorphic imperative to humanize forces that would otherwise remain pitilessly inhuman. Christ, overshadowed by God the Father in *The Awful Rowing*, is back, being a fool again, but human. The animals that are awful in some of the poems are blessed in others. The moose is praised for his "proud body," which the speaker wishes to keep "past your mystery/and mine." Even as the body's "fall from grace" is mourned in "The Big Boots of Pain," a new note of hope occurs in the two final poems of the collection.

In "There You Were" the house of the body breaks out of the sea and onto the shore. This time the "carpenter" is a woman. "The house of my body has spoken/often as you rebuild me like blocks." In the final poem, "The Consecrating Mother," the ocean is a source of nurture, power, force, and comfort. The narrative stance is complex and ambiguous—this is by no means a simply celebratory poem—but a solid sense of feminine strength is imagined in the bodied, naked power of the ocean, "flashing breasts made of milk-water." The damning and beloved mothers of other poems—and this volume includes one as fierce as any other—are incorporated and transcended.

Sexton never, of course, "solved" the mind/body problem. But she wrote from the conviction that if there were any earthly answers, they must be sought from within the "central creature" created through the integration of body and psyche. She expressed the pain and joy of being human by mourning the body's frailty and celebrating its strength. She wrote about loss and love and the poignancy of people. That poignancy is not so much in what they said but in the bittersweet memory of their "dear bodies."

4

Is It True?
Feeding, Feces, and Creativity

Does God Live in Shit?

I hope to end this discussion of beginnings and endings, feces and fruit, in the place of specifically feminine grace made accessible by Stephanie Demetrakopoulos's meditation "The Nursing Mother and Feminine Metaphysics," of which more later. But I will begin earlier in the feeding cycle at a moment that is by its nature far less graceful. Although I confine myself to Anne Sexton, whose extremes might be aberrant, let me here record that I think her dilemma belongs to a lesser degree to all women, and certainly to all women poets. The dilemma and its poetic resolution has to do with the development of creativity in infancy and especially with the relationship between feces and language. Sexton employs the oral and anal stages of psychosexual development to explore the uses of oral incorporation and anal defiance as primary sources of poetic power. In Sexton's version of the emergence of poetic consciousness, the infant's ambivalent attachment to feces becomes a metaphor for the literal fertilizing of the imagination. This journey of creative growth ends with power and good but begins with impotence and evil.

Anne Sexton believed that evil crawled into her, "something I ate" ("Is It True?"). The process of ingesting evil begins with birth, with the lactation and feeding process whereby "all my need took you down like a meal." Her speaker needs the white love of mother's milk, but because this feeding depletes the mother, she ingests evil, becomes the body of evil in the act of feeding. It all comes out the other end:

> When I tell the priest I am full
> of bowel movement, right into the fingers,
> he shrugs. To him shit is good.
> To me, to my mother, it was poison
> and the poison was all of me
> in the nose, in the ears, in the lungs.
> That's why language fails.

> Because to one, shit is a feeder of plants,
> to another the evil that permeates them
> and although they try,
> day after day of childhood,
> they can't push the poison out.
> So much for language.
> So much for psychology.
> God lives in shit—I have been told.

"Is it true?" she asks. In "The Hoarder" (*The Book of Folly*), "there is something there/I've got to get and I dig/down." She finds the objects and sins of her past as she digs—the aunt's clock she broke, the five dollars belonging to her sister that she ripped up—until she reaches "my first doll that water went/into and water came out of," yet what she must find is deeper still:

> Earlier it was the diaper I wore
> and the dirt thereof and my
> mother hating me for it and me
> loving me for it but the hate
> won didn't it yes the distaste
> won the disgust won and because
> of this I am a hoarder of words
> I hold them in though they are
> dung oh God I am a digger
> I am not an idler
> am I?

If the problem begins at birth and deepens with the enculturation process embodied in toilet training, it becomes endlessly cyclical, for we must all eat and shit, are all bodily creatures. Sexton identified with and loved that creature—"body, you are good goods"—yet was so ambivalent about it that the struggle between creatureliness and creativity ripped her apart. (See chapter 3, "The Zeal of Her House," on attitudes toward the body.) "Is it true?" became a central question of her quest as spiritual seeker, as poet, as woman. Is it true that God blesses shit and lives in it, that the smell of it is the smell of life rather than of death? Is it true that God can love the rat? (Is it true that God *is* the rat and that the rat accomplishes and keeps the miracle, as in "In the Deep Museum?") If only she could be sure. But she is not. There is no certainty, and Sexton craved absolutes as she craved the sun that shone on her like a "dozen glistening haloes."

The parable of maturation from infancy centers around the feeding-digesting-excreting cycle that makes us so entirely creaturely. In her story of it, as in psychoanalysis's, the infant loves her own feces, is proud of its production, naps in the ooze of its warmth, is most able to move toward imaginative invention when she's got shit in her pants. (More of this oddity later.) When the infant discovers that this dear production in the aura of which it ruminates for lonely hours is suddenly distasteful to the parents, its emerging concept of clean and creaturely identity is forever betrayed. And where does the shit come from? From feeding, the process by which the infant gains its life sustenance through the mother's breast. Although it will be years before the human knows about this cause-and-effect relationship—before, in other words, it is fully introduced into the symbolic order—its body may well "know" it from the start; surely the mother knows and can communicate her acceptance and/or disgust through the nursing process. Henceforth, the connection between nourishment and waste will be ambivalent at best. Ironically, almost embarrassingly, this is Sexton's version of the ideal moment before experience teaches its brutal lesson: this moment of the unity of feces and creativity. The God that is said to be all soul—and also, heretically, all immanence—embodies that same ambivalence. The Trinity's division of spiritual from bodily and human aspects of Godhead becomes emblematic of that division in the civilized human creature. Even God, it seems, is not able to endure the body. At death Christianity projects the reunion of soul and body into the last moments of time, relegating it to an eternity that begins, tellingly, with the Day of Judgment.

Thus the question, "Is it true?" is central to Sexton's spiritual quest. I have said it is also central to her dilemma as both poet and woman. Juhasz, Ostriker, Lauter, and Middlebrook have detailed the ways in which Sexton's femininity became her central preoccupation as poet-person.[1] According to Ostriker, "She gives us full helpings of her breast, her uterus, her menstruation, her abortion, her 'tiny jail' of a vagina, her love life, her mother's and daughters' breasts, everyone's operations, the act of eating, . . . even the trauma of her childhood enemas."[2] Middlebrook's review of *The Complete Poems* includes the thesis that Sexton's lasting importance as a modern poet "lies in her bold exploration of female sexuality and female spirituality." Beginning with *Live or Die*, Middlebrook finds that Sexton "begins to explore the suspicion that what she suffers from is femaleness itself, and is probably incurable."[3] Is it true? Can God love her less or not at all or just as much, because she is a woman? Can she love herself? Is it true that "we must all eat beautiful women," that self-sacrifice is the condition and the mandate of femininity? Is it true that she is defective because female, or is it true, more hopefully, that although woman is more rat than man is, God will take that rat in his arms and embrace her? Or might it be true that woman's nurturance, her concrete creativity in the body, makes her more beloved of God? Does the Father-God love his own image best—that of man—or does he crave that "other," not only human and bodied but also female?

These are questions Sexton answered continuously and contradictorily throughout her personal and poetic lives. If the relationship between nurturance and creativity is of the reciprocal and imaginative sort emblemized by the serpent of eternity with its tail in its mouth, then she will be blessed. But Sexton suspects that the shit with which she is sullied soon after birth, once dear and now evil, is specifically female; that mother and father, and therefore God, find female waste the really messy stuff, the manure of the universe. If "shit is the evil that permeates them" to some, and the feeder of plants to others, it will be, ironically, the nurturant and re-creative female who will most likely experience it as permeation. If the body's unruly creatureliness is the antithesis of what is valued by civilization—famous for its discontents with anything messy—then what body is indeed the messiest, the most bodily, the most creaturely? That body is woman's, "fastened to the earth, listening for its small animal noises," pulled by the tide of sea and moon, bringing forth humanity between piss and shit, in blood and ooze. Neither God nor man will ever forgive woman his ignominious source between her thighs—nor may she forgive herself in Sexton's world, no matter how hard she tries, "day after day of childhood," to "push the poison out."

That, says Sexton, is "why language fails." The direct connection between feces and language made so explicit in "The Hoarder" and "Is It True?" is implicit throughout Sexton's canon and is peculiar to her dilemma as female *poet,* that double bind. To "hoard" words, as the human infant sometimes hoards bowel movement, unable to push it out, filled with it to the lungs and fingertips, is to curse oneself; in Blake's metaphor, it is to "murder an infant in its cradle." If your mother and father—your culture—hate you for smelling up the hearth, then you will try to keep it in. By analogy, the effort to push it out, to speak, will meet with equal contempt, because the woman's shit, her special evil, is the bodily reminder of mortality and creatureliness.

When I say that this was Sexton's dilemma as poet, I mean that literally. The contempt reserved for Sexton and "her kind" is special indeed, quite different from and more vitriolic than that first dispensed in careful and restrained doses to the male confessionals. If the sneer derives from fear, as Ostriker says—and certainly she is right—that is warmer comfort for critics than it must have been for the poet. For the living poet I have noted that the process began immediately, with the special and almost haunted contempt of her teacher, John Holmes. Bear in mind the scatological foundation of this discussion while I cite a few of the positions taken by Sexton's critics, both friends and enemies. Holmes "distrusts the very source and subject of a great many of your poems." He is deeply bothered "that you use poetry this way. It's all a release for you, but what is it for anyone else except a spectacle of someone experiencing release?"[4] James Dickey's now famous review of *Bedlam* is perhaps the most appropriate: "One feels tempted to drop them furtively into the nearest ashcan, rather than be caught with them in the presence of such naked suffering."[5] More recently, Rosemary Johnson, who approaches Sexton with some sympathy and respect, still feels obliged (only partly ironically) to wonder whether "such messy preoccupations will remain to stain the linen of the culture for long or whether good taste bleaches out the most stubborn stain eventually."[6]

To underscore the obvious: A woman of "her kind" is more than invited, is indeed required, to feel that "infantile" connection between feces and words. If she hoards her words, then she is full of shit to the fingertips. If she shares them, the critics declare that she has messed her pants in public, that such "confessions" are indeed nothing but waste matter, smelly soil that belongs—where else?—in the ashcan, furtively dropped there by the reader lest he be "caught with them." The male critic wants to drop the shit in the can, while the female critic, in womanly fashion, wonders rather how we will get out the stain left on the linen of culture, what tastefully applied bleach might take care of the blot created by such "messy preoccupations." Holmes, first and foremost poetic father withholding approval and manifesting disgust—recall that he advised other workshop members to stay away from Sexton, believing her influence to be dangerous and pernicious—speaks for many readers in his "distrust of the source and subject" of her poetry: her own very bodily, excruciatingly female, madness. He finds it only a release for *her;* all this can be for anyone else is the unspeakably crude spectacle of someone else taking a public dump.

One way of reading Anne Sexton's poetic dilemma is through anthropologist Mary Douglas's cultural categories in *Purity and Danger.*

Douglas analyzed ancient Hebrew responses to "dirt," defined as "matter out of place."[7] The seemingly arbitrary abominations of Leviticus make sense in an analysis that takes into account the social structures established by the Hebrew tribes to pattern their sense of order and chaos. In our culture Sexton's poetry was doubly perceived as dirt, as "matter out of place," twenty-five years ago; it still is. Her subjects are "inappropriate" for poetry, appropriate only for the priest or analyst. In their proper place, these revelations are sacred; out of place, they are a profanation of the sacred. The function of poetry in twentieth-century America still retains its ritual roots in the sacred, and Sexton's poems appear radically profane. By tampering with established mediation devices, she crossed boundaries between the sacred and the profane that are artificially high precisely because the two are so closely akin. Sexton recognized not only their close proximity; she often insisted upon their identification. The categories of the sacred and the profane are inevitably connected to gender and to sexuality, so that when a woman stained the cultural linen with her messy and bodily preoccupations, the critical establishment could not help but perceive it as "dirt."

If psychoanalytic theory sometimes seems silly because of the attention it pays to the process of toilet training and to its symbolic meanings and lasting influence on our lives, the reaction of many critics to Anne Sexton's poetry seems to prove its case. Perhaps, after all, the source of a great deal of our enduring conflicts, joys, suffering, and confidence or lack of it emerges from this first encounter with enculturation. And perhaps, indeed, it all has something fundamental to do with language, imagination, and creativity. And why should these concerns not be within the domain of our poetry? Why do we get so all-fired mad about it? Why has writing these pages had a temporary influence on my eating habits and my digestion? Because when I write this book I am a critic rather than a poet, I will refrain from staining the critical linen with any enlightening details.

Swallowing Magic, Delivering Anne

I locate the central poem for the relationship between infancy and creativity, and between feces and language, in the "Third Psalm" of "O Ye Tongues," where Sexton employs what Middlebrook calls "that most nurturant rhetoric: praise."[8] I want here to employ that same rhetoric to suggest some of Sexton's finest poetic accomplishments. I consider this poem significant for its mythic and prophetic qualities and for its place in Sexton's radical retelling of the story of humanity's creation, fall, and renewal in the poetry that begins with *Transformations* and includes "The Jesus Papers," "The Death of the Fathers," and the "Furies" and "Angels" sequences.

"O Ye Tongues" begins with a tone reminiscent of the Psalms; its subject is Genesis:

> Let the waters divide so that God may wash his face in first light.
>
> Let there be pin holes in the sky in which God puts his little finger.
>
> . . . .
>
> Let there be seasons so the sky dogs will jump across the sun in December.
>
> . . . .
>
> Let there be a heaven so that man may outlive his grasses.

A tonally nonviolent flood—"Let Noah build an ark out of the old lady's shoe and fill it with the creatures of the Lord"—is conducted by a largely benevolent God who is presented only once in a slightly ironic light when the ark of salvation serves to "notch his belt repeatedly." The joyous bulk of humanity imagined at its daily tasks and delights is finally particularized in the "Third Psalm" with an "I" not quite or only Anne Sexton; she is the human infant in civilization. That this infant is American and urban is specified by her coming "from the grave of my mama's belly into the commerce of Boston."

Here Sexton achieves the perfect and delicate balance between telling her own story and telling the story of us all; this is, as Middlebrook points out, "an eerily, beautifully sustained account of the emergence of the symbol-making consciousness in infancy" and a "parable of liberation from confinement by means of invention."[9] I am especially interested here in the part played in that drama by eating and defecating. Sexton envisions for us an infant, alone with herself in the new universe for many more hours each day than she is accompanied by adults (the "big balloons"), a baby full of human intelligence and not yet able to occupy her mind with the mental activity that precedes articulated identity:

> For I could not read or speak and on the long nights I could not turn the moon off or count the lights of cars across the ceiling.

What does such a one do, alone in the universe, newly birthed from one kind of grave? In Sexton's story she begins to engage in mental creativity, a "reproduction" that is at the same time a splitting. Such a process has been long surmised and theoretically posited by psychoanalysis to take place only with and through the infant's contact with the mother figure.

> For Anne and Christopher were born in my head as I howled
> at the grave of the roses, the ninety-four rose crèches of my
> bedroom.

The imaginary brother, or other self, functions in Sexton's parable as a kind of animus figure, who prior to the formation of a fully recognizable "I" is united (and split) into a "we," a "kind of company when the big balloons did not bend over us." Here Sexton implicitly locates the source of both wholeness and fragmentation in the emerging psyche, dependent crucially not only upon the *presence* of the big balloons (alienating, even if needed for nurture and as a reference point for the emergence of identity) but on their sustained and frequent *absence*. With no one to talk to, to gaze upon and therefore gain a sense of reality and identity from, Sexton posits that the infant creates its own companion within the psyche. We have long recognized that the "imaginary companion" of very young childhood emerges from such a need to fill up lonely hours and to communicate, but popular mythology and formal theory alike place its birth later in the process. Sexton presses back the boundaries to the birthplace, supposing that the infant will engage in the process it has just been through: a birth that sunders it from connection, yet ironically brings it from death into life. Both imitative and inventive by nature, Sexton's infant makes an analogy of the birth trauma, compensating for its loss and celebrating its life. In an analogy to the psychoanalytic concept of penis envy in the female, Sexton conflates developmental stages into this creative act of the brother's mental birth: Christopher is her twin, "holding his baby cock like a minnow."

When the balloons appear, then the infant lapses into passivity, even if that passivity is sometimes angry.

> For I lay as pale as flour and drank moon juice from a rubber
> tip.

And what else does the infant do? It wets its pants, and it shits; and when it does, "Christopher smiled and said let the air be sweet with your soil." Here Christopher becomes that self-affirming voice of confidence, assuring Anne that she is altogether good. She can listen to

Christopher, "unless the balloon came and changed my bandage." The body that experiences the cleansing and feeding rituals is the female body, in this case, so it is "she" who first experiences humiliation and distaste from the balloons. Christopher, entirely mental, escapes censure and confusion. As I read him here, Christopher is not only the aspect of self that infuses one with self-confidence but also the infant and imaginative forerunner of Sexton's later Christ as "ragged brother" and fellow traveler, the human figure of Godhead with whom she can identify, and whom she eventually lost; for Christopher in enlarged form will later change from self-brother to Father-God.

> For I lay as single as death. Christopher lay beside me. He was living.

Christopher takes care of her when the balloons disappear, and they talk together. In answer to her question, "Where are we?" (she is experiencing the "boundaries of the closed room"), Christopher says, "Jail." When Christopher sleeps and is not there to answer the questions or to reassure her, the infant "Anne" learns to rely on herself, surmounting the frustration of the fingers that "would not stay" and that "broke out of my mouth":

> For I was prodding myself out of my sleep, out the green room.
> The sleep of the desperate who travel backwards into darkness.

Momentarily alone, she knows she must be her own awakener, must bring herself out of sleep even while Christopher sleeps, "making a sea sound."

What "Anne" figures out alone, and develops with Christopher when he reawakens, is the final lesson of the parable, and a fair account of the ambiguous polarities of Anne Sexton's subsequent life; perhaps, read another way, it speaks of all of our lives:

> For birth was a disease and Christopher and I invented the cure.

> For we swallow magic and we deliver Anne.

Considering Anne Sexton's life and death, and the context of such imagery in the rest of her poetry, we can only read these lines as ambiguous. Sexton apparently did consider even her very birth, her existence in the world, as a disease; the invention of "cure" in "swallowing magic" has ironically defeating references to her dependence upon drugs and her repeated efforts to commit suicide by means of pills. In "Wanting to Die" she writes:

> Twice I have so simply declared myself,
> have possessed the enemy, eaten the enemy,
> have taken on his craft, his magic.

"The enemy" can be either life or death; in either case, to take on the craft and the magic refers to killing oneself through a parody of normal nurturance, through ingestion that fixes once and for all the disease of life sustained from the beginning by that other ingestion of food which results in the shit one cannot get out of one's fingers or one's soul.

But whatever the echoed allusion here to previous and future sources of disease and cure, the function of "magic" in "O Ye Tongues" is the creation not only of a sustaining self but of a creative impulse. The "Anne" delivered in the rest of the sequence is the heroine of her own story of coming of age into womanhood, motherhood, and poetry. From her beginnings, lying in quiet and in soiled diapers, talking to herself, inventing Christopher, surrounded by her own sweet soil and its smell, she rises into yet another birth, this one meant to correct the flaws of the first. In the "Fourth Psalm" Anne and Christopher "come forth" from "soil" and make "poison sweet." The mole who comes from the ground—that "artificial anus"—into the light is capable of "swallowing the sun." Every image in the "Fourth Psalm" is natural, earthly, and regenerative: daisy, orange, snail, squid, cauliflower, rose, daffodil, dog, carp, leopard, even cockroach, all are blessed. Given little praise for her creatureliness or her femininity either by culture or by its designated enforcers in the persons of parents, "Anne" celebrates that feminine creature from soil and sea, as she does in so many poems throughout the canon. In the "Seventh Psalm" she takes on the female function of reproduction as an embodiment of "a magnitude," a "many," each of us "patting ourselves dry with a towel." At the same time she is a solitary figure, "in the dark room putting bones into place." Seeing the large design, she births her baby into "many worlds of milk."

The progress from her infancy to her own motherhood marks a transformation of the meaning of the feeding cycle; that transformation is from psychoanalysis to myth, a journeying I will expand upon in Part III of this study. Sexton always placed herself in the middle and mediating positions of mother-daughter constellations. Understanding what went awry between herself and her mother, she endeavors to ensure that she will not do to her daughters what was done to her; in the terms of this discussion, she will try to experience nursing not as psychic depletion but as spiritual abundance. The terms of this transformation are theoretically outlined in antithetical essays by Freud ("On the Transformation of Instincts") and Stephanie Demetrakopoulos ("The Nursing Mother and Feminine Metaphysics").[10]

"To begin with," says Freud, "it would appear that in the products of the unconscious—spontaneous ideas, phantasies, symptoms—the conceptions *faeces* (money, gift), *child*, and *penis* are seldom distinguished and are easily interchangeable." While I agree with the feminist contention that what women "envy" is "power," I support the psychoanalytic contention that the metaphor is grounded in an always bodily reality—i.e., that *penis envy* is a valid term. Sexton's infant conjures up a penis of her own in Christopher, "holding his baby cock like a minnow." It is through the mediation of fecal matter that the infant first feels the desire for "power," experienced in Sexton's poem as invention and creativity. The infant engages in that other "birthing" in which she does indeed deliver a child. In Freud's scenario this process will take place over a period of years and will normally end with the female's relinquishment of the desire for the penis in the substitute "child." In Sexton's, the process in the early psalms of "O Ye Tongues" is entirely imaginative; she has already begun to transform the terms of psychoanalysis into mythic structures. Freud is concerned in his essay to trace adult character traits that have their sources in the anal stage, and among these traits are obstinacy, stubbornness, or defiance. The process of defecation affords the infant and young child its first occasion to decide between "a narcissistic and an object-loving attitude." He or she can offer up feces as a gift or else retain them as a means of "asserting his own will." Because he is concerned to trace the etiology of neurosis, Freud's language is censorious; failure to relinquish the gift results in defiant, obstinate attitudes that spring from a "narcissistic clinging to the pleasure of anal erotism."

Anne Sexton has been called "narcissistic," and in other poems she does speak of withholding feces; but I want to transform the meanings of the Freudian terminology. The story of Sexton's infant may indeed be that of a developing neurosis, yet it is also a description of another and creative kind of "defiance," a primary source of energy and power in Sexton's poetry. The early formation of an individualized, courageous stance in art may be connected to this infant drama of giving and withholding. Sexton's infant wants to keep that penis, that power, that child. It belongs to her, more especially since it is rejected rather than welcomed by the mother because of its female character. The nursing experienced as depletion by the infant's mother results in this product she will also despise, and Sexton's infant makes of this situation the best that could be hoped for. In the contest of wills between resentful mother and defiant infant, the infant cuts her losses in the real world by compensating in her imaginative life. What Freud mourns as symptom, Sexton celebrates as power.

When Sexton's infant grows into maternity herself, she tries to perceive the nursing process differently, aware that her perception of it will have vast consequences for the child:

> For the baby suckles and there is a people made of milk for her
> to use. There are milk trees to hiss her on. There are milk beds
> in which to lie and dream of a warm room. There are milk
> fingers to fold and unfold. There are milk bottoms that are wet
> and caressed and put into their cotton.
>
> For there are many worlds of milk to walk through under the
> moon.

Stephanie Demetrakopoulos uses Sexton's psalms to forward a thesis about nursing: If Lévi-Strauss's metaphor "The Raw and the Cooked" is a central image for raw nature turning into culture, then "woman cooking, woman gestating, woman nursing" are all images of that process: "Woman's alchemy changes blood to milk; her body is a transmutation system that has the power to change her very body to food which becomes in turn the physical and psychic energy of her child. She is creating an incarnate soul, assisting its growth." Demetrakopoulos sees Sexton's imagery of nursing in the "Seventh Psalm" as a sign of specifically feminine grace. She experiences it as the "connective tissue, the flow, the indisputable plenitude of a loving ground of being, a goddess who seems to amalgamate Demeter with Sophia."

This movement from compensatory struggle to assisting the growth of an incarnate soul was clearly conceived by Sexton as midwifed by the mother who governs the tone of the feeding cycle:

> For the baby grows and the mother places her giggle-jog on her
> knee and sings a song of Christopher and Anne.
>
> For the mother sings songs of the baby that knew.

"Anne" herself, now become a mother, is the "baby that knew" what we all know in some private reach of unconsciousness inaccessible to many of us, accessible to Anne Sexton throughout her life: the loneliness *and* the companionable creativity of infancy is the double source of all we are, all we might become. "For the mother remembers the baby she was and never locks and twists or puts lonely into a foreign place." This is, after all, a hopeful fiction, a myth, for motherhood precipitated Anne Sexton's first mental breakdown, and her illness later did compel her to "put lonely into a foreign place." She acknowledged in many poems that despite her efforts to make it so, love has no simple, "uncomplicated hymn."

Thus the mother of the ninth and final psalm sees that motherhood cannot be her only creation. She must "climb her own mountain." For this woman the mountain is poetry:

> For I am placing fist over fist on rock and plunging into the altitude of words. The silence of words.

Even as the mother does so, the daughter "starts up her own mountain" to "build her own city and fill it with her own oranges, her own words." The image of the orange functions in "O Ye Tongues" as an embryo of the human form: the expectant mother "has swallowed a bagful of oranges and she is well pleased." Now the same orange is equated with language, especially the language of poetry that operates by the creation of metaphor and images—another gestation, another birthing. Sexton has come full circle from feces to fruit, from language to babies, in the regenerative cycle. Sometimes her false pregnancies have filled her with waste. But she bears ripe fruit in moments of genuine conception, of greater grace. The child is mothered by the woman, but the poem arises from the imaginative impregnation of the self.

Part III

Person, Persona, Prophecy

5

Sexton's Speakers: Many Kinds of "I"

Poetic truth is not necessarily autobiographical. It is truth that goes beyond the immediate self, another life. I don't adhere to literal facts all the time; I make them up whenever needed. . . . I would alter any word, attitude, image or persona for the sake of a poem. As Yeats said, "I have lived many lives, I have been a slave and a prince. Many a beloved has sat upon my knee, and I have sat upon the knee of many a beloved. Everything that has been shall be again." . . . I believe I am many people. When I am writing a poem, I feel I am the person who should have written it. . . . When I wrote about the farmer's wife, I lived in my mind in Illinois; when I had the illegitimate child, I nursed it—in my mind—and gave it back and traded life. When I gave my lover back to his wife, in my mind, I grieved and saw how ethereal and unnecessary I had been. When I was Christ, I felt like Christ. My arms hurt, I desperately wanted to pull them in off the cross. When I was taken down off the cross and buried alive, I sought solutions; I hoped they were Christian solutions.

—Anne Sexton, in Barbara Kevles, "The Art of Poetry xv: Anne Sexton"

When I read the book, the biography famous,
And is this then (said I) what the author calls a
     man's life?
And so will someone when I am dead and gone write my
     life?
(As if any man really knew aught of my life,
Why even I myself I often think know little or
     nothing of my real life,
Only a few hints, a few diffused faint clews and
     indirections). . . .

—Walt Whitman, "When I Read the Book," *Leaves of Grass*

"Diffused Faint Clews and Indirections"

The confessional poet *appears* to offer the poem as unmediated object, which is finally a contradiction in terms. If the so-called confessional school embodied a deeply revolutionary break with tradition—and I think it questionable that it did—that break did not consist of doing away with mediation. The confessionals' contribution to the aesthetics of poetry was, rather, an alteration of the American audience's perception of mediation. Theirs was, in part, a return to other sources from which American poetry emanates: the Romantics in England, Whitman and Dickinson in America.

The confessional impulse, in whatever guise it assumes at a given moment, is surely among the bases of all art in all cultures. What our culture insists upon in order to credit "confession" as art is that ritual mediation, often called "aesthetic distance," often achieved in poetry through the use of a persona, that ostensibly transforms the merely personal into the universal: tired old terms for a tired old argument, one that has never been quite resolved because mediation is somehow definitive of "high art." But Lowell and Plath, as well as Sexton, are dead. The confessional furor died down years ago. Lowell is canonized, and Plath seems assured a place in the pantheon. The most casual reading of *Poetry* or the *American Poetry Review* in the 1980s confirms anyone's sense that this should be a dead issue. American poetry by 1980 had assumed as its own the personal voice it disdained a short twenty-five years earlier. Yet when it comes to Anne Sexton and "her kind," critics and fellow poets are capable of resuscitating the tired terms that have long since lost their authority in the discussion of other poets. The reasons for this have something to do, it seems certain, with gender.

The contemporary woman poet is Anne Sexton's double inheritor. Not only was Sexton among the original members of the confessional school; she might legitimately be said to be its mother. Her first collection, *To Bedlam and Part Way Back*, was finished while Lowell was completing *Life Studies*, the publication of which is usually said to mark the beginning of the confessional movement. Sexton was studying with John Holmes during the gestation and writing of *Bedlam*, and from him she received no encouragement at all for her subjects and her style. By the time she entered Lowell's workshop, *Bedlam* was substantially complete, and she read none of Lowell's own new work while working with him. (He did, of course, read hers.) The primary male influence on Sexton's first book was, as she repeatedly acknowledged, W. D. Snodgrass.

Snodgrass gave her "permission," as she phrased it, to write about her own life in her own voice, and that permission included the discussion of crisis, loss, neurosis, even madness. Anne Sexton understood the critical response to such revelations in these terms in *45 Mercy Street*'s "Talking to Sheep":

> Yet even five centuries ago this smelled queer,
> confession, confession,
> and your devil was thought to push out their eyes
> and all the eyes had seen (too much! too much!).
> It was proof that you were a needle
> to push into their pupils.
> And the only cure for such confessions overheard
> was to sit in a cold bath for six days,
> a bath full of leeches, drawing out your blood
> into which confessors had heated the devil in them,
> inhabited them with their madness.

No degree of insight could have prepared Anne Sexton for the peculiar form of distaste expressed by many critics. Louis Simpson, kinder than most, said that "a poem titled 'Menstruation at Forty' was the straw that broke this camel's back."[1] The permission from Snodgrass to write about one's personal crises could not include the permission to write about a feminine experience from within a female body. For that bold stroke there was no modern precedent. If the response of her contemporaries to "confessional poetry" was sometimes sharply negative, it was specially inflected with contempt for "her kind." When Lowell confessed, at first we slapped his patrician hand and told him to shape up and put back the stiff in his upper lip. When Sexton confessed, we sharpened the knife and heated the pot. In chapter 4 I moved toward the thesis that Sexton is the textbook case of the woman poet devalued for speaking in her own feeling, bodily, feminine voice.

Many feminist critics contend that gender shapes not only the way readers read but the ways writers write. Recent research and debate on the question of possible differences between male and female "imaginations" indicate that the argument is still lively, both within and outside of feminist critical circles.[2] Whether differences between men's and women's poetry are due to nature or nurture, the concept of the persona, according to Marilyn Farwell and others, is an inadequate critical tool for the evaluation of women's poetry because the persona is by definition founded on the culturally masculine attributes of separation and intellectual "objectivity"; the culturally feminine attributes of relationship, intimacy, and involvement with the concrete and the personal result in a more empathetic and subjective approach to poetry. The mind of the female poet does not necessarily aspire to the "shred to platinum" of Eliot's ideal. The overvaluation of separation between "the man who suffers and the mind which creates" makes inevitable the undervaluation of the feminine voice in our critical tradition.

Isolated from and even antagonistic toward the value system we have inherited from New Criticism, which represents the extreme of the masculine-scientific aesthetic, the woman poet's *I*, in Farwell's and other feminist critical scenarios, will more likely diminish the distance between the person who suffers and the mind that creates. Her *I* will likely result from a combination of her enculturation, her psychology, and her lack of tradition; "she will tend to speak from personal experience because she is socialized in that way and because the 'universal' literary experience is not hers."[3]

I have said that Sexton is a textbook case of the fate of such a poet, and her insistent positions in interviews and letters support this. She regularly turned aside questions about where she fit into the poetic "tradition"; she did not know, she says. That tradition is not hers, she says. No, she has not read this or that poet; no, she is not aware of this or that theory; no, she was not deliberately taking up the position of Stevens — or Blake or Donne or Whitman. "It was not a planned thing to come into English poetry, which I didn't even know — I was just writing, and what I was writing was what I was feeling, and that's what I needed to write." She had her own "theory" about some of the purposes of poetry: "If you could document the imagination, experiences, everything, even some wit, whatever, of one life, one life, however long it may last, it might be of some value to someone someday just to say, well, this human being lived from 1928 to whenever, and this is what she had to say about her life. And that's really all I know."[4] And about the particularly "feminine" perceptions of women poets, Sexton had this to say: "I talk of the life-death cycle of the body. Well, women tell time by the body. They are like clocks. They are always fastened to the earth, listening for its small animal noises."[5]

So the example of Anne Sexton supports a feminist objection to the persona and the extreme of the masculine scientific aesthetic definitive of it. We must find other "evaluative tools" with which to deal with women's poetry; or we must give up "evaluation" altogether, at least as we have defined it, a position taken by many feminist critics and by other outsiders such as Leslie Fiedler. Sexton's own poetics are founded on the image, which she maintained was the heart of the poem.

Yet the creation of an image requires some "distancing" or separation between the person who suffers and the mind that creates. The structure of metaphor is the emblem of a paradox: identification in the psyche or the poem is dependent upon a prior discontinuity, may even involve a splitting in the act of fusion. And many feminists have been dissatisfied with any feminist aesthetic that would posit a fundamentally gendered concept of consciousness and imagination. The male poet whose work is intimate and concrete and concerned with relationship is not necessarily "feminine" in outlook; nor should the female poet whose images depend heavily upon abstraction be jerked out of the fullness of her humanity by a literary theory that will call her "masculine." Even "androgyny" is similarly limiting as a literary concept. Perhaps, as the Lacanian view has it, language itself constitutes, is definitive of, separation from the man who suffers—and the woman, too.

These are thorny issues, and no one has claim to definitive answers. Anne Sexton's poetry supports polar positions and provides a clear case that feminist readers must be selective about what they discard. Some quality, inadequately expressed by terms such as *distancing* or *objectifying,* is certainly definitive of any creative act. Perhaps we should call it *shaping* or some other (preferably commonplace) word. The danger that "art" will degenerate into "mere statement" has always seemed to me a straw man. What is mere statement anyway? We all suspect we know it when we see it, even if we do not know anything about art but know what we like. Since what we like and do not like is stupefyingly diverse, even among our experts, I suspect it is at the heart of any definition of art. Why we like what we do like or do not like what we don't like, is indeed a legitimate matter of concern, since from such intricate psychic structures arises any culture's hierarchy of values. Subjective and transactive models teach something worth knowing that it seems literary criticism will not happily accept: each person's relationship to any work of art is an elaborate transaction among the text, the author, and the identity of the perceiver; some of the perceiver's responses will be unique, and others will be common to many people on the basis of their psychic structures. Get enough perceivers sharing enough common psychic structures and a system of hierarchical values develops. Male and female readers and writers encode and decode differently, as Annette Kolodny says, and literary values have been shaped by male decoders responsive to male encoding and unresponsive to female encoding. Certainly we have all had enough of the results of this sort of solipsism. Beyond that, I am sure of nothing.

If Anne Sexton demonstrates a clear case of the woman poet whose works should not be judged by the traditional masculine measure—if she often writes in the first person and means her reader to perceive the identity or at least the continuity of herself and her speaker—she also provides a case for careful qualification of any such assumptions. Sexton was an adept at the use of the traditional persona, and among her autobiographical poems, the range of purposes and effects stands comparison with any modern poet's. We should recognize the distinctions she clearly meant and made throughout her career among her *I* poems; and I exclude from detailed discussion here the body of third-person poetry she also produced from beginning to end of her writing life. Her use of the traditional persona is often characterized by that persona's close attention to interior events; perhaps that is why critics have so often assumed the identity of poet and speaker.

Even the most nakedly autobiographical poetry involves a shaping process that is in some sense fictional; that fiction need not consist of ordinary distancing or objectifying procedures. But to create is, in some sense, to make up. While the use of tight metrical forms such as Sexton frequently employed in her early poetry is in itself a formal fiction, it is not the only kind. Autobiographical poetry in free verse [*sic*] or in form is never mere statement. Sexton speaks at length in several interviews about the process of writing "The Double Image," among her earliest autobiographical forays. The tight formalities by which the poem proceeds— metrics, complex rhythmic structures, intricate constellations and juxtapositions of imagery and ideas, ironies both subtle and intense— constitute an elaborate fiction as well as an artful truth; the two may come to the same thing. Poets need not engage in the extremities of internal separation required by an aesthetics in which the person who suffers and the mind that re-creates that suffering are schizophrenically split; neither, I think, should we assume that women poets will always want to speak only in their own voices—even when those voices are, among other possibilities, their own.

Consider, for instance, the speaker of "Suicide Note" in *Live or Die,* a poem to which I give extended attention in the following chapter. Certainly the speaker of "Suicide Note" is Anne Sexton. But this is Anne Sexton the poet *creating herself as character.* The *I* of this poem is both self-reflective and self-reflexive, a formally constructed persona of the kind we find in "Wanting to Die." Because she was a poet who wrote primarily in some form of personal voice, she was extraordinarily subtle in her achievement of range within that voice. In "Suicide Note" we are given the formal framework that is all artifice, the pretense of a suicide note that is *not* a suicide note but rather a deliberate re-creation of a state of mind that the speaker could hardly be in at the moment of composition, else she could not compose. The very form is artful ruse, the kind of lie we may need to hold in check such intensely emotional content.

Worksheets of "Suicide Note" published in *New York Quarterly* give us a clearer than usual indication of the composition process and address the very problem at issue here. Sexton took the poem through at least five drafts before the final one, in late May and June 1965. The revision, expansions, and cuts are extensive—the first draft is a mere twenty lines, written in crayon. Says Sexton: "I never heard of anyone committing suicide with a crayon in their hand, but then I wasn't committing suicide, was I, I was only writing about it." Whatever ironies she may have intended with this comment—perhaps she means us to realize that the poem grew out of a real attempt, and perhaps she means to say that it did not—she speaks wryly here of the misconceptions that can arise even in a sophisticated poetic audience. Three drafts end with, "I am only Anne,/coward, Anne," or variations on that. I consider it important that these lines appear nowhere in the finished draft.[6] In several Sexton poems "Anne" remains, but here she is deleted. The effect is not so much a depersonalized excision of self but the creation of a larger space for us to envision the speaker, who *might* be Anne and might also be someone else, not only this woman but any suicide with fantasies of identification with Christ, a catalogue of justifications, a need to be understood.

Walt Whitman said that the most seemingly complete and elaborate story of a life in poetry is a fiction behind which even the poet only glimpses at the completion of a lived and living truth. Many years after he published *Song of Myself* and the sexually explicit *Children of Adam*, he remarked with gentle, slightly acidic irony, "As if any man really knew aught of my life." Even he knows "little or nothing" of his "real life," only "a few hints, a few diffused faint clews and indirections." The truths anyone may confess are partial and hidden, even from the self. While the object of the poet's pursuit may be truth, the most confessional poem is more than half artifice, more than half the "complicated lie" of Sexton's "For John, Who Begs Me Not to Enquire Further." The poet knows very little and can confess to less than she knows. "I'm hunting for the truth," said Sexton. But that truth is always "poetic," not just "factual." Isolated member of no tradition that she declared herself to be, Anne Sexton is in Whitman's tradition not only when she sings of herself but also when she acknowledges that "behind everything that happens to you, every act, there is another truth, a secret life."[7] The poem can only grope in the direction of the secret life. Its inevitable failure constitutes the achievement of yet "another truth."

Many Kinds of *I*

In "Four Kinds of *I*" Maxine Kumin addresses the attacks on confessional poetry by differentiating among four diverse, if overlapping, categories of the first-person poem. Poetry critics have often behaved, she implicitly suggests, as if there were only two kinds of *I:* the persona and the autobiographical or "confessional." Finding these categories not finely enough tuned to the diverse effects that can be achieved by the *I,* she suggests at least two other categories: the lyric *I,* and the ideational *I.*[8]

While Kumin does not intend her four categories as either comprehensive or mutually exclusive, they are useful reference points. The use of the lyric *I* is among the most venerable and ancient of poetic traditions, dating at least to the Greek lyrics that are our earliest literary artifacts. No one has ever known quite how to define or limit the lyric, so Kumin mentions its most consistent characteristic: the communication of personal emotion in a voice and in rhythms appropriate for singing. Dylan Thomas's "If I Were Tickled by the Rub of Love" is a modern example.

The persona *I,* which Kumin discusses through Ransom's "Piazza Piece" (with obligatory mentions of Browning's "My Last Duchess" and Yeats's Crazy Jane poems), is generally characterized by a first-person narrator, distinct from the poet, who reveals things about him or herself that he understands less well than does the intended audience. I find this definition limiting; although the ironic gap between self-knowledge and the perception of the other is among the salient characteristics of many persona poems, it is not the only one. As I have implied, it could be argued that all first-person poetry involves either as conscious strategy or unconscious accident the creation of a persona, a fiction constituted in a text.

The ideational *I* is Kumin's third category, and among the toughest either to define or point to by example—yet she has made a useful distinction here. "In these poems," she writes, "the use of the first-person voice seems to me to be subordinate to establishing the intent of the poem itself, the making of a statement." Using Frost's "Design," Kumin points out that the introduction of a perceiver "serves to introduce a deliberately personal note, partly to bring mankind—human life—into this philosophical orbit, and particularly to anticipate and prepare for the essentially human conclusions of the sestet."[9] Auden's "September 1, 1939" serves as another example in this difficult category.

For the autobiographical *I,* an "ancient and honorable" tradition exists. In the autobiographical poem the reader is invited to break down that respectful distinction between speaker and poet; often a full reading of such poetry requires that the reader take up the invitation. It is this category that is equated with the confessional movement of which Anne Sexton was a part, and Kumin uses her friend's "The Double Image" to point to the kinds of control required and maintained by a good autobiographical poem. She points out, but does not labor, that the best confessional poetry is not in the least devoid of artistry, nor is it "merely" personal or selfish. The confessional poem invites the reader in by enlisting her sympathy and identification. The experiences of the confessional poet embody to some degree the national crisis, which need not be political, nor even objectively observable; it can represent an inner and psychological dilemma faced by large numbers of people.

The four categories, Kumin concludes, frequently overlap. And in a great poem, "the distinction is purely academic."[10] Although I would not say that all of the Sexton poems I will cite here represent her best work, they are all poems for which distinctions are worth making, and many of them do overlap. In Sexton's first several collections, *Bedlam, All My Pretty Ones, Live or Die,* and *Love Poems,* third-person poems are so common that I am newly surprised at the critical focus that treats her as though she never employed anything but the *I* in its autobiographical form. But among the first-person poems for which she is best known, the range of narrative strategy is wide. I will exclude the autobiographical category here, because it needs no further demonstration in Sexton. Instead I will point to her uses of ideational, persona, and lyric forms of *I,* confining myself to Sexton's first four collections.

Bedlam's "Torn Down from Glory Daily" exemplifies Sexton's ideational first-person poem in which *I* becomes an unidentified "we" who are watching the beach gulls "striking the top of the sky," up there "godding the whole blue world/and shrieking at a snip of land." While "we" watch, a single gull goes for the crumbs of dinner roll left on a

97

stone for it, then brings back its flock, like a "city of/wings that fall from the air." The beach becomes

> a world of beasts
> thrusting for one rock.

But there is not enough for all of them, and "just four" go "swinging over Gloucester" with their booty.

> Oh see how
> they cushion their fishy bellies
> with a brother's crumb.

The first-person voice here is clearly subordinate to establishing a thematic statement. As in Frost's "Design," the introduction of the *I* (here the "we") is crucial, if only implicitly, to that thematic statement; the poet could have presented the gulls without the humans, fighting for a fish or a clam or for bread left by anonymous hands. But the fact that "we" have left the bread implicates "us" in the unstated analogy with human greed thereby established.

"The Road Back" is similarly constructed on the ideational pattern, employing another "we," adults who drive a car "heavy with children/ tugged back from summer" at the end of a vacation trip. At such moments "there is no word for time," although mutability is the ideational core of the poem. The situation, the counting of cows along the road to pass the time for frustrated children who want summer never to end, the quietly responsible adults, all exist to embody the poem's statement that the children's sense of timelessness (which "tells them nothing ends") is entirely at odds with the adults' knowledge that everything ends—yet ironically, the adults, too, "ignore our regular loss" of time in the long parenthetical moments here illustrated by the car trip:

> Today, all cars,
> all fathers, all mothers, all
> children and lovers will
> have to forget
> about that thing in the sky,
> going around
> like a persistent rumor
> that will get us yet.

All My Pretty Ones continues the ideational strategy in such poems as "Lament," "Ghosts," "Old," "The Black Art," and "For Eleanor Boylan Talking with God"; sometimes the *I* is also a persona, while at other times we may guess it is autobiographical. In "Lament" an unnamed "someone" is dead. Everything in the air, even the trees, "knows" it. The speaker (possibly Sexton, possibly a persona—the subordination of the *I* to the poem's thematic statement makes certainty both impossible and irrelevant) hesitates before taking on a secret guilt:

> I think . . .
> I think I could have stopped it,
> if I'd been as firm as a nurse
> or noticed the neck of the driver
> as he cheated the crosstown lights;
> or later in the evening,
> if I'd held my napkin over my mouth.
> I think I could . . .
> if I'd been different, or wise, or calm,
> I think I could have charmed the table,
> the stained dish or the hand of the dealer.

While this *I* has all the characteristics of Sexton's own neuroses, the poem is primarily ideational. We are given no personal details of who has died or how, no sense of the connection, if there is any, between the deceased and the *I;* it does not matter who either character is, in a personal sense. Sexton is speaking of the human tendency to take on magical guilt and of the ironically animistic and primitive movement of the modern and civilized mind that hopes, through rituals of appeasement, to swerve fate.

In "Ghosts" an *I* who does not enter until the second stanza, and then only in one line ("I have seen others"), describes ghosts that are women, ghosts that are men, and finally child ghosts,

> curling like pink tea cups
> on any pillow, or kicking,
> showing their innocent bottoms, wailing
> for Lucifer.

Here the *I* of the second stanza seems all but gratuitously added to what might have been a third-person poem; but while the *I* is radically subordinated to the idea here, its presence in that line serves to add an implication that would be absent without such an intrusion: the insertion of the living observer into what would otherwise be only a description of types of ghosts serves to unite the world of the living and the dead suggested obliquely throughout the poem. We suspect that the ghosts being described, then, are actually other living men and women and children, and we wonder what kind of ghost the *I* herself is, especially since she "sees" them.

In "The Black Art" three sections characterize the female writer, the male writer, and the relationship of the writer to other human beings, especially other writers. Spies and crooks, subject to trances and portents and spells and fetishes, they are incapable of loving themselves yet are capable of the greatest love for the reflection of the self and its intimate inversion in each other. When they "marry,"

> the children leave in disgust.
> There is too much food and no one left over
> to eat up all the weird abundance.

The *I* here is the female writer, and we may suspect she is Anne Sexton: "Dear love, I am that girl." The unidentified male writer—"Dear love, you are that man"—is the addressee. But again, their personal identities are entirely subordinate to the primary aim of the poem, which is to forward a complex hypothesis about the writerly personality and its connection to sexuality and fertility.

Live or Die's "Wanting to Die" embodies the distinction between the ideational and autobiographical strategies and also constitutes an ideal combination of the two. The *I* becomes the mediator between the audience and an idea utterly foreign to it. *I* is crucial to the transmission or translation of the idea, because it concerns the internal economy, the psychology, and even the fundamental philosophy of the suicide. Certainly this poem is also autobiographical, yet its central purpose is to convey to a "you" the suicidal approach toward life. Thus *I* is less concerned to present tragic personal detail or to tally up specific losses than to present to the reader a translation of a "special language" in which the ordinary values of words and of concepts are inverted. Because detachment from life is the suicide's primary attitude, the tone remains detached and impersonal, the *I* never quite "alive," reflecting her "stillborn" stance. This idea could not be as effectively conveyed in the third person, in which case it would entirely lack the ironies on which the poem's richness depends. But the particular identity or story of the *I* is entirely subordinated to the intricate explanation of an idea. Sexton employed this combination of the autobiographical and the ideational *I*, usefully differentiated from the autobiographical *I* who has other primary purposes, from the very beginning of her poetic career in such poems as "Said the Poet to the Analyst," "Her Kind," "The Lost Ingredient," and "For John, Who Begs Me Not to Enquire Further." In "For John" the autobiographical *I* becomes a spokesperson for the poetic and personal authenticity of the confessional stance.

While all of Sexton's (of any poet's) first-person poems might be said to employ personas, a number of her works are constructed on a limited definition of the persona as a constructed poetic self who may clearly be differentiated from the poet, even when she is the poet's blood relative. "The Exorcists" (*Bedlam*) is an early example, in which the female speaker, pregnant with an unwanted baby, submits to an abortion and disowns the love that spoke what she will now "unsay." While critics have assumed that this poem and "The Abortion" in *All My Pretty Ones* depict her own experience, Sexton never specified that she had one; and even if she did, the *I* of both poems is clearly a persona, a constructed character who tells her story in a rhythmic and allusive narrative ("I know you not") that indicates considerable formal distance between poet and speaker. Consider the ritual distance between the tone of this section of "The Exorcists" and the one that follows, from one of Sexton's most autobiographical poems in the same volume, "The Division of Parts." Both excerpts deal with forms of denial:

> And I solemnly swear
> on the chill of secrecy
> that I know you not, this room never,
> the swollen dress I wear,
> nor the anonymous spoons that free me,
> nor this calendar nor the pulse we pare and cover.
>
> ("The Exorcists")

> The clutter of worship
> that you taught me, Mary Gray,
> is old. I imitate
> a memory of belief
> that I do not own. I trip
> on your death and Jesus, *my stranger*
> floats up over
> my Christian home, wearing his straight
> thorn tree. . . .
>
> ("The Division of Parts")

If the difference between the tones, themes, and imagery of these two poems seems less clear to my reader than to me, perhaps it indicates that far from being unable to achieve the artistry of the "impersonal," Sexton was able to make both her autobiographical and her persona poems equally convincing and persuasive.

Other less ambiguous persona poems in *Bedlam* include "Portrait of an Old Woman on the College Tavern Wall," in which the speaker is the painted woman in the portrait; "Where I Live in This Honorable House of the Laurel Tree," spoken by Daphne to Apollo; "The Expatriates," in which expatriation is both literal and metaphorical; "For Johnny Pole," spoken by a soldier's sister; "Unknown Girl in the Maternity Ward," wherein a young girl speaks to her illegitimate child; and "The Moss of His Skin," rendered in the quasi-mythic voice of a young girl buried alive with her father's corpse. *All My Pretty Ones* is similarly studded with persona poems both traditional and radical in their approaches and assumptions—it is here that Sexton first speaks in the voice of Christ ("In the Deep Museum"), one she would later assume in a number of poems that constitute the use of yet another kind of *I*. The speaker of "Old," which I have also called ideational, is an eighty-year-old woman, while "The Hangman" speaks of the tragedy of retarded children from the perspective of the child's father. In "Wallflower" the diminished and pathetic female speaker lends her cynicism and irony to a (probably young) listener; and the personas of "Doors, Doors, Doors" include an old seamstress and a young girl.

In *Live or Die* Sexton speaks in voices not limited to Kumin's four categories; I will simply mention here that "The Legend of the One-Eyed Man" and "To Lose the Earth" are, whatever else they may be, persona poems. Other personas in *Live or Die* are poetically and thematically conservative by comparison: the unhappy couple of "Man and Wife," the lonely and abandoned mother of "Two Sons," even the elaborately constructed "self" of "Suicide Note." Perhaps because it touches upon the spiritual subject that would come to obsess Sexton in later years, "Protestant Easter" seems exceptionally vibrant, even if its speaker is an ordinary eight-year-old child rather than a legendary one-eyed man.

Lyric poetry is notoriously difficult to define. Several of the poems I have already categorized elsewhere might belong here, but the lyric voice is so slippery and anyone's sense of it so intuitive that I have saved for this group only a few "songs" that seem to me to satisfy even the most musically exacting ear. Among Sexton's lyrics I include *Bedlam*'s "Where I Live in This Honorable House of the Laurel Tree," sung by Daphne to Apollo, with its refrain of "wooden legs and O/my green green hands";

and perhaps "For John, Who Begs Me," which is so spacious a poem that it embodies at once all of Kumin's kinds of *I*. In *All My Pretty Ones,* "The Starry Night"—"Oh starry starry night! This is how I want to die."—is balanced between lyric and dirge, while "I Remember" is a sheerly celebratory song to the past. "From the Garden" praises quite another impulse in relation to time: the enjoyment of the present in a simple *carpe diem* motif that ends in the tones of the sweetest pastoral: "Come here! Come here!/Come eat my pleasant fruits." The "time of water, time of trees" evoked in *Live or Die*'s "Three Green Windows" has the tonal flavor of lyric poetry, and the elegy "Somewhere in Africa" approaches chant. *Love Poems*'s "In Celebration of My Uterus" is pure lyric, as is my personal favorite among all of Sexton's love poems, "Us," in which the speaker is transported, and transports her reader, into a harvest song, "acre after acre of gold."

The Prophetic *I* (Eye)

> Prophets in the modern sense of the word have never existed[.] Jonah was no prophet in the modern sense for his prophecy of Ninevah failed. . . . A Prophet is a Seer not an Arbitrary Dictator.
>
> —William Blake[11]

> It is the dream of every poem to become a myth.
>
> —Galway Kinnell[12]

To Kumin's four kinds of *I*, I will add a fifth. I am hampered by the lack of an adequately inclusive yet not overblown word and neverthe-less compelled by the sense that there is something here worth the distinction, a kind of *I* first Americanized by Whitman and most frequently associated with William Blake. I will call it the "prophetic" *I*, to designate those poems in which the poet's voice transcends the personal by becoming mythic or collective or archetypal. The prophetic *I* transmutes the other categories by including them; thus it employs a persona and is at once lyric, ideational, autobiographical, as well as collective and archetypal. It must include a form of the persona in order to speak for many people, yet it must probably also be autobiographical if it is to ring true. Who would listen to disembodied prophets who do not personally know whereof they speak? (People listened to Teiresias not because he was neither man nor woman but because he had been both.) The prophetic voice is lyric, even if it sings in haunting and disturbing tones in order to touch us with the muted music of our collective hearts. Among our contemporaries, I associate the prophetic *I* especially with Galway Kinnell. In poems such as *The Book of Nightmares*, Kinnell speaks in voices that include and transcend the personal *I*. It is not accidental that Kinnell traces the sources of his *I* to Whitman's *Song of Myself*.

The poet as prophet: William Blake. Sexton mentions in a late letter to Rise and Steven Axelrod that she has not read Blake. I infer from the context that the Axelrods had compared her work with Blake's in some respects. Alicia Ostriker points out that only one other poet has attempted in English the revision of Christian myth attempted by Sexton. That poet is William Blake. Sexton's convictions about reaching the holy through art and sensuality are reminiscent of Blake's. The difference in emphasis is that Blake claimed to have found what Sexton continued to pursue. Although Blake and Sexton have been longtime pals of my desk, to borrow a Sextonism, I did not perceive similarities of real consequence between them for many years. I now see similarities in the structure and development of their poetic visions, as well as in what Blake would have called "minute particulars." The early works of both poets are marked by the productive tension of the contraries Blake called innocence and experience. (See "The Girl-Child and the Middle-Aged Witch.") The later work of both Sexton and Blake shares the prophetic voice, modulated by centuries, gender, style, disposition, personality, and geography—all trivialities in the face of a voice crying in the wilderness of Boston or London, in the early nineteenth century or the mid-twentieth, with and against an inadequate and patriarchal God, an uncomfortable and hostile public. Both Blake and Sexton are "mad" poets; both were the victims or recipients of spiritual visions; both quested after the living God. They were equally accused of inappropriate style and off-the-wall imagery, partly as a consequence of both poets' insistence on a peculiar vernacular that included references to people, places, even streets, familiar to themselves but not to us, or terms appropriate to the print shop (Blake) or the kitchen (Sexton), but not to the sacred grove. Sexton and Blake did not confine their impudence and inappropriateness to style and imagery, for their subject matter was far more forbidden. They talked of the psyche and of sex in anatomically specific ways. Both were anatomically specific about the cultural malaise as well and analyzed the sexual etiology of the neuroses by which, they well knew, they were themselves victimized. Both were feminists without quite knowing it. And both, it might be argued, after becoming wild spiritual revolutionaries who dreamed they could "piss in God's eye," lapsed into virtuous and slightly desperate belief at the ends of their very different lives.

The prophetic voice need not "prophesy" in the sense of prediction, but it must sound the seer's note of insight into large cultural stuff. As Ostriker says of *Transformations*, Sexton seized and cracked open folk-tale material, maintaining the continuity of the tradition even as the healthy meanings we are used to enjoying are "held up to icy scrutiny." In the fairy tale universe, we are accustomed to thinking that all mean-hearted realities and hierarchies are turned upside down; the poor become rich, men and women live happily ever after, bad guys get theirs. But Sexton's retellings expose the fact that such reversals are superficial, and that the moral universe of the fairy tale is exceptionally conservative rather than radical, especially as regards its primary (if repressed) sexual subject matter. Her ironic narrator, the "middle-aged witch, me," suggests to us that the meanings we have been enjoying all along are indeed "healthy"—i.e., rigorously conservative and disap-pointingly normal. "Were we to look at these poems as moral texts, we would have to see in them a demand for some transvaluation of social values."[13] While I agree that their primary appeal is not moral and that Sexton's versions retain the psychic impact of the originals, turned in on themselves and us in a horribly funny and badly cracked mirror, I do experience them as moral texts—and in this they are not different from the originals, which inculcate the very moral lessons that Sexton explodes. What is the moral lesson of *Little Red Riding Hood?* Stay home, little girl. Do not stray from the appointed path. Sexton enlarges this into a parable on deception in its many guises.

Transformations freed Sexton more fully to speak in the prophetic voice that is an amalgam of the mythic, the archetypal, and the transpersonal. Hers becomes, as Lauter says, an earnest quest of "soul-making" characterized by impudence and heresy. In "The Jesus Papers," "The Death of the Fathers," "O Ye Tongues," "The Death Baby," and "The Furies," she rewrites both Christian myth and the history of her gender, more than incidentally connected. At one moment she seems to move toward a visionary insight into how things might be different, how she might tell the story of the woman poet in ways that could change her life through changing her *perceptions* and those of others. In "O Ye Tongues," for instance, she reimagines her entire history as a means to experiencing it creatively. At another moment her visionary eye is more bent on telling the story that *is* as opposed to the one that we think it is, or even the one that might transform us; in these works, such as "The Death Baby," penetrating analysis is its own form of prophecy, and that prophecy participates in prediction even as it goes beyond it: this is how it has been; this is how it will be if we are not careful, she says of our self-destructiveness in "The Death Baby."

I have said that one way to define the prophetic *I* is as an amalgam of the four forms of *I* designated by Kumin. The whole is more than the sum of its parts, for the combined lyric, ideational, autobiographical, and confessional *I* transcends the authenticity and the resonance of any of the other types. The prophetic *I* might be called another kind of *over-I,* with ironic correspondences to the customary English translation of that term in psychoanalysis as "superego." If the superego is the harshly restraining internalized voice of the parents and of cultural sublimation, it is still, as Freud always insisted, a part of the id, and takes its ravenous character from that source. The psychoanalytic superego is a moralistic inversion, perhaps, of this other "over-I." While the superego has the narrowest possible vision, the vision of the prophetic eye is all-encompassing. The superego is a petty moralist, while the prophetic *I,* in the poets with whom we most readily associate it (Blake and Whitman) tends toward what some might call hedonism. The superego's sense of the "right" is rigorously normative, but the prophetic *I* tends to reverse normative values—or at least to expose their inadequacy. The superego refrains from discussing sex or religion in public; the prophetic voice cannot shut up about either. Impudence, heresy, humor, and wit, especially regarding the most ultimate matters— these qualities so frequently associated with Anne Sexton always combine in the prophet-poet, than whom no one could be more genuinely reverent.

I discuss elsewhere in this book many of the Sexton poems I am here calling prophetic: "The Death Baby," "O Ye Tongues," "The Death of the Fathers," "The Consecrating Mother," sections of *Transformations.* Alicia Ostriker, Estella Lauter, Suzanne Juhasz, and Diane Middlebrook have claimed similar achievements for Sexton's late poetry, especially "The Jesus Papers." While *Transformations* declared her full emancipation from restrictions, Sexton announced her intentions to speak in the prophetic voice long before its publication. *Bedlam*'s "Where I Live" and "The Moss of His Skin" try out mythic and cross-cultural female voices; and "In the Deep Museum" (*All My Pretty Ones*), the first of Sexton's Jesus poems, remains a major achievement in the prophetic mode. The speaker of "Museum" is Christ himself—a bold stroke for any poet, and especially a woman. The Christ of this appropriation of a man-god's voice is the ragged human brother, trapped in his tomb after crucifixion, buried alive, and knowing he is no god. "Surely my body is done? Surely I died?" he asks plaintively, knowing that "I lied." Joined by a rat, this immensely needy and completely human Christ considers his companion's purpose: "His teeth test me; he waits like a good cook." Sorry for the lie of his incomplete death and the betrayal of his followers, he invites his brother rats to eat his body, committing "my prophecy and fear" to their bellies and jaws. "Far below The Cross, I correct its flaws./We have kept the miracle. I will not be here." While "Museum" irreverently imagines a biological rather than spiritual explanation for the disappearance of Christ's body, it does so in a way that can only be called religious. This first of Sexton's Christs has no selfish motives, wishes only to help his fellow humans, and has been forsaken by his God just as generations of his followers will feel sometimes forsaken. The perfections of the scriptural Christ yield to the identification of the poet with her own utterly human God. Without once straying toward clichés, the poem tests the relationship between humanity and one of its gods, created in its own image, and suggests how we might first have come to announce a miracle.

In another poem from *All My Pretty Ones*, "Water," Sexton makes an early reach toward a mythic and collective voice:

> Water is worse than woman.
> It calls to a man to empty him.
> Under us
> twelve princesses dance all night,
> exhausting their lovers, then giving them up.
> I have known water.
> I have sung all night
> for the last cargo of boys.

But *Live or Die* provides the most extensive early evidence of Sexton's desire to speak in the mythic and collective voice of a culture. A spirit of generous power presides over "Somewhere in Africa," Sexton's elegy to her teacher, John Holmes, the censorious Jocasta of "For John, Who Begs Me Not to Enquire Further." This poem reaches toward prophecy with confidence and clarity. For four of its eight stanzas, "Somewhere in Africa" is a powerful elegy to a dead teacher who has lost his power not only to death but to a passing time and an unyieldingly pedestrian world. "Dead of a dark thing," he has been mourned as father and teacher with "piety and grace" and blessed with the prayers and psalms of a colorless and bloodless religion. The critics have ignored his last book, and the doctors have abandoned him to cancer. Most ironic, he has been "praised by the mild God" who leaves him "timid, with no real age,/whitewashed by belief, as dull as the windy preacher!" The world into which he is commended, and which robs him of all force and power, is ironically the one he has worked to protect in its literary form: one of decorum, reason, restraint, institutionalized authority. Yet there is no edge of triumph in the speaker's voice.

Just as it appears we are going to leave John Holmes's "small eyes" to the nurses that carry him "into a strange land," we are transported to the primal and exotic domain of the prophetic poet, in which the God is "some tribal female who is known but forbidden." Sexton seizes the spirit of Holmes from its death in the catacomb of the fathers and takes it to a wild, unbridled place where rituals of power will resurrect it into dream and mystery, incantation and fertility, presided over by "a woman of some virtue/and wild breasts." Diane Middlebrook concludes, after examining the details of Sexton's confrontational, troubled relationship to Holmes, that Sexton is claiming Holmes for the eternity reserved for poets, in contrast to the institutional world that had earlier claimed him in health as well as in sickness; these two states or places are respectively feminine and masculine. The prophesied and forbidden world of poetry is that of libidinous, passionate expression, disclosure and reinvestment of mystery, and of primary process—no doubt, no naysaying, no dry restraint here. The poem is wet not only with water but with palm oil, sweat, and the juice of fruits. It concludes with the speaker's advice to the spirit of Holmes:

> John Holmes, cut from a single tree, lie heavy in her hold
> and go down that river with the ivory, the copra and the gold.

"Somewhere in Africa" begins as an earthbound elegy, moves toward a parable of the domain of poetry, and is spacious enough to read as a prayer of incantation for and to the dead—any dear dead, poet or not—that invokes the most fundamental spirits of life.

That Sexton felt herself to be in touch with such prophetic spirits during the composition of poems in *Live or Die* is also clear in "Consorting with Angels," in which she begins as a woman "tired of my mouth and my breasts," of "the gender of things." The woman weary of gender journeys into a dream to find the answer to her predicament. There she finds a city made of chains, "where Joan was put to death in man's clothes," and where no two creatures are of the same species—meaning,

I assume, that here there is no sexual reproduction and therefore no gender. "You are the answer," the speaker cries to this dream and enters the city, where she loses "my common gender and my final aspect." With Adam on one side of her and Eve on the other, she rides under the sun, free of her femaleness. The final section begs several questions of tone and intent:

> O daughters of Jerusalem,
> the king has brought me into his chamber.
> I am black and I am beautiful.
> I've been opened and undressed.
> I have no arms or legs.
> I'm all one skin like a fish.
> I'm no more a woman
> than Christ was a man.

The return of gender in the city of its absence, and in a sexually explicit scene, both reinforces and undercuts the "answer" the dream has claimed to provide the speaker. The final two lines are a nearly comic disclaimer for which I see at least two possible readings. Christ was not a man as ordinary men are: he was beyond gender; he included both genders. But Christianity claimed him as God in the form of man; given her perception of Christianity, Sexton might also mean us to notice that Christ was, in some of his incarnations, nothing *but* a man. Tonal consideration requires us to allow for at least two sharply conflicting possibilities: a woman, a man, can escape gender in a dreamworld where gender is transcended or included, a heaven of angels whose nature "went unexplained"; but the genderless place is a city of chains where one loses one's "final aspect" and becomes "all one skin like a fish." The poem also affirms that the dream is a lie, that there is no escaping gender, here or beyond, waking or in dream.

Another prophetic voice in *Live or Die* is the speaker of "To Lose the Earth," who inhabits a cave by the sea in the bowels of the earth, where a musician plays a flute. "This is the music that you waited for/in the great concert halls,/season after season,/and never found." The side of the flute grows into the wall and extends, perhaps, as far as the sun. Like "Consorting with Angels," this poem concerns itself with the visionary meanings of gender; the musician is both man and woman, the undefiled aspect of all humanity, "the eternal listener/who has cried back into the earth." In this place of utter purity, the visitors are appalled to find the Other, the dwarf whose instrument is not a solar flute but rather an extension of his tongue. "He plays his own song, cursing the wind/with his enormous misshapen mouth." Each one who sees him jumps up and shouts, "It is you!" and is forced to acknowledge what he or she knew from the moment of entry into the cave: even eternity, even primal purity, has its dwarf with the misshapen mouth.

"The Legend of the One-Eyed Man" demonstrated the close alliance the prophetic poet may claim to material she utterly transmutes from its personal form. Sexton's theme here was the repression and sacrifice of the feminine that constitutes Christianity's other "betrayal"; through this story central to our culture, she characterized our spiritual and sexual dilemmas. The poem's speaker is male, and the "crime" he is guilty of is peculiarly masculine, but the Oedipal situation at the thematic core of the poem was Sexton's own. The one-eyed man, as I argued in "Oedipus Anne," presents the male counterpart of the feminine dilemma that Sexton saw as her own and that of women in her culture. Along with "In the Deep Museum," "Somewhere in Africa," "Consorting with Angels," and "To Lose the Earth," Sexton's "Legend of the One-Eyed Man" announced her decision to speak of the deepest secrets of her era and her location in the civilized world. It is the poet-prophet's purpose to "see" what we have "overlooked."

6
Innocence and Experience: The Girl-Child and the Middle-Aged Witch

> I dream of falling dolls
> who need cribs and blankets and pajamas
> with real feet in them.
> Why is there no mother?
> Why are all these dolls falling out of the sky?
> Was there a father?
> Or have the planets cut holes in their nets
> and let our childhood out,
> or are we the dolls themselves,
> born but never fed?
>
> —"The Falling Dolls," *45 Mercy Street*

In her haunting evocations of childhood, Anne Sexton joins company with Wordsworth, Vaughan, Traherne, and especially with the Blake of *Songs of Innocence and Experience.* While he wrote collections with these titles, deliberately juxtaposed, she wrote continually pulled by such contraries. The world of Sexton's innocence, like Blake's, is radical and therefore dangerous. The child who wishes to be unrestrained and free must come to terms with the imperatives of experience. Sexton remained a champion of the embattled child within, but, like Blake, she always wrote about the light from the dark perspective of experience. The child's natural exuberance is immediately compromised by contact with the adult world of restrainers who project their guilt and anxiety into the child's perspective. Her poems of innocence are shadowed by the loss that relegates them forever to a dreamed past yet are lightened by the determination to keep the child within alive against all odds. It is always the speaker of *Transformations,* that "middle-aged witch, me," who writes in the child's voice, revitalizing the dreamworld where sexuality is innocent, death does not exist, time is eternity, and "God can really see the heat and painted light." Yet also as in Blake, the wise and corrupted perspective from which Sexton writes does not destroy the authenticity of the child-speaker's vision. It is only that we, the readers, and she, the poet, have lost the power to believe it as true. (Is it true? she asks, knowing the answer.) In this she is also in the tradition of Wordsworth, hers the same straining after innocence that we find in sections of *The Prelude*, structured by a similarly articulated notion of "spots of time" by which she might mark her intimations of immortality. Wordsworth "knows" it is not true, but he would make it true with the force of his dreamed language. So would Sexton. But within her battled, as within Blake, contraries whose juxtaposition created progression but did not offer final solution. She could see a world in a grain of sand and eternity in an hour, but she knew that she, that we all, continually fall back into the prosaic planes of time and space. Throughout the canon, from poems such as "Young" in *All My Pretty Ones* through the "Death Baby" sequence in *Death Notebooks,* Sexton created a child both innocent and corrupted, who has a hole where the heart should be that enables her to "hear the unsaid more clearly."

Perhaps her attraction to the Grimms' fairy tales that form the basis of *Transformations* is in part accounted for by how alive Anne Sexton remained to the voice of the child within. The speaker of the tales is indeed the "middle-aged witch," but her mouth is wide open, receptive to magic. She has come to "remind you,/all of you," of the child within. In a handy bit of trickery, the introduction to *Transformations* allows us to picture children gathering around the witch: "Alice, Samuel, Kurt, Eleanor,/Jane, Brian, Maryel,/all of you draw near." But these are not children after all. The middle-aged witch is speaking to her own generation: "Alice,/at fifty-six do you remember?" The witch tells children's stories to adults she knows are still internally young. It is their own wishes and dreams and fears she will expose, just as she delineates the fearfully mature wisdom of the child. She conjures up a boy, sixteen, who wants some answers: "He is each of us./I mean you./I mean me."

Sexton's detractors have been pleased to turn her gift of communion with the child-self into an accusation—her poems and her personality are "childish"—while those of us not sure we have outgrown our own large child, or not sure we want to, have nodded in delighted recognition at the child of "elbows, knees, dreams, goodnight," in painful identification with the one whose body was "the suspect in its grotesque house." The adult who cannot sometimes still hear "how parents call from sweet beaches anywhere, *come in, come in,*" inhabits a world impoverished by lack of contact with a state of mind I often call July—or, at its most richly ripened moment, August.

Certainly Sexton's preoccupation with childhood was part of her illness, and she knew it. In "You, Doctor Martin" (*Bedlam*), Sexton sees herself and the other mental patients on her ward as the "foxy" and "large" children the doctor must visit after breakfast. Like children, the mentally ill will manipulate their father-doctor to get the attention they want. "Kind Sir: These Woods" (*Bedlam*) remembers that "this is an old game/that we played when we were eight and ten," turning around with eyes shut tight deliberately to become lost, to trick the world into turning upside down. The mad speaker, "lost and of your same kind," has played that trick on herself. In a double parody of herself and of psychoanalysis, the speaker of "Cripples and Other Stories" (*Live or Die*) twits her doctor with this rhyme: "Each time I give lectures/or gather in the grants/you send me off to boarding school/in training pants." But we have seen that the joke is not funny, because she is really thirty-six and "one of the lunatics." When her child-self harms her, she tries to do it in: when there is "rust in my mouth,/the stain of an old kiss," she knows "it is only the child in me bursting out/and I keep plotting how to kill her" ("The Lost Lie," *45 Mercy Street*).

Yet no one knew more surely than Sexton that the sources of pain and delight are identical, that they arise from the unconscious in dreams and in poems. Infancy is the scene of "dreaming the breasts," in which the infant "ate up" the strange goddess, her mother. The infant's guilty greed will cause the adult to make lifelong reparation. "The Death Baby" explores the still-born aspect of the psyche beyond the pleasure principle in the "dumb traveler" we carry lifelong, that ice baby with "still eyes like marbles." Yet infancy is also the source of invention and imagination, as the baby "swallows magic" and delivers herself into life.

The ambivalence of the life into which the young child is delivered is expressed in two poems that record very differently the experience of being five and six years old. In the "May 5, 1970" poem of the "Dr. Y." sequence, the child plays under stiff and sturdy pines, "sifting the air/like harps, sifting over that fifth me." Under the "dark green" of this "different order . . . different sign," she is safe and happy. It is equally true that at six Sexton's speaker lived "in a graveyard full of dolls,/avoiding myself." Both "suspect" and "exile," she "sat all day/stuffing my heart into a shoe box." The bodily indignities of anyone's childhood are grotesquely summarized, if not parodied, in the "bedtime ritual"

> where, on the cold bathroom tiles,
> I was spread out daily
> and examined for flaws.
> —"Those Times . . . " (*Live or Die*)

Reflecting on her "Baby Picture" taken at age seven, Sexton notes the "good-bye-bow in the hair" and the "clerical collar of the dress" and sees through the peeling paint "a child bent on a toilet seat." Who were you? she asks. Her answer—"merely a kid keeping alive"—relinquishes her own, and anyone's, need for uniqueness and acknowledges our commonality. ("Your fear is anyone's fear. . . . ")

The eight-year-old speaker of "Protestant Easter" is beset by uncertainties, but she is a happily inquiring and insightful girl who can penetrate the hypocrisies of the adult world. She is also the speaker (or the one spoken of) in the best of Sexton's childhood poems in *Bedlam*, *All My Pretty Ones*, and *Live or Die*. Her parents have told her that when Jesus was a little boy he was "good all the time." No wonder, she muses in church, that he grew up to be someone who "could forgive people so much." She wonders where he went between crucifixion and resurrection—"Maybe he was only hiding?/Maybe he could fly?"—and realizes how important it is for her to "get him straight." A great deal depends, she knows, on doing so: "Who are we anyhow?/What do we belong to?" Looking to the adult worshippers around her on Easter morning, she suspects they do not know the answers any more than she does. "*Alleluia* they sing./They don't know." The ending, in its wryly eight-year-old yet wise way, pins contemporary suburban Protestantism to the cross of its own hypocrisy, and its hope:

> And about Jesus,
> they couldn't be sure of it,
> not so sure of it anyhow,
> so they decided to become Protestants.
> Those are the people that sing
> when they aren't quite
> sure.

Innocently wise and lovable, this child speaker is perhaps the one we would all like to remember ourselves having been. She is the same child spoken of in what is perhaps Sexton's best single childhood poem, "Young" (*All My Pretty Ones*). Here Sexton recalls herself lying at night in the grass "a thousand doors ago" when it was summer "as long as I could remember." Clover "wrinkled" under her, wise stars "bedded" over her, and "probably a million leaves/sailed on their strange stalks" as she lay in the secure atmosphere of her parents' bedroom windows.

> And I, in my brand new body,
> which was not a woman's yet,
> told the stars my questions
> and thought God could really see
> the heat and painted light,
> elbows, knees, dreams, goodnight.

Not a woman's body yet: Sexton captures with extraordinarily skilled precision this moment before sexuality will change everything. The child's world is not without intimations of this knowledge, however. "In the Beach House" (*Live or Die*) places the child in her little cot, where she listens in "all night long" while her parents are at "the royal strapping," balanced so finely between aggression and tenderness that we do not quite know if they are arguing or making love. One line makes us, and the child listener, sure:

> My loves are oiling their bones
> and then delivering them with unspeakable sounds
> that carry them this way and that
> while summer is hurrying its way in and out,
> over and over,
> in their room.

Most of the time, however, she can deny this knowledge, even while one part of her knows everything. In "Love Song" (*Live or Die*), the speaker on the brink of adolescence is "the girl of the chain letter" and the "wrinkled photo and the lost connections" who kept saying "*Listen! Listen!/We must never! We must never!*/and all those things." Yet while "all those things" are going on, she is aware of "an old red hook in her mouth" that bleeds into "the terrible fields of her soul." She is able to ignore her wound by transforming the repressed knowledge of the forbidden into a harmless kind of fun she will never know as an adult:

> Oh! There is no translating
> that ocean,
> that music,
> that theater,
> that field of ponies.

Poised on the delicate brink of childhood and adolescence, Sexton's speaker remembers her feelings for her parents in two poems that celebrate passionate innocence. In *Bedlam's* "The Bells," she asks, "Father, do you remember?" The girl and her father went together to the circus, where "I, laughing,/lifted to your high shoulder,... was not afraid." Bells trembled as the "flying man" breasted the sky and climbed the air, while "love love/love grew rings around me." What she will always remember from this special moment is "the color of music/and how forever/all the trembling bells of you/were mine."

The mother of "Three Green Windows" (*Live or Die*) does not spread her daughter on cold bathroom tiles to examine her for flaws but tells her a story to "keep me asleep/against her plump and fruity skin." Now middle-aged and half awake in a Sunday nap, the speaker has "misplaced the Van Allen belt" and "forgotten the names of the literary critics" in her childhood reverie:

> I know what I know.
> I am the child I was,
> living the life that was mine.
> I am young and half asleep.
> It is a time of water, a time of trees.

Water and trees are ironically and appropriately the medium for the girl's initiation into fertility and sexuality in "It Is a Spring Afternoon" (*Love Poems*). Because "everything here is yellow and green," because "everything here is possible," a young girl has taken off her clothes and "placed herself upon a tree limb/that hangs over a pool in the river." It is her own awakening into her womanly body that causes the very ground to cure its sores and the trees to "turn in their trenches/and hold up little rain cups/by their slender fingers."

> The face of the child wrinkles
> in the water and is gone forever.
> The woman is all that can be seen
> in her animal loveliness.
> Her cherished and obstinate skin
> lies deeply under the watery tree.
> Everything is altogether possible
> and the blind men can also see.

Nothing will remain so simply pure for long. The "Nana-Hex" that overtakes her at thirteen will make her feel that her own sexuality has introduced evil into the world: "You did it. You are the evil" (*Book of Folly*). The uncompromised innocence of "The Bells" will be replaced by a sexual relationship to the father that has its own ritual dangers in "Oysters" and "How We Danced." Her mother and "Jack," the stand-in for her father in the primal scene of the summer house, "fill up heaven" and "endorse my womanhood," but Mother is dead, and Jack is now a man of the cloth. As Sexton says to her daughter Joy, "I look for uncomplicated hymns,/but love has none" (*Live or Die*).

Sexton personalizes and complicates the initiation into genitality of the adolescent female in "Little Girl, My String Bean, My Lovely Woman," written for her other daughter, Linda. The celebration of womanhood links this famous poem with "It Is a Spring Afternoon," but "Little Girl" ripens the simple lyric moment of "Spring Afternoon" into high noon—"the hour of the ghosts." The tone is correspondingly complex; "Spring Afternoon" is pure celebration, while "Little Girl" strikes notes at once festive and mournfully haunted. Here Sexton is the mother rather than the adolescent daughter, so she knows the complications that await the young girl when young men "come to you,/someday, men bare to the waist, young Romans/at noon where they belong,/with ladders and hammers/while no one sleeps." As is true of all of her poems to her daughters, "Little Girl" is suffused with Sexton's own memory, rendered with immediacy and intimacy, of how it feels to be just such an age, feeling just such urges:

> Oh, funny little girl—this one under a blueberry sky,
> this one! How can I say that I've known
> just what you know and just where you are?

The remembering mother cannot help but mourn the loss attendant upon the worthy gains of achieving sexual maturity, for she knows that her darling, "born in that sweet birthday suit/and having owned it and known it for so long," must now relinquish its innocent joys forever. Speaking in the tones and rhythms of nursery rhymes the daughter is about to outgrow, the mother evokes at one moment the child and the child's passing:

> *Oh, little girl,*
> *my stringbean,*
> *how do you grow?*
> *You grow this way.*
> *You are too many to eat.*

The occasion for the poem is a ritual passage, but its purpose transcends either celebration or mourning. "Little Girl" is a gift from mother to daughter, a blessing full of needful information. The mother had no such ritual messenger to ease her own passing—"I was alone./I waited like a target"—and she must be sure to give her own daughter the timely blessing she lacked. "Mother and Jack" endorsed her own womanhood too late. "Let high noon enter," and "let your body in," she says; but before the naked men come to her, delightful and dangerous as young Romans, there will have been this prior assurance that *"your bones are lovely"* from the hand that formed them. She would have her daughter understand this as another birth, for "women are born twice." Just as the first birth is true, "there is nothing in your body that lies./All that is new is telling the truth." "Little Girl" ends with the sweetest and strongest blessing of mother to daughter in any language, any poetry, any myth. It could come only from a woman who remembers the same moment in her own life and knows how much difference it might make:

> Darling,
> stand still at your door,
> sure of yourself, a white stone, a good stone—
> as exceptional as laughter
> you will strike fire,
> that new thing!

The poet who can remember every resonant moment of the past can also project herself into the final moment of anyone's future. "Old" is spoken by an eighty-year-old woman "afraid of needles" and "tired of faces that I don't know." Her death starts like a dream, "full of objects and my sister's laughter."

> We are young and we are walking
> and picking wild blueberries
> all the way to Damariscotta.

Kenneth Koch's nursing-home poets in *I Never Told Anybody* reveal how keen was Anne Sexton's sense of what matters most to older people.[1] If there is an overarching theme for the poets represented in Koch's anthology, it is their distant pasts, and in particular their childhoods. Sexton's "Old" might speak for any number of them. But I will let them speak for themselves. This is Mary Tkalec, remembering her girlhood on a beloved farm:

> I was a farm girl
> always on the field.
> You always got a shower

> it washed you down.
> I love the feel of it
> and how clean it smells afterward.
> We never had a bathtub,
> we had a brook.
>
> . . . .
>
> We also had a deep swimming hole—
> I swam like a fish.[2]

If Mary Tkalec breaks into the present tense only once in this excerpt, Margaret Whittaker's memories are rendered entirely immediate by the sense of her continuously present past:

> Kevin and Billy are eating tunafish sandwiches and
>   Southern Fried Chicken.
> Night is like popcorn popping, or getting the butter
>   from Grandma.
> The woman on the porch is filling a dish with homemade
>   taffy candy.
> My mother is picking Norwegian Salt Berries.[3]

You know how parents call from those sweet beaches anywhere, *come in, come in,* even if you have long since grown into the parent who calls instead of the child who tries not to hear. Sexton remembers those sweet beaches, those voices, more clearly than most people do, and she gives them back to us, a gift "caught back from time." The "image we did forget" is the one she remembers; the "half a bell" now silenced for most of us, she hears.

> What else is this, this intricate shape of air?
> calling me, calling you.
> —"What's That" (*Bedlam*)

Sexton's ability to be enveloped by that intricate shape of air made her happiest when she was; it also caused her to be vulnerable to a special sort of sadness: "in my heart I am go children slow."

Part IV
Wanting to Die

7
"The Violent against Themselves"

> Anne, I don't want to live. . . . Now listen, life is lovely, but I
> CAN'T LIVE IT. I can't even explain. I know how silly it sounds . . .
> but if you knew how it FELT. To be alive, yes, alive, but not be able
> to live it. AY that's the rub. I am like a stone that lives . . . locked
> outside of all that's real. . . . Anne, do you know of such things, can
> you hear???? I wish, or think I wish, that *I* were dying of something
> for then I could be brave, but to be not dying, and yet . . . and yet to
> [be] behind a wall, watching everyone fit in where I can't, to talk
> behind a gray foggy wall, to live but to not reach or to reach
> wrong . . . to do it all wrong . . . believe me, (can you?) . . . what's
> wrong. I want to belong. I'm like a jew who ends up in the wrong
> country. I'm not a part. I'm not a member. I'm frozen.
>
> —Anne Sexton, from a letter to Anne Clark, October 13, 1964

Attitudes toward Suicide

Dante places the "violent against themselves" in Circle 7 of *The
Inferno*, where their souls are encased in thorny trees and the Harpies
feed upon their leaves, opening wounds from which come "words and
blood together." Only as long as the blood flows may the souls speak, so
that this torturous feeding gives them "pain and pain's outlet simultaneously." Because they have thrown away their bodies—"betrayed the
body," as Anne Sexton writes in "Wanting to Die"—they will not be
permitted to regain them even at Judgment:

> Like the rest, we shall go for our husks on Judgment Day,
>   but not that we may wear them, for it is not just
>   that a man be given what he throws away.
>
> Here shall we drag them and in this mournful glade
>   our bodies will dangle to the end of time,
>   each on the thorns of its tormented shade.[1]

Even though Dante himself cannot speak upon hearing the fate of
the suicides—"such compassion chokes my heart"—there is no room in

his theology for extenuating circumstances, wrinkles in the DNA, chemical imbalances, the overthrow of justice by love. Is there such room in our "theology," our eccentric amalgam of psychology, social science, humanism, and codes of ethics? I sometimes think that there is not. For what other deaths do we reserve such a pietistic, bastard mixture of pity, contempt, disapproval, and fear?

In a culture that dedicates itself aggressively, even if not successfully, to the sanctity of life, we do not like to deal with the fact that some people want to die. Despite all the alterations that the last decade may have brought about in humane attitudes toward suicide, a hard-jawed resistance persists toward accepting the wish to die, an unwillingness to permit that wish to anyone. Such resistance and unwillingness may be born of tenderly humanistic impulses; even so, those impulses undergo a mean transformation when they are codified in culture. The euthanasia and living-will movements may have altered American attitudes toward the desire to die under some circumstances; but those circumstances— the only ones that sufficiently compel social, moral, and sometimes legal compassion—are always extreme and always physical. That is, arguments for changing attitudes toward the voluntary ending of one's life are still restricted to cases involving terminal physical disease or unendurable physical agony. For all the theoretical efforts to establish the legitimacy of mental agony comparable to physical agony—efforts, in other words, to banish simplistic mind/body dichotomies that are nearly definitive of Western culture—fear and disapproval of the desire to end emotional pain by means of suicide still seem utterly undisturbed. Perhaps this is as it should be, in many respects. Any culture that begins tampering with boundaries between life and death must proceed cautiously. But even if such conservatism is well advised, one may regret the cruelly antihumanistic face often worn by the human need to protect its own.

Antipathy toward suicide is not as deep as it once was, but most people still think of suicide as ethically and morally reprehensible— even sinful, although many of us are not comfortable with the word. Perhaps we no longer bury suicides separately, hang their already dead bodies, or say that they are going to hell; at least those of us who consider ourselves enlightened do not say such things. But our compassion and sympathy are inflected with reprobation at the very least and with repulsion in many instances, especially when the suicide occurs for other than "legitimate" reasons. In the case of people whose emotional or mental illness has remained intractable to medication and to human love for years, even decades, for whom the mental agony of staying alive is indeed intolerable and unendurable, and for whom the best that can be said of their mental state is that their dis-ease with life is subject to occasional remission, even of considerable duration—why do we so automatically assume that they should endure, stick it out, to the bitter and "natural" end?

The question is only partly ingenuous. Certainly we all know the answers, or some of them. Our bias in favor of life is to some extent self-explanatory and needs no justification. This places the burden of justification on the potential suicide, who, according to Allen Alvarez, may always have felt he or she was born to die as soon as possible. And when the living of life is itself a nearly unendurable burden, this extra burden, of disapproval or uncomprehending sympathy, of the need to explain and justify to people who cannot understand why one would not want to live, who assume that it is better in all circumstances to be alive than dead, who assume this so utterly that even their deepest sympathy is threaded with repulsion and disapproval, this extra burden, I think, must be heavy beyond endurance. Even the death-radicals among us, those responsible for the formation of euthanasia societies, must show insensitivity for strategic reasons to the legitimacy of suicide undertaken because of emotional agony or depression.

Contrary to the common assumption that suicide is never rational unless it takes place in the presence of racking physical pain or terminal physical illness, Alvarez in *The Savage God* presents what is still the clearest recent explanation in prose of the suicidal stance toward life. Speaking of the majority of suicides, he says:

> For them, the act is neither rash nor operatic nor, in any obvious way, unbalanced. Instead it is, insidiously, a vocation. Once inside the closed world, there seems never to have been a time when one was not suicidal. Just as a writer feels himself never to have been anything except a writer, even if he can remember with embarrassment his first doggerel, even if he has spent years, like Conrad, disguised as a sea dog, so the suicide feels he has always been preparing in secret for this last act.[2]

To such a one, whose "memory is stored with long black afternoons of childhood, with taste of pleasures that gave no pleasure, with sour losses and failures, all repeated endlessly like a scratched phonograph record," admonitions to live courageously for an indefinite period of time seem absurd.³ Most terminally ill people, in the restricted sense in which we have come to use the term, have at least the comfort of an end in sight, which they wish legitimately to hasten. The suicide Alvarez describes, one he considers to represent most achieved and potential suicides, has no such comfort if he or she is in decent bodily condition— using "bodily" in the further and similarly restricted way we do. Few people would consider saying to the lucid person afflicted with terminal throat and jaw cancer, "Well, at least you have your mental health. Be thankful for that." But we say the reverse equivalent to the seriously and chronically depressed person whose condition may be just as beyond her control, and just as "terminal."

Wanting to Die

In the interim between Anne Sexton's first suicide attempt and her final and successful one, an interval of some seventeen years, she wrote at least twenty poems primarily dedicated to explaining what it feels like to want, or need, to die. These poems translate into understandable idiom the language, so foreign to most people, of the suicide. As poems, their degree of success varies. Those that are poetically skillful are also polemically persuasive—if this can be called a polemic, and I think it can. Sexton's finest single poem on the subject is *Live or Die*'s "Wanting to Die,"⁴ which begins:

> Since you ask, most days I cannot remember.
> I walk in my clothing, unmarked by that voyage.
> Then the almost unnameable lust returns.

The speaker answers a question asked outside the poem's frame. It is not possible to know exactly what that question was, but a reasonable inference is that the questioner has inquired about her feelings toward life. She has been asked, in other words, to explain herself. The reader should not lose sight of the implicit audience whose question is the occasion of the poem; that outsider *is* the reader, who comes to such a poem with predictable assumptions and resistances. The first two lines are distant, detached, calm, as well as open and frank. The speaker is answering the question as directly as she can. But the lines are end-stopped, clipped, flat, almost tired. Each day is a trip, a voyage, but one the speaker moves through rather than participates in. The third line shifts abruptly from the weary business of life to the desire for death. The diction suggests intense, passionate, almost sexual involvement, but even this line is still explanatory in tone. The speaker explains the sequence of emotional events:

> Even then I have nothing against life.
> I know well the grass blades you mention,
> the furniture you have placed under the sun.

This could be an institutional lawn where the speaker might be talking to her doctor. But the questioner could as well be any person who cares about the speaker: a husband, a friend, a lover. In any case, an attitude has been conveyed from outside the frame of reference in the poem, and that attitude says, "See how good life is." The simple diction points to forces of fertility and evokes the comfort of man-made things as well. The furniture under the sun recalls warmth, human company, even perhaps domesticity, things that ordinarily make life worthwhile. Again, the tone of her response is detached and assessive:

> But suicides have a special language.
> Like carpenters they want to know *which tools.*
> They never ask *why build.*

The speaker has shifted here from acknowledging the argument for life to asserting the desire for death. To effect this she is forced to use metaphorical language, an analogy with something ordinary that the hearer will understand. Now the speaker must begin the arduous task of translating from a foreign language. This job becomes the central work of the poem, the subtle and controlling metaphor on which the poem stands—or falls. The effectiveness and precision of the translation, the communication of nuance and idiom into words the hearer will understand through his or her own language, are measures of the poem's success. The "language" of the suicide, to make the matter conceptually and practically tougher, is essentially nonverbal and has to do with act rather than word. The speaker is trapped doubly: not only must she translate into words the hearer can understand; she must deal with the problem that the only words at her disposal are in a language whose structure emphatically asserts life. The connotations of the words she must press to her service are all loaded against her: life is good, death is bad. The moral imperatives of this language censure her position from the outset, for its values are as foreign to her as are the values of her speechless language to the hearer. She will be forced literally to overturn the structure of the hearer's language.

The speaker begins with an elementary analogy, a concrete simile easy enough to understand. In order to explain this "lust" of hers to someone who does not feel it, she chooses a dry, uncharged, explicit image to convey a state of mind whose essence is passionate. The carpenter comparison implies an unmentioned third element, the architect or planner who *does* ask "why build," as contrasted with the carpenter whose job it is to arrive at the site and begin to work. Suicides are like this, says the speaker. There is no word for them that translates into "why"; there is only "how," because it is definitive of a carpenter that she find the way to build, and just as definitive of the suicide that she find a way to die. The irony is effective and underscores the reversal of connotative value that the poem has begun: carpenters are creators and builders. Suicides, as normal perception sees them, are destroyers. The hearer, if she is to enter into the linguistic universe of the suicide, must begin to see that for the suicide, killing oneself is a kind of building, a kind of creating. A final advantage of this simile is that its detached, apparently logical construction will mark the suicidal speaker as reasonable, capable of explaining irrationality in a rational, credible manner.

> Twice I have so simply declared myself,
> have possessed the enemy, eaten the enemy,
> have taken on his craft, his magic.

The speaker characterizes her two previous suicide attempts as totally integrated declarations of self. But who is the "enemy?" Is it death or the means to death, perhaps some kind of drug? If she is using language in an ordinary sense, the enemy is obviously death. But consider the speaker's linguistic dilemma; in the special language of the suicide, everything has duplicitous and paradoxical meaning. The enemy may, then, be life itself. When she takes the drug she mentions later, she finally possesses life completely, eats it up, burns it out, ends it. The ambiguity of the grammatical and thematic referent is a problem only if the reader demands that the language of the poem be irreducible. That ambiguity represents the central problem of the poem, the attempt to balance between two paradoxical versions of linguistic and intellectual reality.

From this point on, the "double language" of the poem becomes increasingly important; words and images are always both double and connotatively contradictory. With this stanza Sexton introduces another mediator between the two languages. Ritual and magic are invoked, just at the moment when the reader is asked to make a leap that abandons logic. The suicide has already made that leap. The poem has gently led to this, carefully remaining within the realm of the rational until now; it is time to listen to the suicide talking as much in her own terms as in the listener's. We have been well prepared by the poem for this reversal of values.

> In this way, heavy and thoughtful,
> warmer than oil or water,
> I have rested, drooling at the mouth-hole.

The tone here is subtly but decidedly positive. The speaker might be talking about taking a good nap. But "warm" and "thoughtful" are yoked to other words not easily understood in a positive way. She is "heavy," and she "drools," not from the mouth but from "the mouth-hole." That phrase manages to objectify the self and the body, making both a vacancy, an absence, a hole.

> I did not think of my body at needle point.
> Even the cornea and the leftover urine were gone.
> Suicides have already betrayed the body.

The speaker grows bolder and less apologetic, more trusting of the hearer's understanding. She remains direct and unwavering in the presentation of details, but now they are unmitigated by helpful analogy. Instead, the speaker shifts to a cryptic explanatory line with the statement that suicides have always already betrayed the body, even, by implication, before they try to leave it. This kind of assertion is considerably distant from the language and the tone of the first stanzas of the poem, a long way from the sun and grass and lawn furniture and reasonable explanations.

> Still-born, they don't always die,
> but dazzled, they can't forget a drug so sweet
> that even children would look on and smile.

The image of a child in happy contemplation of the sweetness of death is difficult to stomach; somehow, it is especially objectionable to think of children half in love with easeful death. Why does this poem insist on the complicity of children? Why would the poet risk arousing our passionate defense of innocence? According to the speaker, her particular kind of suicide is figuratively stillborn, always close to that thin line between life and death first differentiated in the womb. The implication is that such people should have been born dead, and since they were not, they naturally spend their lives trying to return to the security of the womb, nexus of the boundary between life and death. The use of "children" attempts to communicate the purity and innocence of that feeling, from the suicide's perspective.

As the speaker moves further into the experience and language of the suicide, she maintains minimal but vital contact with the listener:

> To thrust all that life under your tongue!—
> that, all by itself, becomes a passion.

"Life" is perhaps the drug, the agent of death; this stanza presents the same kind of ambiguity as in stanza 4. The issue of control versus loss of it is the paradox: the speaker does the "thrusting" in an act of will. To gain control over life and death becomes a passion. But that passion is also the desire utterly to lose control.

> Death's a sad bone; bruised, you'd say,
>
> and yet she waits for me, year after year,
> to so delicately undo an old wound,
> to empty my breath from its bad prison.

Death is a sad bone, and it is, by implication, in her bones—bones can signify both the skeletal outside and the very core or essence. "You'd say" that death is a sad bone, "bruised" in the sense that the desire for it results from a wound that can be healed. "You" refers directly back to the listener. For the last several stanzas, the poem has involved itself so totally in rendering the suicidal experience that the reader, if the poem has achieved the proper effect, is taken far away from the sun, the lawn chair, and the sympathetic questioner of the first stanza, even if the reader began by identifying with that questioner. "You'd" say—you, who do not want to admit that death waits from the beginning, that a person can be born sad. If the "old wound" is life, death undoes that by emptying the breath from her body and releasing her. But the poem has taught its readers to expect ambiguity; the old wound may be the unsuccessful suicide attempts the speaker mentioned earlier. In that case, death is still there, waiting to open the wound again, break open the scars, pull out the stitches, and let her die.

> Balanced there, suicides sometimes meet,
> raging at the fruit, a pumped-up moon,
> leaving the bread they mistook for a kiss. . . .

This use of language is bewildering no matter what you do with it. The poem has now progressed almost entirely into that "special language," and it is here that it will leave behind any reader who has not listened closely to the suicidal idiom. This stanza speaks of the suicide's nearly complete isolation from the comforting world of human touch, the total breakdown of predictable relationship between the human and the natural, the alienation from all people and objects, with the exception of the accidental "meeting" that can occur between one suicide and another. All the moorings of ordinary life are gone when the suicides are "balanced there," in a limbo of distortion and hallucination, on the boundary between life and death. To reflect this state of spirit, the poet "balances" the poem "there," on the boundary between intelligibility and incoherence. It is exactly at this point that "reading" the poem in the formal sense stops working; the process of translation fails. This is purely the suicide's language. The speaker has turned inward to other suicides and away from her listener,

> leaving the page of the book carelessly open,
> something unsaid, the phone off the hook
> and the love, whatever it was, an infection.

The speaker has become part of the recollected experience, and it is now through her disappearance from the world of the listener that the poem persuades. True to its subject, the poem has become a kind of suicide attempt. I saw this only after teaching it to an excellent class, which had begun with sharp, moralistic disapproval of the poem's imperatives.

In my experience college students are rigorously normal in their response to suicide. In a discussion before we looked at this poem, the class in which I first taught it asserted positively that wanting to die because you are suffering physically is understandable; wanting to die without what they called "a real reason," by which they meant a physical one attached to disease, is sad—not merely sad but bad, reprehensible, morally irresponsible, and ethically debased. Depression, unlike cancer, said my students, must be reasoned with and always cured. One may never simply give over the struggle. My students almost uniformly denied the legitimacy—even the credibility—of an attitude that says from the beginning, "I would rather not live." (I think of Bartleby, who would always prefer not to, and who, by God, does not.)

I did not discuss these issues with my students as they relate to Anne Sexton's personal agony. Whether or not Sexton's own desire to die could be traced to situational factors or to chemical imbalances in the

DNA is irrelevant to the assumptions and commitments of this poem. We concentrated on the poem as poem, and in the world created by this poem, it is useless to say that the speaker "shouldn't" feel like dying. My class, full of good students who were also good people, wanted to engage in humane and helpful and therapeutic argument with the absent speaker.

But through an explication of the kind I have reconstructed here, my students came to an uneasy, genuine understanding of the suicide's "special language." When we reached the final two stanzas and came up against the limitations of explication, I still felt obliged to "finish the poem" by examining the remaining imagery and anatomizing the language. That had proved, after all, to be the right way into the poem, a poem that concerns itself with translation of language. To end here would be, I thought, to "leave the page of the book carelessly open, something unsaid." I was met with blank faces, but not the kind a teacher meets with when students are uninterested, bored, or even confused. This was the silence of compassionate insight. Finally, one student said, "It's idiomatic." Another said, "It doesn't translate." A third said, "There's nothing left to say." The class simply ended with a fourth comment: "The phone is off the hook." "Wanting to Die" ends in the silence of suicide because, for me and for the students to whom I taught it, the poem is a successful attempt. As one of my students said, "This poem self-destructs."

Perhaps successful suicide attempts, figurative or otherwise, are strange things to celebrate. I do not mean to suggest that there were any converts to suicide in my class. That was not the intention of the poem, and it certainly was not the purpose of my class discussion. The speaker of this poem asks only to be understood, to explain herself; she does not recruit company for her agony. Clearly, I did and do find something here to celebrate. "Wanting to Die" taught my students more about poetic process than any other single poem. It is one thing to learn that language is a powerful tool. It is another but related thing to know that language can be a mediator of this kind, that it can work either to alienate people or to bring them together in an understanding of their disparate and painfully separated selves.

That Ride Home with Our Boy

The anatomy of her speaker's urge to die provides Sexton's readers with many explanations in the form of relationships with people in her life, particularly with parents or parental figures of her childhood. Anna Ladd Dingley is the Elizabeth of "Elizabeth Gone" and "Some Foreign Letters," the beloved great-aunt whose namesake Sexton was, and most of her poems to Anna are generous, moving, sisterly. Sexton brings her aunt back to life as a young woman, wearing "your nickel-plated skates/in the skating park in Berlin" ("Some Foreign Letters"). She records her love affair with a married count and her European adventures as a "yankee girl" abroad. Anna Ladd Dingley came home eventually to live with the Harveys, and there she grew old and deaf and finally mad. Sexton mourns "your apple face, the simple crèche" ("Elizabeth Gone") and imagines what it must have been like for this exceptional woman to come to "the suburbs of Boston,"

> to see the blue-nose
> world go drunk each night, to see the handsome
> children jitterbug, to feel your left ear close
> one Friday at Symphony. . . .
>
> ("Some Foreign Letters")

In "The Hex" Sexton explores other dimensions of this close relationship, which deteriorated from intimate visits in her aunt's rooms to a curse "Nana" put on Anne when the former was finally taken away to a nursing home while Sexton sat on the stairs, a bewildered thirteen-year-old girl, wondering what was happening. (Middlebrook's biography of Sexton will undoubtedly fill in some of the details left unexplained by the poems; Sexton's unpublished play, *Mercy Street*, suggests possible sources for the "curse.") This is the poem of the "Nana-song,"

> sour notes calling out in her madness:
> You did it. You are the evil.

Now, every time the speaker feels happy, "the Nana-hex comes through."

> Birds turn into plumber's tools,
> a sonnet turns into a dirty joke,
> a wind turns into a tracheotomy. . . .

The speaker feels as though she has not been entitled to be happy since that moment on the stairs when she felt blood in her mouth, "a fish flopping in my chest," and "doom stamping its little feet." Nana may be dead, but "the dead take aim" against the living. After all these years the speaker is still the criminal. Yet there is always a part of her that knows she is not guilty. She is willing to be taken to the station to go out on the "death train" with her aunt, but it is her "double" who should get the ticket. That "double," the aspect of herself always eager to take on guilt, who accuses her whenever she says "life is marvelous," is the subject of another poem in *The Book of Folly*, "The Other."

"Mr. Doppelgänger," she calls the other here: brother, spouse, enemy, lover. He is the embodied need to destroy the self at any cost, the voice that in other poems says, "Kill me, kill me." The urge to die can be as alien and unaccountable to the person experiencing it as it is to the reader.

> When the child is soothed and resting on the breast
> it is my other who swallows Lysol.
> When someone kisses someone or flushes the toilet
> it is my other who sits in a ball and cries.

This speaker is a radically different aspect of the self from the one who speaks in "Wanting to Die." She is possessed by an alien presence within herself, and she experiences this presence as male enemy and stranger, instead of as an integrated and accepted part of the self. In this respect, the urge to die experienced as the desire for wholeness and peace, as in "Wanting to Die" or "Leaves That Talk," might actually be preferable to the suicidal person. The "other" sits within the speaker and cries

> until I put on a painted mask
> and leer at Jesus in His passion.
> Then it giggles.

Satanic in its intensity and perversity, the other torments the "I" until it capitulates, until its motives are identical with those of the "other"—or until the "I" can convince the "other" of its complicity: "I" put on a "painted mask," so the inner fragmentation persists, successfully disguised. The speaker resorts now to magic rituals in the attempt to exorcise the demon other, "signing" over "the house, the dog, the ladders, the jewels,/the soul, the family tree, the mailbox." Only then can she go to sleep, "maybe." As an explanation of possession and attempted exorcism, "The Other" is a disturbing success.

"The Silence" suggests the place of poetry in the poet's struggle for life and its ultimate failure as a means of salvation. In a 1965 letter to Charles Bowman, speaking of herself and Sylvia Plath, Sexton said, "Suicide is, after all, the opposite of the poem." She liked the formulation enough to repeat it and expand on it in interviews. Perhaps she believed it. If she did, she was at odds with popular and scholarly beliefs about the purposes and directions of extremist art. I think she wanted, even desperately needed, to believe in the saving power of poetry. It is possible that poetry delayed her death, that every poem she wrote provided another temporary respite from the death demon that pursued her from within. Sexton seems to have believed in the magic of words, in their ritual utility as incantation; but words failed her as often as they saved her. "Sometimes the wrong ones kiss me." She was painfully aware that her poetic and personal life were marked by words "I might have said . . . but did not." She was as full of the unsaid as the said, and silence overwhelmed her speech in the end.

Published in 1972 in *The Book of Folly,* "The Silence" foreshadows the failure of poetry to save her life. It begins:

> My room is whitewashed,
> as white as a rural station house
> and just as silent;
> whiter than chicken bones
> bleaching in the moonlight,
> pure garbage,
> and just as silent.

Sitting alone in this white room of her life, where her hair and beads are black, the poet is "filling the room/with the words from my pen./Words leak out of it like a miscarriage." But however much she speaks, "zinging words out into the air," silence is still the fundamental statement. It is "like an enormous baby mouth," the frozen, silent, "dumb howl" of the later "Death Baby." Odd that the silence should be characterized like this; from a baby's open mouth comes sound, not silence, as we usually conceive it. But that sound is preverbal in the symbolic sense, inarticulate, powerless. In Sexton's sense the baby's "howl" is always "dumb." And she is always that baby, as surely as she is a self-assured woman poet in middle age. By the time the baby grows old enough to symbolize, conceptualize, and articulate, it is always/already too late to speak the words that save. The silence, she says, is death, now transformed from an enormous baby mouth to a "white bird," which sits on her shoulder to "peck at the black eyes/and the vibrating red muscle/of my mouth." This is a painting in white and black and red, a confrontation of ambiguous purities: life, death, blood. White is the primary presence but only the presence of absence. Black, normally associated with evil and with absence of color, is here the aberrant presence of life, offensive, vulgar, conspicuous, and inconsistent with the white that surrounds it.

The white bird that pecks at the "vibrating red muscle/of my mouth" is the triumph of silence over speech, death over life. We are not given the image of the poet's mouth speaking words of efficacious magic. The "red muscle" is the poet's parody of the baby mouth, just as inarticulate, leaking only the poet's own silence, now silenced by the bird of death. If the baby's mouth is one form of death, the poet's failure to speak words that deafen silence—her words are a "miscarriage" of genuine birth—is another death: both mouths are her own, and she is again at the business of killing herself. That she fights against this daily, "filling the room/with the words," makes no difference to the final outcome.

This is a harsh reading of the poem. I am tempted toward a more generous and less self-destructive reading, one that pits the poet in noble, if losing, battle against a silence imposed only from without. But Sexton has taught me how to read her. She does not let herself off the hook here, nor am I inclined to do so. The juxtaposition of the two mouths, that of the silence that is death and that of the poet, is no careless accident. Whatever her apparent activity—"I am zinging words out into the air"—the poet's stance here toward the white bird of death is essentially passive. This white room is, after all, her own.

If Anne Sexton was ever guilty of the self-serving poetic sins she has been accused of so often, it is in "Sylvia's Death" (*Live or Die*). Reading this poem, and this one only, I feel I am overhearing a pathetic competition between suicides, one accomplished and one potential, full of petty jealousy and envy masquerading as eulogy. It is the masquerade I find unsuccessful, even offensive, not the open admission of envy that Sylvia got "that ride home" first. "Sylvia's Death" is a failure barely salvaged by a few good images and a rhythmically haunting line or two. What is wrong with this poem may illuminate what is right with so many of her other forays into the hinterland of suicide.

Although "Sylvia's Death" is ostensibly "for Sylvia Plath," it might more accurately have been dedicated "for myself on the occasion of Sylvia's death." After a strong start that places Plath in her London apartment with her two children

> wandering loose in the tiny playroom,
>
> with your mouth into the sheet,
> into the roofbeam, into the dumb prayer,

and then in Devonshire among her potatoes and bees, the poem moves quickly toward self-pity and self-aggrandizing with the half-ironic accusation that Plath is a "thief" for having crawled down alone "into the death I wanted so badly and for so long." Now Sexton travels back in Plath's and her own life to the poetry workshop days in Boston, where they toasted death with three extra dry martinis. The haunting refrain of the poem, caught in a fine and dismal image, might be enough to save it:

> (In Boston
> the dying
> ride in cabs,
> yes death again,
> that ride home
> with *our* boy.)

Dickinson's "Because I could not stop for Death" is the subtext, with carriage updated to cab. But death is not Dickinson's gentleman here—he is a mere boy, a plaything, a trinket worn by two smart women. She acknowledges the pathetic dimension of the picture she presents of two grown women courting a boyish death and being courted by him. The competitive and cooperative aspects of their individual urges toward death are effectively cast as flirtatious romance: he is "*our* boy," yet it is Sylvia who first got to ride home with him alone. It might be said, then, that the competitive edge of "the death I wanted so badly and for so long" is vindicated as necessary to the structure of the poem. As a metaphoric structure, the romantic competition and coopera- tion work well.

But the control over her material is too tenuous here, and she does not resist banal sentiments: "And me,/me too." Wrenching herself back to Sylvia, she understands Plath's death as "an old belonging,/a mole that fell out/of one of your poems," and in this image she offers her perception that Plath's death was in some respect inevitable—or certainly her own business. (In a 1965 letter to Lois Ames, she insists on Plath's death as a personal belonging: "Everyone runs around condemning her for it and I say She had a right!") The poem ends with empathetic evocation of the desperation of Plath's final days and a poignant memory of her friend's happier self; the sense of loss of a friend, as opposed to martyred whimpering about coming in second, changes the tone. She under- stands that for Plath the "moon" had gone "bad," and she mourns the departure of this "funny duchess" and "blonde thing," whose wit and appearance so belied her heartache.

But this is not enough to make up for the self-serving hunger for me-first martyrdom that has tainted the poem. If Sexton had created a persona here to show us a state of mind, the poem would have been a success, in the manner of narrative monologue. If this were a "My Last Duchess" of the selfishness of suicide, I would analyze it quite differently. But Sexton gives me no choice here; the speaker *is* Anne Sexton, and I can only conclude that she did not know what sort of character she created of herself here—or that she did not care. Sexton's suicide poems usually bring me closer to sympathetic insight and do so by means of superbly modulated poetic controls. She almost always has in mind in these poems a reader who may begin alienated from her and who must be brought to understanding through skillful manipulation of emotion and intellect. I find no such subtle care for the reader here, but merely a desperate harangue disguised as eulogy. It is not that I do not learn something here about suicide, or about extreme states of heart. I learn that sometimes the poet so close to her material does lack restraint. I learn that naked begging for pity inspires in me exactly and only that: pity.

But primarily I learn, by an unexpected contrast, just how well and subtly controlled Sexton's poems on suicide usually are. On first or second readings of such poems as "Wanting to Die," I was not sufficiently aware of the degree of control she exercised, over both her material and her reader's responses. I was not sufficiently aware of how quickly offended I may become, and thus of how skillfully the poet manipulates my sensibilities, playing with the defensive edge any reader may experience when the subject is desire for the ultimate taboo. Perhaps this explains why there may never be any consensus on the worthiness of Sexton's poetry on death; individual readers will vary widely in their capacity to accept this stance toward life.

Keats's "Now more than ever seems it sweet to die" strikes no one as repulsive, but only human. Clothed in abstraction, the sentiment is powerful yet safe. But that was a poem for another age, and Sexton's is for ours, where the passion for anatomizing detail is schooled into our critical sense of what good poetry is. If she is to write good poetry on suicide, it will have to give us a clear, cold look at the facts yet still stop short of crossing certain boundaries. The challenge is bigger, I think, than we have realized. In place of "ceasing upon the midnight with no pain," Sexton gives us the white bird of death that pecks at the "vibrating red muscle/of my mouth." This is more Crashaw or Swinburne than Keats, and readers' degree of openness to such imagery will vary dramatically.

I have my limits, as my reading of "Sylvia's Death" demonstrates. I like to think those limits are dictated by my critical faculties, that all of this has to do with good poetry and bad; I hope that this is in part true. But a whole truth would have to include my private accommodation of wish and fear, my personal relation to the boundary between life and death, the distance between myself and the demons that pursue me. That is true of any poet, and any reader.

Suicide Note

"Suicide Note" is the only death poem Anne Sexton cast in this form, and the decision creates formal peculiarities of expectation and response. In many respects it is like the other suicide poems, all of which are written from slightly differing perspectives, all of which tell this suicide's story from a new narrative angle, all of which provide new images for understanding this state of mind. But the carefully constructed multi-stanza "note" is alone among the poems in that it purports to be a communication left to a "dear friend" prior to the speaker's suicide.

Situated as it is in *Live or Die,* a collection shaped by the decision implied in the title, "Suicide Note" is part of the group of "Die" poems that includes "Wanting to Die," "Sylvia's Death," and "The Addict," among others. These poems anatomize the desire to die, the ways of doing it slowly, the postattempt explanations; but no other poem is situated in time just *before* a planned attempt, whether that attempt is fictive, really about to take place, or real but remembered.

It is an odd experience to read an artfully constructed, cool, restrained note to one the speaker assumes will have survived her, one who will want to know why. It would feel peculiar even if the poet were not now dead. But the actual ironies are denser than that: this is a 1965 poem, published in a collection that concludes with the decision to "Live," the title of its final poem. Anne Sexton, the poet and *perhaps* the speaker, killed herself nearly ten years after this poem was written. Reading it about ten years after her death and almost twenty after its composition, I find it difficult to refrain from experiencing it as what it purports to be and yet is not: a suicide note.

Having been content to collapse speaker and poet in many other poems, I am wary of the ease with which I might do so in this case. "Suicide Note" is, in fact, among her most aloof and "literary" productions, entirely different in tenor from, say, "Sylvia's Death," in which Anne Sexton the potential suicide nearly overwhelms Anne Sexton the poet and craftsperson. This poem, which presents itself as a "note" before killing oneself, is actually a highly formalized poetic epistle, written to a textually constructed self as much as to a similarly constituted addressee. In other words the *I* is partly autobiographical but primarily an ideational persona.

> Better,
> despite the worms talking to
> the mare's hoof in the field;
> better,
> despite the season of young girls
> dropping their blood;
> better somehow
> to drop myself quickly
> into an old room.

The beginning is presented as a conclusion reached after consideration. It is "despite" the worms and the young girls' blood that the speaker finds it "better" to die. The worms and the girls' blood are both ambiguous in their emotional content and their relation to life and death: while one seems primarily death directed and the other life directed, both are at the intersection of fertility and decay. The worms "talking to the mare's hoof" are the rich yeast of the soil on which the horse walks and from which it gains sustenance, yet the worms will ultimately speak not only of nurture but of decay. The season of menarche is the season of greatest potential for life, but bloodletting is also symbolic of destruction. "Despite" the mares and the girls, whose being at this time of year (it is June) affirms life as well as death, the speaker wants to escape into the "old room" of her death. For she has decided that it is better "not to be born" at all; and "far better/not to be born twice," as women are ("Little Girl, My String Bean," *Live or Die*).

Now, having already presented her conclusion, the speaker introduces the "dear friend" to whom she speaks, telling him or her that "I will enter death/like someone's lost optical lens." In contrast to her own sense of smallness—"I will be a light thing"—she says that "life is half enlarged." Describing her own distorted vision, she speaks of life tilting "backward and forward." Close to the natural world of mares and blood, she feels the fierceness of fish and owls on this portentous day. Having made her decision to die, she observes these portents unaffected: "Even the wasps cannot find my eyes." Nothing can sting her now, for she is immune, and her sight has turned to vision by means of distortion and reduction. Once those eyes were "immediate," and "truly awake"; now they have been "pierced."

Recalling her old "hunger" for Jesus, whom she has loved as suffering man more than as God, she thinks of him as a fellow suicide, who "rode calmly into Jerusalem/in search of death" *before* he grew old. She has tried this herself before, but failed. This time, she does not ask for understanding,

> and yet I hope everyone else
> will turn their heads when an unrehearsed fish jumps
> on the surface of Echo Lake;
> when moonlight,
> its bass note turned up loud,
> hurts some building in Boston,
> when the truly beautiful lie together.

These rich lines begin with a disclaimer that the ensuing lines seem to renege on: "I certainly/do not ask for understanding/and yet. . . . " What is it that she "hopes?" That everyone will be sorry she has died? That the natural and man-made world—fish, moon, buildings, people—will take note of the moment of her death? Perhaps. But the lines are larger than that; they may mean almost the opposite: that everyone who has not "dropped quickly into an old room" because of the inability to stand the pain and beauty of life will respond to that beauty and pain. This is the "understanding" she solicits: that she cannot deal with an "unrehearsed" fish breaking the surface of still water in a surge of life-force; that she cannot bear the "bass note" of moonlight bursting on walls; that she is unable to be, or to see, the "truly beautiful" who lie together. Like the images with which the poem begins, these are tonally poised, tilting "backward and forward" as life does for the speaker, refusing a readerly desire for definitive emotional form and statement. (Were her eyes "pierced" so that she could see "the whole story?" Or does that piercing render them unable to see at all?) Ambiguous as this series of images is, the weight of the lines that follow presses toward the more generous appraisal of motives and meaning:

> I think of this, surely,
> and would think of it far longer
> if I were not . . . if I were not
> at that old fire.

She has reminded herself of the painful beauty of life, and the memory might make her hesitate, if she were not "at that old fire," needing

141

death. She knows, she says, that she is "only a coward," but she feels compelled to this death as moths are forced to "suck on the electric bulb." She offers what defense she can. Now that defense takes a form similar to "The Death Baby," a poem Sexton was to write years after "Suicide Note":

> But surely you know that everyone has a death,
> his own death,
> waiting for him.
> So I will go now
> without old age or disease,
> wildly but accurately,
> knowing my best route,
> carried by that toy donkey I rode all these years,
> never asking, "Where are we going?"
> We were riding (if I'd only known)
> to this.

If everyone has his own death waiting anyway, if we are all only riding "to this," the speaker will choose her own moment, without the infirmities of old age or disease, just as she earlier suggests Christ did when he rode into Jerusalem "in search of death." And like Christ, she will ride on a donkey. Three years before the composition of "Suicide Note," Sexton had ridden her donkey out of madness and out of "this sad hotel," the mental hospital, in "Flee on Your Donkey," the third poem in *Live or Die*:

> Anne, Anne,
> flee on your donkey,
> flee this sad hotel,
> ride out on some hairy beast,
> gallop backward pressing
> your buttocks to his withers. . . .

Now she rides the same beast out of life, into a madness that has much method: "wildly but accurately,/knowing my best route." That she has never asked, "Where are we going?" has the same content as never asking, "Why build?" in "Wanting to Die."

The final stanza is an attempt to assure the addressee that the speaker has no illusions about the effect of her death on either the world she leaves behind or the one she goes to. No guitars playing, no kiss from her mother's mouth, no major disturbance in the natural world ("The snakes will certainly not notice") or in the man-made world

("New York City will not mind"). She will die in June, "so concrete with its green breasts and bellies"; the "note" ends where it began, with the abundance of life that the speaker cannot endure. Only the bats will take notice, beating on the trees, "knowing it all,/seeing what they sensed all day." Sexton takes into herself, and sometimes equates with herself, only such animals as bats and rats. (The rat was her favorite poetic animal, and she chose as her epitaph a palindrome: RATS LIVE ON NO EVIL STAR.)

Sexton elaborated her connections to bats in two later works, in both of which the bat is a creaturely representation of the speaker's death. In the "Bestiary" section of *45 Mercy Street*, written between 1971 and 1974, Sexton sounds like Roethke, whose "The Bat" ends with: "Something is out of place/When mice with wings can wear a human face." Sexton's "Bat" envisions the webbing between fingers that seems vestigially to survive in the human hand. Constructing a fantasy of her own prebirth night flight, she writes:

> In August perhaps as the trees rose to the stars
> I have flown from leaf to leaf in the thick dark.
> If you had caught me with your flashlight
> you would have seen a pink corpse with wings. . . .

The bat partakes of death in life, just as does the speaker of "Suicide Note." "Bat" ends on an easy-to-miss note of identification with the bat. Dogs sniff at "me" because

> they know I'm something to be caught
> somewhere in the cemetery hanging upside down
> like a misshapen udder.

It is "me" the dogs sniff, "me" who inhabits the cemetery. The identification of speaker and bat is complete. Written between six and nine years after "Suicide Note," "Bat" serves as a gloss on the ending of the earlier poem. The bats will be the only ones to notice the speaker's death because she is one of their own kind.

In 1974, not long before her death, Sexton wrote a short story titled "The Bat, or to Remember, to Remember," which is among the oddest of her works generically and thematically. Kafkaesque in tone and barely coherent in point of view, the story centers on a speaker who finds himself in a court of judgment after death. The verdict of his judgment is reincarnation as a bat. But this bat will have partial memory of his other nine lives, all of which were human. The memory of past lives comes back as a series of movie images interrupted by ads. The bat remembers its life as a daughter being beaten by her mother, a disappointed man urging his son to stay in college, a male lover about to have intercourse with his lady, a female baby at her mother's breast.

Recurring intermittently as an "ad" throughout the staging of scenarios from other lives is "one drama that repeats and repeats." A man (another incarnation of the bat narrator) saves a young woman from another man who is threatening her on the street. She wants to go home, but she cannot remember where home is, nor can she remember her name. The man takes Miss No-name to his room and tries to comfort her while she weeps, until the voice of the man who had been pursuing her on the street calls into a bullhorn, instructing the narrator to take a hammer and nails into his hands. He does. Then the girl is instructed to go into a closet and flatten herself against the wall. She does. Both the girl and the man follow all instructions, sensing that they are commands from the director of "His play." The instructions are for a paint-by-number crucifixion:

SPREAD OUT YOUR ARMS LIKE A SCARECROW.
TWIST YOUR ANKLES AROUND EACH OTHER.
TAKE ONE NAIL AND HAMMER IT INTO HER PALM.
TAKE ANOTHER NAIL AND HAMMER IT INTO HER OTHER PALM.
DRIVE YOUR HUNTING KNIFE THROUGH HER CHEST.

The narrator opens and shuts drawers, looking for his knife. Even in the midst of a harrowing crucifixion scene, Sexton is funny: "I pull the bed over on top of me and still he calls for the hunting knife." But he cannot find it. "IT'S IN THE MEDICINE CABINET," calls the man with the bullhorn. He finds the knife—in the medicine cabinet, of course—and thrusts it in the girl. "Sideways to slip between the ribs." Miss No-name dies for twenty hours, gasping. "Cut!"

It is the bat who remembers all this, sensing that his incarnation as the murdering man was his last human life. Now he returns to scenes from other lives, and in them the reader recognizes a scene from Anne Sexton's own biography: "the Great Aunt pouring tea from the Spode pitcher." The bat wishes now to remember nothing, "but I do. I am locked into it." The narrator-bat is a Frankenstein, as created by Mary Shelley rather than by Hollywood: he pursues only because he is pursued, victimizes only because he is a victim.

> I wish I could peer into your window at night, and speak in the
> human voice I had nine times and say something to your

snuggling pillowy head of this, this damnation. But you would wake and scream, then with a shaking hand take a pill and at last go back to sleep again, not knowing that the nightmare at your window is living, and reliving, his upside-down lives and maybe, poor sleeper, even one of yours.

Like all of Sexton's short stories, this one is a parable for the life of the poet. The bat is evoked at the end of "Suicide Note" years before this because the bat, whose locale in the modern psyche is the cemetery or catacomb, whose business is death, whose body is alien, whose face is human, is the speaker's animal double. In the later story Sexton is herself all the incarnations of the bat; that is the point. She is baby and adult, human and animal, male and female, and, most especially, murderer and victim in the central scenario, played out as an "ad" between other lives. In this strange choice of metaphor, Sexton is canny about video, in which the fundamental raison d'être is the advertisement, not the programming. It is the ads that stick in our minds awake or in sleep, the ads we hum while making love or bread.

Whatever her lives have been, whatever other forms her particular energy may have taken, this is the central fact: a murder, a crucifixion, carried out on one incarnation of the self by another incarnation of the self, with instructions from yet another self. Just as Sexton is all of these characters in the story, she is the sleeper at the end; unlike most sleepers, she has wakened and not returned to sleep. She has looked out the window and seen the bat's face, recognized it as her own. If the entire story reads like a particularly unhinged dream, this is because of another fact that only seems contradictory: all of life is a dreamed nightmare for the suicide. "Suicide Note" and "The Bat" were written almost ten years apart, but they are one poem, started in 1965 and completed, in prose form, in 1974. This personal journey toward death recurs, uncannily, in exactly the sense in which Freud defined "the uncanny": the return of something familiar that has been repressed.

8
Leaves That Talk
and Green Girls

I infer that "Letters to Dr. Y." were of special significance to Anne Sexton, in part because they constitute the only finished work that Sexton permanently set aside for posthumous publication.[1] It is impossible to know precisely why these long-finished poems, written between 1960 and 1970, remained for years in the private files of a poet who seemed to withhold nothing of her joy, or her pain, from her public. My own conjectures about their significance to the poet arise in part from a 1968 *Paris Review* interview. In response to the interviewer's questions about her religious experiences, Sexton speaks about her "ritualized visions" of God, Christ, and the Saints: "I feel that I can touch them almost . . . that they are a part of me. . . . It's reincarnation, speaking with another voice . . . or else with the Devil. If you want to know the truth, the leaves talk to me every June." When the interviewer asks if Sexton tries to communicate her visions to other people, she answers, "I refuse to talk about it, which is why I'm having a hard time now."

The interviewer is tireless. She tries to elicit further response from Sexton on the nature of her visions, sacred or demonic. Finally, Sexton cuts her off: "I find this very difficult, and I'd just as soon leave it, if you please."[2] Although the emphasis in this portion of the interview is on religious visions, Sexton has alluded to the "talking leaves" that form the core of the suicide poems in the Dr. Y. sequence, and she has spoken of them immediately following a reference to "the Devil." In the "May 5, 1970" Dr. Y. poem, the analyst asks her what the leaves say to her, and she answers, "I am not allowed to repeat it./There are rules about this." It is possible that Sexton was uncomfortable about publishing during her lifetime poems that would certainly "break the rules" imposed by her demonic voices. And these are poems that break the rules of the poetry world as well.

Although Sexton had in her earlier collections included poems to and about her doctors (such as the superb "You, Doctor Martin" and "Said the Poet to the Analyst," in *To Bedlam and Part Way Back*), she had never dealt directly with the therapeutic process in poetry. Even the most openly confessional poets usually refrain, it seems, from violating the therapeutic session. In the "Letters to Dr. Y." sequence, she does just that, and the result is remarkably, uncomfortably intimate; the reader is in the doctor's office, invading, albeit by invitation, a space as sacred as the confessional booth. "Letters to Dr. Y." bring close to a contemporary readership a ritualized human relationship unique to our time and our social structures, that between a healer of the mind and his or her patient. Mind healers have probably practiced in every society in civilized history in one guise or another, but the psychoanalyst is uniquely our own: twentieth century, post-Freudian, European and American. And although mental illness and artistic achievement are not causally related—I agree with those who would caution against our tendency to view the former as necessary to the latter—the psychoanalyst is pre-eminently a healer of the imagination, whose methods are metaphoric, imagistic, and poetic. "My business is words," writes Anne Sexton in "Said the Poet to the Analyst"; and "your business is watching my words."

The patient-analyst relationship is by its nature little explored, even if much alluded to, in our poetry. The achievement of "Letters to Dr. Y." is the concrete interpenetration of poetry and psychoanalysis. The analytic situation has always been "poetic" in method and in aim; Freud himself granted that "our poets" had anticipated the major tenets of psychoanalytic theory. But poetry, as differentiated from the critical anatomy of poetry, has reverently declined the opportunity to put the analytic encounter on the poetic couch. "Letters to Dr. Y." translates into poetry this special collusion of imaginations. In delicately honed images and rhythms, Sexton shows us how free association works in the analytic situation, how information is exchanged between patient and analyst, how therapy progresses. More important for my purposes here, the recurring theme of the speaker-patient's sessions with the analyst is suicide. In concert with her earlier poems on the subject, the Dr. Y. sequence constitutes a body of poetry on suicide that is unique in modern American verse.

Scattered throughout half a dozen collections, Sexton's earlier published poems on suicide are isolated, singly shaped attempts to convey the speaker's state of mind during suicidal depressions or suicidal highs. ("The Death Baby" sequence in *The Death Notebooks* is a partial exception, but it is not only, or even primarily, a suicide poem.) Although only three of the twenty-three poems in the "Letters to Dr. Y." sequence take suicide as their main subject, they represent the core of the speaker's "safe psychosis" throughout the series. Separated in time of composition by several years, and by position in the sequence by intervening poems, they form the nucleus of the skeletal case history that unfolds in ten years of "Letters." I will refer to the poems by date rather than title, since Sexton titles none of them.

"February 16, 1960" opens the sequence and sets the tone for the patient-poet's treatment by Dr. Y. Here Sexton speaks of the tiny internal voice that says, "Kill me." Between this suicide poem and the second one are ten poems and seven years of treatment. The intervening poems deal with poetry, word association, the speaker's mother's death, her relationship to Dr. Y., her religious quest. On "June 6, 1967," the voice resumes, this time as a grotesquely multiple chorus line: "What do the voices say?" Dr. Y. asks. The poem is her answer. Three years and six poems later, the series picks up the theme like a dropped stitch on "May 5, 1970," with "What are the leaves saying?" Like *Live or Die,* the sequence ends with the decision to live, with the safe psychosis "broken"; the speaker is "happy today with the sheets of life," hung out on the line to dry with "all the oxygen of the world" in their windy lift and slap, just as she was happy with the new Dalmatian puppies and the "excitable gift" of sun in "Live." But the therapeutically successful shape of the "Letters" sequence—Sexton certainly intended a progress from sickness toward cure—is not my main subject here. I am concerned with the hard core of suicide poems at the sequence's conceptual center, through which I want to suggest two related hypotheses about Sexton: the connection of the death wish to a specifically feminine desire for power and control; and deeper still, an ironic relationship of the death wish to a protest against human mortality.

Green Girls and Santa Claus: Death as a Woman, Death as a Man

In the first Dr. Y. poem the speaker begins by telling her doctor she needs his "Rescue Inc. voice" to keep her from "going underfoot" and "growing stiff/as a yardstick." The emotional situation she goes on to describe is indeed desperate; while the first stanza speaks to Dr. Y., the following ones make Dr. Y. privy to another private conversation, that between the patient and death:

> Death,
> I need your hot breath,
> my index finger in the flame,
> two cretins standing at my ears,
> listening for the cop car.

The speaker recognizes her "need" and conveys it in images that might make it familiar to a reader not personally acquainted with the desire to die. Who has not played with an index finger in the flame? Who will not recognize that urge, in perfectly "normal" people, if not in oneself? Who has not known the fear of (and wish for) getting caught—if not at suicide, then at some slighter self-destruction?

> Death,
> I need a little cradle
> to carry me out,
>
>   . . . .
> and no kiss
> on my kiss.

Sexton would later more fully explore the relationship between death and infancy in "The Death Baby" sequence of *The Death Notebooks.* In the "March 14, 1964" poem of the Dr. Y. sequence, she extends the connection between infancy and death in stanzas dealing with her mother's death from cancer. Her mother becomes deformed in her illness, and the speaker, bending over her bed, imagines her physical transformation as the "ugliness" of a new baby, "growing back to your first skull."

> A baby just lies there
> having come from its bath;
> lies there getting used to being outside the bath,
> lies there getting used to being outside of something,
> while you, death-child, lie fitfully
> waiting to go inside.

"No kiss/on my kiss" may refer to the guilt and lovelessness that is likely to be the suicide's internalized legacy, even if she has been worthy and lovable in others' eyes. But perhaps "no kiss" is also of positive worth; the speaker may be weary of the kiss, the human touch that binds her to this world.

The final stanza of the first letter recalls Sexton's best translation of the language of the suicide in "Wanting to Die" (*Live or Die*). After acknowledging that she needs "my little addiction to

149

you," she brings the force of that need to bear in a single, startling image:

> I need that tiny voice who,
> even as I rise from the sea,
> all woman, all there,
> says kill me, kill me.

Where does that voice come from? In later Dr. Y. poems she will speak of other voices within, those of her "green girls," the homunculae in her soul. But here the voice is singular, and it says enough: a beautiful woman comes out of the sea, alive in every respect, risen from the source of all life. Probably she is smiling. Perhaps she is speaking to her children, her friends. The sun is shining. But behind her smile, another voice speaks, just as much herself as this healthy creature rising from the waves.

Here, as in "Wanting to Die," her strategy suggests a reader or hearer who will not immediately comprehend, for whom this is foreign and frightening territory, and to whom she can only hope to translate. She is trying with considerable restraint to explain the suicide's passion, and the vehicle, as it often is for Sexton, is sexuality:

> To die whole,
> riddled with nothing
> but desire for it,
> is like breakfast
> after love.

In "Wanting to Die" Sexton tried similarly to shock the reader into understanding and to make unfailingly clear that the desire to die is erotically charged with life. In the earlier poem the desire to die is an "unnameable lust," a "passion." Here the sexual allusions are more specific. Both poems attempt to make understandable the innocence of such a passion as well as its corruption, its purity as well as its infectedness. "Breakfast/after love" suggests nurture and conversation following sexual release, perhaps the comfort of plumped pillows and folded coverlets. If this image conflicts grotesquely with a normal person's sense of what it must be like to die, so much the better. It is not, she tells us, what we would have it. It certainly is as awful, but we know that. The news, to readers anxious to divorce such urges from normality, is the sense of "wholeness" death promises. This conviction or desperate hope that the moment of death will coincide with a moment of wholeness is one Sexton returned to repeatedly to convey her predicament.

"June 6, 1967" begins with a question from the analyst: "What do the voices say? Dr. Y. asks." The poem consists of her answer, broken into five voices: leaves, rock, white clown, razor, and whip. They are, she says, "as real as books." They tell her, while she is doing normal daily activities—this time eating soup, as last time rising from an ocean swim—that she is "on trial" every moment. The razor voice says what one might expect: "Have you ever thought, my single one,/that your hands are thorns to be cut to the quick?" The razor's "language" is, appropriately, "a thin whine." While this is the only suicidal reference to razors in Sexton's poetry, the whip is a more familiar image: "You have seen my father whip me./You have seen me stroke my father's whip" ("The Death Baby," *The Death Notebooks*). Like many suicides, and especially women, Sexton both meant and did not mean every attempt. The shape of "June 6, 1967" suggests that not all of her suicidal voices are equally lethal. The whip is the fifth and final voice, emblem of father-daughter sexuality, of pain as pleasure, of psychic obliteration, but not of genuine death. "I will mark you all over with little red fish./You will be almost killed, a delight."

But the male voice is not always less lethal than the female. Voices number one and two illuminate a mystery rooted in paradox. Voice number one is the leaves: "I am forty young girls in green shells./Come out of your house and come unto me...." The leaves are always feminine girls who speak with sisterly seductiveness to the speaker. But voice number two, "the rock in front/of your window," who tells her to "choke on me," is male, a "sword blade," a "Mr. Gobblegook."

Examined in concert with the last suicide poem in the Dr. Y. sequence ("May 5, 1970") and several other poems in Sexton's canon, the voices of "June 6, 1967" present a clearly gendered imaging of death. Anne Sexton seems to have been well aware of this peculiar characteristic of her suicidal urges and to have used it consciously in her poetry. In a 1964 letter to a friend who also happened to be an analyst, Sexton reported on a particularly fruitful session with her own therapist, something she did not ordinarily do in letters: "When (to me) death takes you and puts you thru the wringer, it's a man. But when you kill yourself it's a woman." Suicide becomes a way of claiming power when she feels most powerless. "I guess I see it as a way of cheating death."[3] How this dismally ironic version of feminine power could make psychic sense becomes clearer in the "May 5, 1970" letter to Dr. Y.

"What do the leaves remind you of?" asks Dr. Y., and the speaker answers, "Green. Green!" In a poetic parallel for the technique of free association in analysis, the speaker answers at length when the analyst next asks, "What does green remind you of?" Our culture's collective connotations for green, and any reader's own personal associations, function as an unarticulated subtext: fertility, growth, grass, trees, perhaps money, jealousy. The speaker's list of associations includes both tonally negative and positive objects and feelings, but the negatives are overwhelming—green reminds her of a fisherman, for instance, but with "green fruit in his net." Thus no associations with benignly rich fertility here, and a surfeit of "slime pools" and "drunks vomiting." While "night baseball games" and "Lake Como" sneak into the list, the tally is still startlingly unbalanced. At the end of the list she says, "But those are painted colors./Only the leaves are human."

With this statement she introduces those associations most speakers would have articulated in the first place, images of fertility and life, but for her tainted always with death:

> They are girls. Green girls.
> Death and life is their daily work.
> Death seams up and down the leaf.
> I call the leaves my death girls.
> The death girls turn at the raggedy edge
> and swim another length down the veins
> to the raggedy heart.

English poetry has often associated fertility with mutability—"beauty that must die"—but this speaker turns the worm subtly. She calls the leaf voices "girls," not women, emphasizing their youth and thus, one would think, their liveliness. But having connected them briefly to the obvious—fertility, life—she associates the rest of the description with a specifically feminine death. It is difficult to dislike or to fear the death girls, as one is accustomed to fear and loathe images of death in Western culture—the skeletal old man, the shrouded figure with scythe, even the sexually mature and seductive woman. Sexton means to make the death girls appealing, and she succeeds. "And these death girls sing to you? . . . And does it excite you?" Vibrating now with the charge of erotic excitement, the poem moves toward explanation of the "canker-suicide high," the "sisterhood" she feels with the green girls. Returning to the wish for wholeness, she explains that she needs to be "laid out at last/under them, as straight as a pea pod":

> To die whole. To die as soft and young as a leaf.
> To lie down whole in that green god's belly.

So it is again in search of wholeness, of purity, and of innocence that the speaker leans toward death. Mythologizing a moment of childhood, she answers the analyst's next question, which amounts to "and how long have you felt like this?":

> When I was five I played under pines.
> Pines that were stiff and sturdy.
>
>   . . . .
>
> Dark green.
> A different order.
> A different sign.
> I was safe there at five under that stiff crotch.

Earlier, in the associations to "green," the speaker remembered "the back lawn I danced on when I was eight." But eight was perhaps not young enough. Now she chooses, as emblematic of the moment she first wished to die, the psychically redolent age of five, that "fifth me," the ritual age at which Western and post-Freudian culture fix the first end of innocence. That the ages between birth and five are some of our most troubled and least stable is equally appropriate: the "fifth me" alludes to the huge transformations conflated in those first years. Five is still the age at which our society imagines innocence on the trembling verge of disintegration, the age at which we fix the apex of one kind of wholeness succumbing to the burden of a disillusionment of grand proportions. That disillusionment differs significantly for males and females; for males the fear of castration is said to resolve the Oedipus complex; for females it inaugurates the Oedipus complex. For both sexes Oedipal conflict at about age five erodes the intimacy of the bond with the mother. The female child will henceforth turn to the father in search of such intimacy but will not, in most cases, be able to secure it. For both sexes the psychic and cultural forces summarized by the term *Oedipus complex* constitute the individual's formal introduction into culture, as Juliet Mitchell has shown in *Psychoanalysis and Feminism*.[4]

The speaker notes that the pines under which she played at age five were "stiff and sturdy," just as she said she needed to be laid out under the green girls, "straight as a pea pod." In images laden with sexuality, she makes for herself a "stiff crotch" under the pines of her memory and lays herself out dead there—dead, but whole. The "stiff crotch" is clearly both womb and phallus, both feminine and masculine. Sexton's speaker first experiences the wish to die "whole" at the very moment at which she will otherwise be forced to relinquish that imagined wholeness.

But even though the images suggest a perfect balance of feminine and masculine nurture, of magical union with both parents caught at the last possible moment, this is a primarily feminine and maternal dreamscape. The leaves are always female, always sisters or mothers or images of the self.

As I read it, the poem takes place in the domain of the "phallic mother." I am using the term *phallic* here in the Lacanian rather than the Freudian sense, as an attribute of power associated with the father but that unlike the penis, belongs to neither father nor mother—nor to any speaking being. The phallus symbolizes the unmediated power and protection always lacking in real people, but thought by all of us to exist in the parental imagos of imagination. The mother imago's phallus is veiled behind and before the father's, and her power, thus hidden, is literally boundless. As Jane Gallop writes in *The Daughter's Seduction,* the phallus is "the subject presumed to know, the object of transference, the Phallic mother, in command of the mysterious processes of life, death, meaning, and identity."[5] In exactly this sense, the speaker of Sexton's poem lies in a crotch of stiff pines of "a different order" and "a different sign," where she is protected by an entity "in command of the mysterious processes of life, death, meaning, and identity." However masculine in tenor, this is still a feminine death, presided over by the mother's priestesses, those green girls whose business is not only life but the death that "seams up and down the leaf."

"May 5, 1970" is so intimately connected to "Leaves That Talk" (*45 Mercy Street*) that they read as parts of one poem. In "Leaves That Talk" the same green girls call out their death wish to the speaker: "Anne, Anne, come to us." Concentrating again on their veins, she is beguiled by their "woman apron lives" and their "brown stick branches." The speaker is subject to the voices even while she goes about the mundane, sensible business of daily life. "They call, though I sit here/sensibly behind my window screen."

> They want me. They need me.
> I belong lying down under them,
> letting the green coffin fold and unfold
> above me as I go out.

Sexton explains her death urges in ways that will be familiar to most readers in directly opposite terms: to lie down under a leafy tree and absorb the green is usually an effective evocation of life rather than death. The green voices are determined, consistent: "They steam all summer, . . . and they do not shut up./They do not."

In a remarkably analytic stanza, the speaker tells us as nearly as she can who the green girls are. "It has a body./It has many bodies." She muses upon the possibility that the green girls are her female forebears: "the generation of women, down the line,/the genealogical line right to the *Mayflower.* . . . " Tired of analysis and unsure she is right, she concludes: "whoever my green girls are—/they *are.*" She knows it is vital to discover their identities. She knows equally well that they are veiled, may be veiled from her all her life, speaking to her from behind shrouds that obscure their faces.

But the dramatis personae of death for Sexton are not only or always female, even if always familial. In "Leaves That Talk" she parades her pantheon of family ghosts, especially the male aspect of death represented by her grandfather, infrequent but important visitor to her dream-thoughts. If the green girls sing to her over the common music of life like a "dream in a dream," it is in an equally dreamlike state that she is "having a love affair/with grandfather," who "touches my neck and breast." This unnatural affair, this betrayal of the feminine conspiracy, causes the leaves to fall off, "*clank, clank,*/crashing down like stones, New England/stones, one by one. . . . " A chorus of outraged pain issues from them: "There are one hundred thousand woman cries,/tree by tree. . . . "

No other such naked confrontation between male and female versions of death occurs in Sexton's poetry. It might seem that the male principle here, represented by the grandfather who tells her "Do not be afraid!/It's only the leaves falling!" exerts a force of life in opposition to the feminine force of death, and in one respect that may be true. (See chapter 2, "How We Danced," for other conjectures on his significance.) Grandfather is, after all, making love to her, driving off and offending the green death women, causing the speaker to "scream out in my fear/that my green ladies are leaving,/my lovely obsessions,/and I need them." But for what is grandfather saving her from them? For life, for health? Perhaps. Just as likely, he saves her from the death women in order to claim her for himself. His incestuous love would weave her more tightly into the cyclonic neurosis of patriarchal romance, for which the pattern is woman as victimized daughter. My reading is that while grandfather temporarily represents a life-force in opposition to the death the green girls offer, it is a fragmented and obliterated self he offers, a reincarnation of her grandmother, whereas, to her dis-eased imagination, the green girls call to her to be whole, to be herself. (When death puts you through the wringer, it's a man. When you do it yourself, it's a woman.)

In the "May 30th" poem of the "Scorpio, Bad Spider, Die" sequence in *Words for Dr. Y.,* Sexton identifies death with her father, indirectly but completely. The speaker addresses God: "Don't look now, God, we're all right./All the suicides are eating Black Bean Soup." Her family is happy, even the dog. The poem ends with another plea:

> Please God, we're all right here. Please leave us alone.
> Don't send death in his fat red suit and his ho-ho baritone.

Death as Santa Claus? In "Santa" (*The Book of Folly*), she remembers her dead father's Santa impersonations, telling him that the Santa Claus suit he bought before she was born is "dead," even though she can still hear him "all the time laughing that North Pole laugh." As a child, she once smelled liquor on him: "The year I ceased to believe in you/is the year you were drunk." Playing Santa was over for the rest of her own childhood, to be resumed for her own children. When the speaker was a child, "Mother would kiss you/for she was that tall." Years later, "We were conspirators,/secret actors,/and I kissed you/because I was tall enough." She has grown from daughter into wife, just as in "May 30th" she is her grandfather's lover. "Death in his fat red suit and his ho-ho baritone" *is* her dear and dead father.

"For Mr. Death Who Stands with His Door Open" (*The Death Notebooks*) conflates nearly all of Sexton's personalized images of death as a familiar male. Contrasting time, here feminine, and death, masculine, she creates the dramatic conceit of a lifelong romance between herself and Mr. Death, faceless and yet many-faced. Mr. Death destroys time, "old gal of mine," who was once "all goggle-eyed,/wiggling her skirts, singing her torch song." As time grows short, she remembers it young: "May I say how young she was back then,/playing piggley-witch and hoola-hoop." Evoking an oceanic myth of feminine nurture, as she does frequently from *The Death Notebooks* on, she remembers that when time was young, "the sea washed me daily in its delicate brine."

> Time was when I could hiccup and hold my breath
> and not in that instant meet Mr. Death.

But Mr. Death has been coming to her for many years as the poem opens. He is an actor with "many masks." Envisioning him first as "a kind of Valentino/with my father's bathtub gin in your flask," he is next a death-camp manager who "held out the bait" for her suicide attempt. Now he is no longer the slim suitor, having aged as she has. "Your beer belly hangs out like Fatso./You are popping your buttons and expelling gas." Razzing him as one might a familiar old boyfriend, she asks, "How can I lie down with you, my comical beau/when you are so middle-aged and lower-class." Yet she knows she must lie down with him, that he will "press me down in your envelope." Ironic and comical or not, the romance is still alive, as it must be until she is dead. So she will play the courtship with death to the hilt, as she has played life. She would have her final death slow:

> Let it be pantomime, this last peep show,
> so that I may squat at the edge trying on
> my black necessary trousseau.

Knowing that at last she must marry this outrageous suitor, she savors the courtship for its comic and dramatic potential.

"Mr. Death" is a distant enough figure to merit being called by his surname, but his familiar faces rescue him from the purely abstract. This is the death one may flirt with, even patronize, at least until the wedding night. Not so the incarnation of death as the My Lai soldier in the 1969 untitled poem from the Dr. Y. sequence that begins with the speaker "dreaming the My Lai soldier again." The visitor at her door who first appears to be the Fuller Brush man "lowers me down with the other dead women and babies/saying, *It's my job. It's my job.*"

> I am lying in this belly of dead babies
> each one belching up the yellow gasses of death
> and their mothers tumble, eyeballs, knees, upon me,
> each for the last time, each authentically dead.
> The soldier stands on a stepladder above us
> pointing his red penis right at me and saying,
> Don't take this personally.

Here it is again: the contrary of suicide, in which she takes control, in which she has the power, is murder at the hands of a man, death by unpredictable, undeserved accident, death horribly out of her own control. And this death is accomplished by sexual assault, both here and in "The Death Baby," where angry dogs devour an infant: "They loved me until I was gone." It is more than accidental that this mental condition is divided along gender lines. In a world where women are less powerful, where a My Lai soldier *can* victimize women and babies, where it *is* men who murder women and children, Sexton's gendered imaging of death is not so much shocking—although it is that—as predictably shared knowledge likely to be understood by a woman.

Unfortunately for this poet, who spent the last decade of her life in search of an adequate god, death-as-a-man is ultimately God. However she may have sought his mercy in *The Awful Rowing toward God,* the deity in whom she believed was not one of love and forgiveness but one of judgment, bodily arbitrariness, and abstract male principle. In "Hurry Up Please It's Time" (*The Death Notebooks*), the "power in the Lord" is a symbol of complete victimization for the penitent believer. "One noon as you walk out to the mailbox/He'll snatch you up—/a woman beside the road like a red mitten." The only way Anne Sexton thought she could escape her legacy of powerlessness in a world presided over by this God was to kill herself before He could.

In *Women and Madness* Chesler described the difficulty of suicide for women:

> Women are conditioned to experience *physicality*—be it violent, destructive or pleasurable—more in the presence of another, or at male hands, than alone or at their own female hands. Female suicide attempts are not so much realistic "calls for help" or hostile inconveniencing of others as they are the assigned baring of the powerless throat, signals of ritual readiness for self-sacrifice. Like female tears, female suicide attempts constitute an essential act of resignation and helplessness—which alone can command temporary relief or secondary rewards. Suicide *attempts* are the grand rites of "femininity"—i.e., ideally women are supposed to "lose" in order to "win." Women who *succeed* at suicide are, tragically, outwitting or rejecting their "feminine" role, and at the only price possible: their death.[6]

While Anne Sexton's personality and circumstances differed immeasurably from those of most of the victimized women in Chesler's study, she shared with most suicidal women a complexly ironic version of this uniquely feminine tragedy.

"The End of Fear and the Fear of Dying"

While I think it is true that Anne Sexton's position as a woman contributed to both her illness and her death, I do not want to feminize away, or politicize into resolution, a situation so clearly and fundamentally beyond either gender or politics. Although the particular form of self-loathing she experienced was deeply and enduringly connected to her gender and her sexuality, the desire to die transcends sexual coinage. The tortuous web of psychic processes that ironically led her to perceive self-inflicted death as a way of claiming power as a woman against the overwhelmingly masculine adversary, death inflicted from outside the self, is only one component of her urge to die.

The central paradox of Sexton's suicide poems is the probability that the poems, and the act that ended them, were directed as much against mortality as against life. Sexton spoke of this only once in her letters, to Brian Sweeney in 1970: "You are so right about my fear of death. I think I have embraced it only because I feared it so."[7] And only once did she voice the thought undisguised in her poetry, in two slight lines from "The Death King" in *Words for Dr. Y.:*

> Death will be the end of fear
> and the fear of dying.

These two quotations crystallize the paradox that seems irreconcilable. Anne Sexton was a joyful poet who wrote witty fairy tales, who spoke with such authority about delight that we know her to have experienced it intensely, whose metaphors rose as often from limitless capacity to love and enjoy as from limitless capacity to suffer and to revel in suffering. How could one so open to life, so clearly in love with energy and vitality, choose to kill herself? What sense can it make to kill yourself because you fear death, or because you are angry at mortality?

Ernest Becker contends that if we were in constant touch with the truth of our mortality, we would be terrified every waking and sleeping moment. The terror of death is "all-consuming" to the human animal when he or she looks it full in the face. Repression of this fear "takes care of the complex symbol of death for most people."[8] But certainly there must be some people—and Anne Sexton was among them—who never do accomplish the great human task of primary repression of death, who never thicken their skins enough to block out the anguish of constant awareness. (There are just as certainly a few people who *can* directly contemplate their own mortality without experiencing what Becker calls "terror"—but they are probably as unusual as those who face it fully and cannot endure the resulting agony.) The greatest number of us expend considerable energy in order to avoid thinking about it at all, except in fleeting flashes or in abstract terms. Writing this chapter constitutes a safely abstract way for me to think about it, for instance.

But it is not only an awareness of the power of death that we must avoid. Most people are equally unable to experience life fully. We are collectively nostalgic about the wondrous sense of life commonly experienced in childhood, but that very sense of wonder would be impossible to sustain. We need to diminish it through repression if we are to function at all. Becker hypothesizes that by the time we leave childhood, we have successfully "repressed our vision of the primary miraculousness of creation":

> Sometimes we may recapture this world by remembering some striking childhood perceptions, how suffused they were in emotion and wonder. . . . We change these heavily emotional perceptions precisely because we need to move about in the world with some kind of equanimity, some kind of strength and directness; we can't keep gaping with our heart in our mouth, greedily sucking up with our eyes everything great and powerful that strikes us. The great boon of repression is that it makes it possible to live decisively in an overwhelmingly miraculous and incomprehensible world, a world so full of beauty, majesty and terror that if animals perceived it all they would be paralyzed to act.[9]

It is just this kind of emotional equanimity that Anne Sexton seems never to have experienced, except in brief moments of her life. She was "gaping with her heart in her mouth" daily, sometimes hourly, absolutely filled with a sense of the "miraculous and incomprehensible." This is why she is so effective as a poet of childhood; her child speakers feel immediate and immanent and real because they *are*, because Anne Sexton never did repress the primary miraculousness of creation—nor the primary terror. In the course of normal development, the child represses both the consciousness of death *and* the surfeit of life, so that the human animal is characterized by the "two great fears" we believe other animals are protected from: the fear of life and the fear of death. Anne Sexton was, I think, protected from neither. As Erica Jong put it shortly after Sexton's death, Sexton simply had no skin.[10] I cannot imagine—I mean that literally—what it would be like to experience life in this way. But I can well imagine that for such a one, suicide might be a daily possibility. Life might always seem too much to live through with no definite end in sight—even if, or especially if, that end were what one found most unthinkable in the face of the fierce daily miracle.

We can turn almost anywhere in Sexton's canon and find evidence of her anger against mortality, the terrible fear of death that is sister to the desire. In "The Fury of Sunrises" (*The Death Notebooks*), the speaker travels literally from darkness to light, from night to day, in an anxious chant for life:

> After the death,
> after the black of black,
> this lightness—
> not to die, not to die—
> that God begot.

It is in part *because* she so delights in life, is so consumed by its abundant beauty, that she mourns the necessity of death and thus seeks it out of time. It is significantly the deaths of others, of "all her pretty ones," that are unbearable, and the sense of their loss suffuses almost every volume of Sexton's poetry. Her own death seems sometimes to be the penance she must pay for the fact of death in her universe. In a 1966 letter to Lois Ames, Sexton speaks of "the old need to die, and how it returns under any stress. An old command of my mother's."[11] Death is always her fault, and she is willing to pay with her life. But she would rather not. She would like everyone to live forever. "Yellow," a 1972 poem published in *Words for Dr. Y.*, shares with "The Fury of Sunrises" the central image of unfolding light:

> There will be no poison anywhere, no plague
> in the sky and there will be a mother-broth
> for all of the people and we will
> never die, not one of us, we'll go on
> won't we?

"Won't we?" is childishly poignant, and also maturely ironic. She knows, of course, that we won't.

If the desire for immortality, if infinite sadness at the prospect of death, is finally what her death wish is about, if it is a protest against our being what Becker calls "Gods with anuses" or "worms that think," then we can indeed fault her for childishness, whining, egomania. We can accuse Anne Sexton of an insufficient tolerance for the way things are, an inability gracefully to accept mortality. Certainly we can. But why should we? Do we not, almost all of us, share this protest? Do we not need someone to externalize it, to give voice to that part of us which feels this anguish? So that we can get on with the living that, however troubled it may be, is what we want to do? Forever?

Shortly after Sexton's death, Denise Levertov published an article in *Ramparts* titled "Anne Sexton: Light Up the Cave," in which she expressed deep concern that the response to Anne Sexton's suicide might be like the response to Sylvia Plath's: an epidemic of suicide attempts on the part of young students who supposed that in order to become poets they had to be self-destructive. "Therefore it seems to me that we who are alive must make clear, as [Anne Sexton] could not, the distinction between creativity and self-destruction."[12] I disagree with Levertov's suggestion that Sexton herself could not really distinguish between the two. She did, continuously in her poetry and often in her interviews. "Suicide is the opposite of the poem," as she said more than once. But of course I share Levertov's concern that we not fatally misconstrue the relationship between mental illness and art. I agree with her that although depression may be an occupational hazard, it is not a "prescriptive stimulus to artistic activity." And I would like to agree with her that "while the creative impulse and the self-destructive impulse can, and often do, coexist, their relationship is distinctly acausal; self-destructiveness is a handicap to the life of art, not the reverse." I say I would like to agree; I am not sure one can make any such hard and fast rules. I hope she is right about that one.

But in this frequently reprinted and influential essay, Levertov goes on to say a great deal that I cannot agree with. She asserts that contrary to romanticized notions about the interpenetration of art and self-destruction, "the greatest heroes and heroines are truly those who hold out the longest, or, if they do die young, do so unwillingly, resisting to the last."[13] Levertov wrote this much-quoted and admired article at the height of the most political stage of her poetic career, so she cites guerilla poets of Latin America as examples of artistic heroism. I cannot disagree that artists who hang on to life, who "hold out the longest," are admirable on that account; but she asks me, implicitly, to find the suicidal artist pathetic and reprehensible. She holds out "resistance to the last" as of primary and definitive significance, *in opposition to* a stance toward life that finds unending resistance beside the point. I do not mind being asked to admire dogged persistence and human courage; I do resist being asked to define the quality of art by its correlation to the affirmation of life. And in the end that is what Levertov asks that we do. After quoting several fine lines from Sexton's "Wanting to Die," Levertov writes:

Too many readers, with a perversity that, yes, really does seem to me to be bound up with white middle class privilege and all its moral disadvantages, would sooner remember, and identify with, lines like those than with these, which (in *The Death Notebooks*) she also wrote:

> Depression is boring, I think
> and I would do better to make
> some soup and light up the cave.[14]

To "fittingly honor her memory," Levertov implies that readers should turn away from a poem such as "Wanting to Die" and toward—apparently only toward—poems such as the slight "Fury of Rainstorms" she quotes at the end. I wonder, especially after reading her own later collection, *Life in the Forest*, whether Levertov would still stand by this statement. I hope she would not. The source of Sexton's creativity is closely bound up with both her delight and her pain, and that is probably true of any poet, of any person. Poems such as "Us," "Little Girl, My String Bean, My Lovely Woman," and "In Celebration of My Uterus" deserve to survive and be read because they are fine evocations of the celebratory impulse; poems such as "Wanting to Die," "The Death Baby," and "Leaves That Talk" are just as worthy for their poetic validation of the elegiac impulse. Art should certainly celebrate and affirm. And art at its best also takes life seriously. I agree with Ernest Becker that taking life seriously means something such as this: "That whatever man does on this planet has to be done in the lived truth of the terror of creation, of the grotesque, of the rumble of panic underneath everything. Otherwise it is false."[15]

To read only Sexton's poems of celebration and affirmation is to deplete her poetic legacy and our own capacity to feel. What Anne Sexton achieved from within her subjective energies is poetry written in that lived truth of the terror, and the delight, of creation. Panic always rumbled underneath, and to this she was as alive as she was to joy.[16]

9

Beyond the Pleasure Principle:
The Death Baby

Let us suppose, then, that all the organic instincts are conservative, are acquired historically and tend towards the restoration of an earlier state of things. . . . Every modification which is thus imposed upon the course of the organism's life is accepted by the conservative organic instincts and stored up for further repetition. Those instincts are therefore bound to give a deceptive appearance of being forces tending towards change and progress, whilst in fact they are merely seeking to reach an ancient goal by paths alike old and new. Moreover it is possible to specify this final goal of all organic striving[;] . . . it must be an *old* state of things, an initial state from which the living entity has at one time or other departed and to which it is striving to return by the circuitous paths along which its development leads. If we are to take it as a truth that knows no exception that everything living dies for *internal* reasons— becomes inorganic once again—then we shall be compelled to say that *"the aim of all life is death"* and, looking backwards, that *"inanimate things existed before living ones."*

. . . . Seen in this light, the theoretical importance of the instincts of self-preservation, of self-assertion and of mastery greatly diminishes. They are component instincts whose function it is to assure that the organism shall follow its own path to death, and to ward off any possible ways of returning to inorganic existence other than those which are immanent in the organism itself. . . . What we are left with is the fact that the organism wishes to die only in its own fashion.

—Sigmund Freud, *Beyond the Pleasure Principle*

The soul, is I think, a human being who speaks with the pressure of death at his head. . . . The self in trouble . . . not just the self without love (as us) but the self as it will always be (with gun at its head finally). . . . To live and know it is only for a moment . . . that is to know "the soul" . . . and it increases closeness and despair and happiness.

—Anne Sexton, *Anne Sexton: A Self-Portrait in Letters*

> What does it mean to be a *self-conscious* animal? The idea is
> ludicrous, if it is not monstrous. . . . This is the terror: to have
> emerged from nothing, to have a name, consciousness of self, deep
> inner feelings, an excruciating inner yearning for life and self-
> expression—and with all this yet to die.
>
> —Ernest Becker, *The Denial of Death*

Becker and Freud

Freud published *Beyond the Pleasure Principle* in 1920, and ever
since its publication, Freudians have been trying to beat anti-Freudians
to the draw in the effort to unwrite it. Even classical analysts tend to
consider it erratic and easily dismissible, almost an aberration in the
career of an otherwise authoritative theorist. Indeed, its appeals to
biology seem quaint and easy to patronize. That Freud wrote this
book during his intellectual maturity and that he never refuted it, but
rather made its premises the basis of all subsequent theory, seem not to
matter. It is as though most readers agree that *Beyond the Pleasure
Principle* represents a momentary lapse of concentration and intellectual vitality.

The thesis that so upsets even aficionados is relatively simple: in
Beyond the Pleasure Principle Freud proposed the existence of a "death
instinct," a biologically rooted urge in organic life to reachieve the
inorganic state. Among the factors that led him to this hypothesis is the
"repetition compulsion" he had noted in the course of analytic treatment and of world events, what he later called a "piece of unconquer-
able nature" or a "force which is defending itself by every possible
means against recovery."[1]

No one likes the idea that the enemy has outposts in our heads. The
proposition that there is in all of us an urge toward death competitive
with the urge toward life seems outrageous, even ridiculous. If Freud
had proposed that this was true of only severely neurotic or psychotic
individuals, no one would have argued the point. But he posited that
"we must suppose [the death instincts] to be associated from the very
first with life instincts" in all living beings, and that is simply beyond
the pale, to say nothing of the pleasure principle.[2] In the dramatic battle
he staged between Eros and Thanatos in the germ plasm of all living
creatures, Freud still gave the impression of championing Eros, but he
implied that if "the aim of all life is death," Thanatos will always,
eventually, win out. Between birth and death Freud envisioned the

165

organism vibrating anxiously: "[The sexual instincts] are the true life instincts. They operate against the purpose of the other instincts, which leads, by reason of their function, to death; and this fact indicates that there is an opposition between them and the other instincts.... It is as though the life of the organism moved with a vacillating rhythm."[3]

His conclusions in *Beyond the Pleasure Principle* led to significant shifts in the rest of psychoanalytic theory. For example, he was forced now to consider that there *might* be such a thing as primary masochism, whereas before he had regarded masochism as sadism or aggressiveness turned inward upon the subject. But the fear of death, as opposed to the wish for it, remained for Freud at this time a special case of displaced sexual anxiety associated primarily with the castration complex.

The dismissal of a tract as hypothetical as *Beyond the Pleasure Principle* is inevitable in a culture that represses and avoids death as ours does. In his *The Denial of Death,* Ernest Becker proposes that the fear and dread of death is the primary repression in almost all cultures, and in this he means to contradict Freud: "*Consciousness of death* is the primary repression, not sexuality.... *This* is what is creaturely about man, *this* is the repression on which culture is built, a repression unique to the self-conscious animal."[4]

A psychoanalytic theorist himself, Becker agrees with Otto Rank that Freud was unable to establish "man's continuity and his difference from the lower animals on the basis of his *protest* against death rather than on his built-in instinctive urge toward it."[5] In this judgment he concurs with both popular and scholarly opinion. As Gregory Zilboorg remarks ironically in his introduction to an edition of *Beyond the Pleasure Principle,* the consensus has it that "the book in question is therefore more or less superannuated and deserves but a respectful historical glance before we put it back on the shelf to gather more dust."[6] Becker's own judgment is as damning and dismissive as any qualified opinion could be: "Freud's tortuous formulations on the death instinct can now securely be relegated to the dust bin of history."[7]

Becker refers to "Freud's unfortunate habit of forming polarities in his thought" but fails to see similarly structured polarities in his own thought. Becker may be right that *Beyond the Pleasure Principle* patched up the instinct libido theory into another comfortable duality, but it is just as true that Becker's own theses about death fear are based on polarities and dualities, in this case the unquestioning acceptance of mind/body dichotomies on which our culture may be based, but which are not necessarily productive or "true" on that account. Becker is eloquent in his defense of dualism *as truth*:

> This is the paradox: he (man) is out of nature and hopelessly in it; he is dual, up in the stars and yet housed in a heart-pumping, breath-gasping body that once belonged to a fish and still carries the gill-marks to prove it. His body is a material fleshy casing that is alien to him in many ways—the strangest and most repugnant way being that it aches and bleeds and will decay and die. Man is literally split in two: he has an awareness of his own splendid uniqueness in that he sticks out of nature with a towering majesty, and yet he goes back into the ground a few feet in order blindly and dumbly to rot and disappear forever.[8]

If Becker's repugnance toward the body sounds overly disgusted, he is only reflecting a paradox to which we are all heirs. The most significant thing about Becker's fine book, it seems to me, is that it was regarded as new, radical, and bold when it was published in 1973. He speaks here, after all, of a dualism so commonly held that it is nearly definitive of Judeo-Christian culture's body politic and personal. But I do not quote him here just to argue with him—he is now dead and cannot argue back, at any rate—for I believe he is right, irrefutably so, in his contention that the repression of the knowledge and fear of death is primary to humankind in a sophisticated culture, that we are faced with what seems an impossible paradox: constant fear of death in the biological functioning of our self-preservative instincts, as well as obliviousness to this fear in our conscious life. So awful is the thought of our mortality, contends Becker, that "those who speculate that a full apprehension of man's condition would drive him insane are right, quite literally right." The essence of normality, in the face of this terrible and definitive fact of our lives, is the "refusal of reality." Some people have more trouble with their lies than others, and these people we call neurotic or, depending on the severity of symptoms, psychotic.[9]

As a counter to the Freudian contention that the fear of death is not primary and is not repressed, but is rather only a displacement for the fear of castration, Becker's reminder is necessary. It has always seemed to me ingenuous of Freud to dismiss the fear of death primarily because he believed that the unconscious has no knowledge of its own death. That he altered this position to permit himself to think that we do have unconscious knowledge of our own deaths but that the knowledge can take the form only of an instinct *toward* it or wish *for* it seems to me lopsided, and Becker joins those who point out this lapse of attention to possibilities. There is indeed *no theoretically necessary reason* why Freud should have restricted our relationship to our own mortality in such an intellectually and imaginatively cramped fashion. He need not have insisted that sexuality is the only primary repression, nor that the wish for death is not accompanied by the greatest fear of it.

But I have a similar objection to Becker. Refuting Freud's contention that all primary repressions are sexual in nature, Becker counterasserts that all primary repression has to do with death rather than sexuality. Just as Freud shuts his door on the possibility of a primary death fear, Becker slams his own on the possibility of a primary death wish, as though the primacy of fear could not be mutually compatible with the primacy of wish—or tendency or urge or instinct. These are ironically rigid pronouncements, given that psychoanalytic thought is built upon the accommodation of paradoxes that seem, on the face of it, mutually exclusive. The reconciling of opposites through overdetermination, projection, reaction formation, and other psychic mechanisms is perhaps the greatest contribution of psychoanalytic thought. But at bedrock (which Freud located by definition in biology), the tendency toward either/or structures seems to defeat even the groundbreakers—or especially the groundbreakers.

It is my assumption, and the assumption of this book, that wish and fear, symbolic of our psychic orientation to all primary oppositions, are elaborately intertwined in unconscious mental life. In Anne Sexton's death poetry, wish and fear are often functionally identical. This does not mean that it is useless to distinguish the separable components of wish and fear, to identify one human urge juxtaposed with its opposite, when that is poetically possible; any analysis of tonal complexities must at least attempt to do this. But Sexton's poetry on death absolutely defies the desire finally to sunder wish and fear. Perhaps that is why this poetry is so disconcerting, so uncomfortable to assimilate. It speaks to our deepest identifications and defenses and rouses our need to protest against the blurring of boundaries, the obliteration of distinctions among objects and feelings people need to think of separately. It embodies the anomalies that call up our need for purity and our flight from danger.

The Dumb Traveler

"The Death Baby" (*The Death Notebooks*) is among the most psychoanalytic of Sexton's poems. By this I do not mean that it merely confesses to a neurosis that may be analyzed psychoanalytically or that the critic can dissect as case history. Rather, I mean that in "The Death Baby" Sexton presents in poetry a persuasive case for a controversial piece of Freudian theory, providing a poetic analogue for the hypothesis Freud outlined in *Beyond the Pleasure Principle.* I have no reason to suppose that she set out to achieve this or that she conceived of "The Death Baby" as supportive of any psychological theory. Finding such correspondences is the critic's job, not the poet's. But while Sexton was not a psychoanalytic theorist by any measure, she was preeminently a psychoanalytic poet, and in "The Death Baby" she clearly wishes to convey not only a truth she has lived but something close to a thesis about the workings of unconscious mental life. She proceeds toward her thesis inductively, and my exploration follows that method.

"The Death Baby" is a sequence of six poems interconnected by dreams, dolls, and death. In the first poem, "Dreams," the speaker imagines herself a frozen blue ice baby, "my mouth stiffened into a dumb howl." She has been told this is only a childhood dream, but she knows better than to dismiss it on that account: "I remember that hardening." Without ever refuting that it was indeed a dream, she asserts the authenticity of the experience and the memory. Sexton's use of the dream-state here and throughout the canon insists upon this authenticity of dreams, in exactly the way analytic theory insists upon it. For Sexton the mind dreaming is "she of the origin,/she of the primal crack," and the bed is an "operating table," where dreams "slice me into pieces" ("January 24th," *Dr. Y;* and "The Lost Lie," *45 Mercy Street*). In "Dreams" an unspecified "they" attempt to dismiss the memory by calling it dream, but the speaker knows that the images in dreams are emblems of psychic reality. The first stanza leaves the reader contemplating a double image: the adult speaker superimposed on a howling baby frozen into ice.

The second stanza calls into question whose dream we are dealing with:

> My sister at six
> dreamt nightly of my death:
> "The baby turned to ice.
> Someone put her in the refrigerator
> and she turned as hard as a Popsicle."

This was not the speaker's dream after all, as the first stanza had let the reader assume. Rereading, I am struck by how easy it would have been to reverse the first two stanzas to avoid confusion about the identity of the dreamer. But the ambiguity is purposeful. Sexton wants us to be confused about identities here, and she will deepen that confusion by creating identifications not only between the speaker and her sister but also between the speaker and her mother. Finally, such ambiguity serves to establish that the poem will concern itself with the wish to kill as well as to die, with the hostility and aggression toward others that may be part of our species' urge toward death.

The third stanza is among the most grotesquely powerful in Sexton's canon. The speaker places herself in the refrigerator in her incarnation as ice baby. She remembers "how I was put on a platter and laid/between the mayonnaise and the bacon." As is so characteristic of Sexton's manipulation of the grotesque, the image is softened, or twisted, by the humorous specificity of mayo and bacon. What might otherwise be merely maudlin and shocking is rendered almost funny, yet still terrifying. Readers would soon wilt under the burden of the images that follow— "The tomatoes vomited up their stomachs"—if such wince-making metaphors were not accompanied by others that bring a degree of levity to an unimaginably horrible scenario in which a baby, its mouth stiffened into a dumb howl, is placed on a platter in a refrigerator along with other leftover edibles. Sexton saves the situation, and our sensibilities, with "the pimentos kissed like cupids." This stanza ends with the ice baby moving on its platter, "like a lobster,/slower and slower," suffocated by the "tiny" air.

Next we are taken into the black core of another dream, this one also the sister's dream, but belonging to the speaker as her own lived reality:

> I was at the dogs' party.
> I was their bone.
> I had been laid out in their kennel
> like a fresh turkey.

Just as she "remembers" the hardening in the refrigerator, she remembers "that quartering" by Boston bull terriers, "ten angry bulls/jumping like enormous roaches" over her body. First the dogs lap her "very clean." Then they begin with their teeth, "those nails," to dismember her.

I was coming apart.
They loved me until
I was gone.

In each of these two segments, the speaker has been transformed by the wish of another, her sister, into an object stripped of humanity, a kind of stillborn baby; and in each she is further objectified and transformed into food, first for people, finally for dogs. By the end of the first poem in the sequence, then, the speaker has been born and has died in infancy. Sexton does not explain or labor the Oedipal scenario so clearly enacted by the sister, who, at age six, sees the newcomer as intruder and competitor for the affections of the parents and wishes her dead. She concentrates instead on the degree of internalization the speaker experienced when she was old enough to be told about the dream, and still experiences as an adult. Having learned about the ice baby of her sister's dream, she identifies with that image; or perhaps the ice-baby image corresponds uncannily to the sense she has always had of herself. Someone else's dream has always been true for her, has always been the lived nightmare of her own reality.

Significantly, the adult agents of her transformation are entirely absent in this segment of the poem. No mother or father comes to rescue this helpless infant trapped in the hideous half-light we know not only from dreams but also from fairy tales. This may be Sexton's own private image for the menace of obliteration, but the author of *Transformations* already knew that her own private pantheon of demons belonged to everyone, was derived from the storehouse of cultural nightmare she milked from her own unconscious depths. Sexton's ice baby on a platter draws from the same source of horror in domestic disguise as do fairy tales. The fear of children transformed into food for giants or monsters or wolves or consuming mothers is familiar from *Hansel and Gretel, Little Red Riding Hood, Jack and the Beanstalk;* the kitchen is the right room in which to stage a scenario about fears of consumption, just as it was in "For John," the poem with which I began this journey through Sexton. In this case, the child is helplessly sunk in motor incapacity, without language, reduced to a frozen howl.

Becker says of young children: "In their tortured interiors radiate complex symbols of many inadmissible realities—terror of the world, the horror of one's own wishes, the fear of vengeance by the parents, the disappearance of things, one's lack of control over anything, really." If "to grow up at all is to conceal the mass of internal scar tissue that throbs in our dreams," then Sexton is here engaged in opening the wounds, driving back to the beginning the lack of control epitomized by infancy, exposing the "tortured interior."[10] And although the agent of her trans-formation to frozen food is not named—"Someone put her in the refrigerator"—the absent parents are surely among the suspects. Who puts food in the refrigerator? Usually the mother or, in the case of Sexton's own household, the maid, the mother's kitchen surrogate. Even if the parents did not put her in the fridge—and on a platter—they did not save her. There is no help here; the infant's world is all unmanageable violence.[11]

The "quartering" of the baby's body by the dogs constitutes sexual violation as well as murder. "They loved me until/I was gone." The desire to consume, experienced by every infant, is closely related to the fear of being consumed, and both are connected to the mode of sexuality characteristic of the oral stage of psychic development. Infantile sexual-ity is polymorphous, experienced as far as we can tell throughout the body and not necessarily focused on or restricted to the genitals. (Some of the best anecdotal evidence for the dispersed, polymorphous nature of infantile sexuality comes from adult memories of earliest sexual fantasies. One woman I know describes her earliest sexual fantasy like this: "I am riding on the seat in a train, watching the lights go by. I am naked, possibly about to be diapered. My entire body is vibrating with the train. I don't even know why I call this a 'sexual' fantasy, but it is.") Creating an unimaginably horrible scene of a baby's rape and murder by ravenous dogs, Sexton's poem alludes to unconscious connections between death and sexuality even in infancy and relates such connec-tions to the aggression of orality, of consuming and being consumed.

Before language, prior to the sense of control that develops as a child grows, the possibility of nightmare victimization, of consumption, and of violation and finally obliteration is a fundamental human fear. And the infant—this infant, any infant—can respond only with a "dumb howl." Sexton renders a universal human condition—the helpless-ness of infancy, the fear of obliteration that lives on in nightmares—through the particularities of her speaker's dream life. These are only dreams, only someone else's dreams, not even the speaker's, and yet the poem makes me see that baby on a platter in the refrigerator, see her torn in pieces and eaten by dogs, so clearly that I wonder, indeed, whose dream this is.

The second poem in the "Death Baby" sequence is "The Dy-dee Doll," who, the speaker says, died twice:

> Once when I snapped
> her head off
> and let it float in the toilet
> and once under the sun lamp
> trying to get warm
> she melted.

The matter-of-fact and unapologetic tone emphasizes the shadowy presence of the child whose baby doll this was. (The doll represents an infant rather than a child—a "Dy-dee" is a doll that can be diapered.) The placement of "The Dy-dee Doll," following the "Dreams" sequence, brings the nightmare aura of the earlier poems into the reenacted remembrance of childhood reality. Sexton plays here on the familiar pattern of the doll as surrogate self—children often punish and mistreat dolls in exact reenactments of their own punishments and real or imagined mistreatments by parents. A beloved doll can be literally torn apart in the service of vengeance against the parental powers in whose presence the child herself is helpless.

The degree of malicious motivation differs in the two deaths of the doll. In the first we are told that the speaker "snapped/her head off"; the incident is reported without emotional content. We see a child purposely and determinedly snapping off a doll's head and then casting it in the toilet, enacting a murder that is only vicious play, for the head floats and can apparently be replaced. The second, final death seems less purposeful; the doll was "trying to get warm." But anyone who remembers such play, with pets as well as with dolls, knows how thin is the line between cruelty and carelessness, between innocence and malicious self-deception. Here we cannot judge for certain, but we can suspect. After the flat, toneless relating of facts, the speaker ends with:

> She was a gloom,
> her face embracing
> her little bent arms.
> She died in all her rubber wisdom.

I read a certain amount of irony in the last line. Rubber wisdom? That is no wisdom at all—or no more wisdom than can be attributed to a frozen baby with a dumb howl on its face. But genuine sympathy and regret are present in the description of the dying doll, whose face embraces her arms, melting into rubber soup just as the refrigerated baby froze into ice. In the dreams and the play of children, these first two poems assert, is enacted the business of horror, mutilation, objectification, and bodily obliteration we know perfectly well resides there but like to pretend does not. Just as people know that children are not innocent of sexuality, we know that they are not innocent of murderous thoughts. We somehow relegate these experienced and remembered kinds of knowledge, which we observe again as parents, to a safe place, thinking that the real business of death gets done in hospitals or on battlefields. We repress what we know of the horror of infancy and childhood, the fear of dying, the wish to kill, the fear of being consumed, the wish to consume.

A later poem provides support for connections between the dy-dee doll and the abandoned ice baby of the first segment. In "The Falling Dolls" (45 *Mercy Street*), Sexton dreams that "Dolls,/by the thousands,/are falling out of the sky." She wonders who will catch them and imagines the carnage of doll bodies smashing to earth. Some of them will fall on highways, "so that they may be run over like muskrats," and some will land in national parks, where centuries later "they'll be found petrified like stone babies." The speaker tries to catch as many as she can, knowing that they are "the babies I practice upon." The dolls "need cribs and blankets and pajamas/with real feet in them." She wants to know "Why is there no mother?" and "Was there a father?"—the same questions I asked as a reader of "Dreams." The final stanza serves as a bridge between "Dreams" and "The Dy-dee Doll":

> Or have the planets cut holes in their nets
> and let our childhood out,
> or are we the dolls themselves,
> born but never fed?

Thus far Sexton has restricted the sequence to examination of the *fear of dying* and the *wish to kill*, all placed in the psychoanalytic and poetic context of infancy and early childhood and anatomized through the agency of dreaming. Now she builds outward from that chronology, moving toward another dimension of psychic reality. The third poem, "Seven Times," is a ritual reiteration of the speaker's many deaths:

> I died seven times
> in seven ways
> letting death give me a sign,
> letting death place his mark on my forehead,
> *crossed over, crossed over.*

The experienced Sexton reader is likely to interpret the seven deaths as suicide attempts, half- or wholehearted. But this poem stands on its own without such personal context, and since she does not say that the seven deaths are self-inflicted, I am inclined to honor that ambiguity, or that refusal of clarity. Rather than being an active participant in her own deaths, the speaker assumes a passive role here, so that she might be referring to grave illnesses or psychic deaths. She "lets" death give her a sign and place his mark on her, a mark that says she is *"crossed over."* But these are not final deaths, although they may be real in some sense. They are, instead, deaths of the kind described in the first two poems: dream deaths, play deaths, deaths that can be taken back. If the mark on her forehead says she is *"crossed over,"* it is only temporary, like the dream-state, like the snapped-off doll's head. But the deaths are no less serious for being temporary or partial; rather, the fact that the speaker comes to life again with death's mark still on her forehead, means that she wears the mark continuously throughout life. One wakes from a dream but goes to sleep again, to dream again:

> And death took root in that sleep.
> In that sleep I held an ice baby
> and I rocked it
> and was rocked by it.
> Oh Madonna, hold me.
> I am a small handful.

Now the speaker holds her own ice baby, the stillborn aspect of herself from her sister's dream of many years before. As a child she mothered her doll, whom she also murdered. The central images of both "Dreams" and "The Dy-dee Doll" are conflated in this rocking scene, which takes place in sleep. In a peculiar twist on the ordinary relationship of mother and infant, she not only rocks this alien yet intimate death baby; she is also "rocked by it." Instantly, she transforms it into a Madonna, whom she begs to hold her. If we are to make sense of this unintelligible switch, that sense must be psychoanalytic.

In dreams people and objects transform into their opposites, or merely into other objects or people, through the agencies of projection, displacement, and condensation. Freud originally proposed that all dreams are fulfillments of disguised wishes and that upon analysis such disguised wishes will always reveal their sexual, infantile sources. But in *Beyond the Pleasure Principle* he proposed significant exceptions to this rule. "It is impossible to classify as wish-fulfillments the dreams . . .

which occur in traumatic neuroses, or the dreams during psychoanalyses which bring to memory the psychical traumas of childhood. They arise, rather, in obedience to the compulsion to repeat. . . . "[12]

This "repetition compulsion" is the foundation of Freud's theory on the death instinct. In popular usage it has come to signify any repetitive behaviors that are "neurotic," that keep people from progressing or changing in ways they consciously believe they want to. Freud eventually came to think of such repetitive behavior as inevitable or inescapable. The compulsion to repeat is ascribed by Freud to the unconscious repressed and is thus a manifestation of the power of repressed material to influence the conscious behaviors of normal as well as ill people. Freud found that in analysis patients repeat "unwanted situations and painful emotions" and "revive them with the greatest ingenuity." Eventually, he came to see this force as so powerful that it defended itself against cure at any cost. People in treatment returned to the same traumatic events of their pasts again and again, "under pressure of a compulsion."[13] The clearest way to characterize the tendency Freud is speaking of is to quote his comments on the repetition compulsion in the lives of normal people:

> Thus we have come across people all of whose human relationships have the same outcome, such as the benefactor who is abandoned in anger after a time by each of his proteges . . . and who thus seems doomed to taste all the bitterness of ingratitude; or the man whose friendships all end in betrayal by his friend; . . . or, again, the lover each of whose love affairs with a woman passes through the same phase and reaches the same conclusion.[14]

Most important for my purposes here, Freud relates the repetition compulsion to the kind of dream discussed above and to the impulse that leads children to play. In the first two poems of "The Death Baby" sequence, Sexton has explored exactly these activities, traumatic dreaming and playing. In the first sequence the speaker returns, apparently under force of a compulsion, to a traumatic dream of childhood, which she has erected into a memory she must resuscitate even though it does not bring her pleasure. The dream in question is the sister's, and it is clear how for the sister it would have been a wish-fulfillment dream: it gets rid of the new baby in the house. As the speaker's own dream, vicarious but real, it cannot be said to fulfill any pleasurable wish, as we conceive of pleasure. But the need to repeat overrides what Freud called the dominance of the pleasure principle in instinctual life.

The example of child's play that Sexton produces in the second poem is similarly unpleasurable as a memory, but it must be repeated. Such examples, says Freud, "give the appearance of some 'daemonic' force at work," as do all manifestations of the repetition compulsion when they seem to act against the best interests of the agent.[15] There may indeed be something pleasurable for the child who acts out murderous wishes against her doll, and perhaps the adult remembering the incident is able to recapture the sense of power she felt as a child. But the memory is clearly more unpleasant than pleasant, more traumatic than healing. Speaking of children's play, Freud writes, "Children repeat unpleasurable experiences for the additional reason that they can master a powerful impression far more thoroughly by being active than they could by merely experiencing it passively."[16] The speaker's enactment of the doll's death serves this purpose of attempting to master a traumatic experience, that experience being the dream-state of helplessness in "Dreams." But it is not only for purposes of mastery that the speaker returns and returns to unpleasant childhood memories. The compulsion to repeat embodies urges literally *beyond* the pleasure principle.

The thesis that Freud eventually builds on the foundation of the repetition compulsion is the urge toward death in all organic life, the need to return to the quiescence of the inorganic state. By the third poem in the sequence, Sexton is already synthesizing the same psychic mechanisms that Freud delineated in *Beyond the Pleasure Principle,* by placing herself in the sleep of death with the ice baby in her lap, rocking.

But baby as Madonna? In this dream- and sleep state near to death, the speaker makes identifications out of near opposites. The logic of the poem is circular and cyclical: mother turns into baby in her relationship to daughter. "Madonna," meaning originally "my lady," had the more specific meanings to Sexton of the Virgin Mary *and* her own mother, whose name was Mary. Sexton played with this accident of nomenclature throughout her career. From her many poems about Mary the mother of Christ, it is also clear that Sexton saw Mary as wise but thoroughly victimized and institutionally infantilized, especially in her relationship to her own infant son, who, although he grows up and away from her, is always an infant himself because his human development is sexually arrested. Sexton was also deeply and painfully aware of the exchange of places between mother and daughter when a mother grows into old age and disease. That the ice baby of death has turned into a Madonna is an appropriate juxtaposition of the themes of the first two sections; and the subject of the fourth poem, "Madonna," is the role reversal of mother and daughter:

> My mother died
> unrocked, unrocked.

Beside a hospital deathbed, the speaker relives her mother's death from cancer. She watches her mother "thrust herself against the metal bars," with "vomit steaming from her mouth." The speaker remembers herself

> wanting to place my head in her lap
> or even take her in my arms somehow
> and fondle her twisted gray hair.

Throughout the poem, Sexton intertwines images of mothering and being mothered, nurturing and being nurtured, repeatedly changing places with her mother. In the example above she wants to place her head in her mother's lap, i.e., to be mothered by her; and she wants to "take her in my arms," to mother her mother in her pain.

Playing on the pregnancy that brought her own life forth from her mother's body, the speaker finds "her belly . . . big with another child,/ cancer's baby, big as a football." There is nothing she can do to help, so she must watch the mother diminish into death before her eyes:

> With every hump and crack
> there was less Madonna
> until that strange labor took her.

The "strange labor" is the reversal of ordinary birthing, the birth into death. "Cancer's baby" is a parody sibling of those other infants, the ice baby and the doll. "Cancer's baby" replaces the baby the speaker once was and answers to the speaker's conviction that she, too, was born of death-in-life.

Fifth in the sequence, "Max" refers to Sexton's closest friend, poet Maxine Kumin. "Max and I" are "two immoderate sisters,/two immoderate writers,/two burdeners," whose understanding of each other's relationship to death ended in a "pact":

> To beat death down with a stick.
> To take over.
> To build our death like carpenters.

This poem reverses the trend of passivity toward her own death that has been characteristic of the speaker in earlier poems in the sequence. As the ice-dream baby she was completely passive and helpless and overwhelmed; in "Seven Times" she has let death give her a sign, allowed him to place a mark on her forehead; at her mother's deathbed she has been the passive and helpless observer. Only in "The Dy-dee Doll" segment has she been active in relation to death, and that was only a play death. In "Max" she takes over, protesting the powerlessness of her position. If death is her lot, as it is everyone's, she will not wait for it quietly but will defeat it, "beat [it] down with a stick." But to beat it down might mean to refute it, to fight against it; to clarify, she says she and Max will "build" their deaths like "carpenters" (see "Wanting to Die"). They will struggle against it until they are ready; but then they will take death into their own hands instead of being taken *by* it. (This position bears remarkable similarities to the arguments of euthanasia proponents, who advocate just such active participation in one's own death.) Their agreement is that when they know "the moment" has come,

> we'll talk turkey,
> we'll shoot words straight from the hip,
> we'll play it as it lays.
> Yes,
> when death comes with its hood
> we won't be polite.

The stance of "Max" is courageous and unblinking. Sexton here insists on resisting death before embracing it, creating an adversary as well as a seductive relationship to one's own death.

"Baby," the finale of "The Death Baby" sequence, synthesizes the first five poems and goes far beyond them—and far beyond the separate implications of pain and pleasure principles. "Baby" is addressed directly to death, resurrected from the first poem as a "cherub." Now the infant is more luminous than frozen, more mythic than ordinarily mortal:

> Your milky wings are as still as plastic.
> Hair as soft as music.
> Hair the color of a harp.
> And eyes made of glass,
> as brittle as crystal.

Whereas the ice baby was helplessly fixed into a silent howl of pain, the death baby is an embodiment of power, a delicate and dangerous force field. The speaker rocks the death baby in her arms, staring at its eyes, which are wise with primal knowledge: "Glass eye, ice eye,/primordial

eye,/lava eye,/pin eye,/break eye,/how you stare back!" Like the Homun-
culus in Goethe's *Faust*, this baby contains the essence and recapitula-
tion of all that is peculiarly human, but the knowledge in its eyes gazes
out from the face of a cherub. Its knowledge is not only universal—it
knows what it is to be human and mortal—but particular; the death
baby knows the speaker's own life history. "You know all about me."

> You have worn my underwear.
> You have read my newspaper.
> You have seen my father whip me.
> You have seen me stroke my father's whip.

These intimacies cannot be known by anyone except the self, and
this is the point: the death baby *is* the speaker, what Estella Lauter calls
"the still-born aspect of the self."[17] It is thus the aspect of the self that is
subject to the repetition compulsion, to urges toward primary masochism,
to the fusion of Eros and Thanatos, sexuality and death. The cameo
appearance of the father comes as a surprise in this feminine poem of
mothers, sisters, daughters, babies, and female friends. His function is
to bring the patriarchal order into the self-enclosed circle of women,
infants, and death; it might be said that his earlier surrogates were the
angry dogs who "quartered" the ice baby. Once again the speaker
reenacts or reevokes an experience that cannot have been pleasurable,
in the ordinary sense, but that *is* pleasurable in the perversely erotic
sense experienced by the masochistic daughter in relation to the patriarchal father. The death baby knows all about this kind of pleasure, for
the baby is the literal, infantilized embodiment of the urge to experience pain, shame, and finally death.

The speaker rocks the death baby as they "plunge back and
forth/comforting each other." Together they are a "stone pietà," the
Madonna and child of the earlier poems. In this rocking all else is
obliterated. The world outside may be the scene of larger events, even
"Pakistan is swallowed in a mouthful," but here in the room of rocking,
there is only the self and the self's own death baby, "my stone child/with
still eyes like marbles."

Now the poet swerves without warning or apology into a didactic
mode. The story of "The Death Baby" has a moral, reminiscent of the
morals in *Transformations*, but entirely without the wry tone Sexton
saved for fairy tales. This is the meaning she cannot allow us to
miss—and that, without the admonitory tone, we might easily wish to
avoid:

> There is a death baby
> for each of us.
> We own him.
> His smell is our smell.

Were she speaking here to other suicidal people, our agreement would be easy and immediate. But she is speaking to "each of us." The grotesquely intimate death baby belongs not just to Sexton or her kind but to everyone. She insists that this is not the story only of personal pathology but of a people, a culture, perhaps all cultures, all individuals. The death baby is the clearest possible humanized metaphor for the processes Freud delineated in *Beyond the Pleasure Principle*. Sexton is "supposing," with Freud, that organic instincts are "conservative," that they "tend towards the restoration of an earlier state of things." We mistake matters if we think all of our "instinctual" urges are directed toward prolonging life indefinitely. "Those instincts are . . . bound," Freud writes, "to give a deceptive appearance of being forces tending towards change and progress, whilst in fact they are merely seeking to reach an ancient goal by paths alike old and new."[18]

The stillborn aspect of each life, its glass and ice eye calcified into a stare that peers into the soul of the living self, remains in Sexton's mythopoeic terms a baby we rock, are rocked by, throughout life and into death. This corresponds exactly to Freud's "final goal of all organic striving": "If we are to take it as a truth that knows no exception that everything living dies for *internal* reasons—becomes inorganic once again—then we shall be compelled to say that *'the aim of all life is death.'* "[19] One may, of course, quarrel with the validity of that "truth." Freud carefully specifies that the conclusion he is compelled toward is conditional upon the hypothesis that everything dies for internal reasons. With the exceptions of death by accident from outer agencies, I find Freud's statement one way of stating the facts: if we live to be old enough, we do die for internal reasons. And the extremities of old age are closely united to the extremities of infancy, making the death baby an appropriate image for the ironic circularity of the life cycle.

The "ancient goal" of inorganic quiescence, the "*old* state of things," is emphasized in Sexton's poem in the "primordial" gaze of the death baby's eyes. In the sense that the "primordial" is first in order of appearance in the growth or development of an organism, it is fundamental, present at and participating in the very process of ordering, of coming into being: the death baby is born with and within the "life" baby. Or, as Freud expresses the same principle, "We must suppose [the death instincts] to be associated from the very first with life instincts."[20]

Although the death baby's visage is compelling and even seductive, Sexton does not embrace it without anxiety, nor does she suggest that any of us rock our death babies without being aware of what we thus nurture:

> Beware. Beware.
> There is a tenderness.
> There is a love
> for this dumb traveler
> waiting in his pink covers.

The warning is clear: watch out for your death baby, in whatever guise he comes to you. She tells us that we need beware not only his presence but also our affection for this death-in-life principle. The death baby appears harmless, clothed in the colors of innocence and purity, and therein lies the danger that we will mistake it, not be sufficiently on guard against the seductive tenderness we feel. And we cannot expect the baby to tell us who he is: he is "dumb," without language, before language, even if wise *beyond* language.

The ending of "The Death Baby" sequence imagines the moment when it will be time, when the speaker will know the necessity of finally and completely embracing her own death:

> Someday,
> heavy with cancer or disaster
> I will look up at Max
> and say: It is time.
> Hand me the death baby
> and there will be
> that final rocking.

If she seems to be succumbing here to the seductiveness of the death baby, there are significant qualifications upon that relinquishing of life, and for the substance of them we must return to "Max," and to Freud.

Even after he formulated his death-instinct hypothesis, Freud felt that urges toward self-preservation, assertion, and mastery were still very important; he had merely qualified what had been an exclusive emphasis on their power and significance. To go *beyond* the pleasure principle, where Eros reigns, is not to abandon the pleasure principle but merely to temper it to accord with clinical experience and observation of the behavior patterns of real people. If he could no longer suppose the sexual, or life instincts, to be all-powerful, he still found a place for them even within the death instinct, for they "assure that the organism shall follow its own path to death" and "ward off any possible ways of returning to inorganic existence other than those which are immanent in the organism itself."[21] Readers of Freud have found this a depressing hypothesis; but given that death is inevitable for all living creatures, the idea that "the organism wishes to die only in its own fashion" accords at least the semblance of internal choice. Note that it is not the death instinct itself that governs this choice, in Freud's scheme, but rather the life-preserving urges, engaged in negotiating a compromise between their own single-minded direction and the equally single-minded direction of the death urge. Seen in this light, the choice of the moment of death is a decision, albeit usually an unconscious one, on the part of a living being.

But the "final rocking" that Sexton speaks of involves an element of conscious choice on the speaker's part, in delicately negotiated compromise between Eros and Thanatos. Cancer or disaster may not be her conscious choices, may be the result of a struggle between internal, unconscious motivations, some directed toward living and some toward dying. But Sexton speaks here of her own *conscious* and *rational* decision to take control over both. The decision-making process was described in "Max," where the speaker and Max made the "pact" to "take over" their deaths. When Max had a broken back, the two women "built" her sleep nightly over the phone. Max had not chosen her broken back in any conscious way; but given her pain, undeniable and irrefutable, the building of sleep to ease that pain and to lead toward recovery was the life-affirming choice. Similarly, the "building" of death will take place in the clear-eyed recognition of the facts—this time cancer or disaster— and will affirm the power of the individual to choose her moment, when there is nothing else she can hope to gain by staying alive. In the face of cancer the speaker will not passively await the helpless, "unrocked" death that befell her mother while she watched; she will elect to take the death baby, humanized symbol of her own necessary and always-waiting death, into her arms for that "final rocking." It is better, this poem suggests, to rock your own death baby in your arms than to die, as her mother did, "unrocked, unrocked." For to rock your own death baby, *when it is time*—"I will look up at Max/and say: It is time"—is also to *be rocked by it*, to accept it, to receive comfort, to let go.

I am aware that many readers, many people who cared about Anne

Sexton, will feel the irony inherent in my reading of "The Death Baby." The source of the irony is the manner and timing of Anne Sexton's death, which we are not accustomed to see as a rational, courageous embrace of death at the "right" time, in the "right" way. This poem articulates a thesis about death that is uncomfortable even for people used to seeing the world psychoanalytically, even, as I have said, for Freudians. Yet the poem concludes with a movement, a decision, that militates against the dark, almost demonic direction of the rest of the poem, at least as I read it. The choice to die, in the face of "cancer" or its substitutes, is one that many people now agree or at least sympathize with; and I have suggested that the position Sexton takes here is similar to the positions advocated by euthanasia activists. But we do not extend the same agreement and sympathy to what Sexton here designates as "disaster."

Anne Sexton took the death baby in her arms for that final rocking at a time most people would consider premature. According to her lights, disaster was upon her, if not cancer. It is difficult to see how that could have been so; in 1974 she was a renowned poet living almost anyone's version of the good life. That she was fresh from a divorce seems insufficient cause for such drastic action, and the divorce is the only public indication we have of the straits she was in. Her death was immeasurably painful for her family and friends, premature by any ordinary measure. She responded to the call of her own death baby or her green girls or her Mr. Death before we would have wanted her to. "The Death Baby" can be read as a sad commentary on her own pathology, and to the extent that it is just that, we will distance ourselves from its implications, fail to see what she was in fact saying about everyone.

We cannot judge the depth of Sexton's despair, the manner of "disaster" she was encountering at the time of her death. For her the moment of her death was by definition the right time to rock the death baby—even if, knowing Max might not agree, she could not ask Maxine Kumin to hand it to her. It is certain that Sexton knew her own death baby far better than I know mine, far more intimately than most people know theirs.[22] This is a matter of poetic and personal insight, a mark of her special knowledge, as well as a clinical fact that can be translated into aberration. The timing and manner of the poet's death does not compromise the special knowledge conveyed in "The Death Baby." If the suicidal poet can show us the commonality of our "normal" neurosis and her psychosis, those of us who sometimes respond with cramped and alienated sympathies will have learned something needful about ourselves. Perhaps we will consider our tenderness for our own dumb travelers.

Notes

Chapter 1. Oedipus Anne

1. Juliet Mitchell, *Psychoanalysis and Feminism* (New York: Random House, 1974), xxi. For Freud's central statements on these issues, see *Three Essays on the Theory of Sexuality*, trans. James Strachey, in vol. 7 of *The Standard Edition of the Complete Psychological Works of Sigmund Freud* (London: Hogarth Press; Institute of Psycho-Analysis, 1955), 125–248; especially "Infantile Sexuality." See also Dorothy Dinnerstein, *The Mermaid and the Minotaur: Sexual Arrangements and Human Malaise* (New York: Harper and Row, 1976).

2. Bruno Bettelheim, *Freud and Man's Soul* (New York: Alfred A. Knopf, 1983), 23–24.

3. Ibid., 22.

4. Ibid., 23.

5. Ibid., 24–27.

6. I am grateful to Alicia Ostriker for pointing out to me these further applications of my ideas in this chapter.

7. Diane Middlebrook, "Housewife into Poet: The Apprenticeship of Anne Sexton," *New England Quarterly* 56, no. 4 (Dec. 1983): 493.

8. Ibid., 496.

9. Ibid., 494.

10. The most complete details available on Sexton's relationship to her mother are in Diane Middlebrook's "Becoming Anne Sexton," *Denver Quarterly* 18, no. 4 (Winter 1984): 23–34.

11. Anne Sexton, *Anne Sexton: A Self-Portrait in Letters,* ed. Linda Gray Sexton and Lois Ames (Boston: Houghton Mifflin Co., 1977), 33.

12. William H. Shurr's hypothesis about the source of the "legend" is convincing. He traces Sexton's linking of Judas and Oedipus to the 1911 *Encyclopedia Britannica* entry on "Judas Iscariot" (eleventh edition), which cites a "medieval legend" that Judas's mother had a dream that her son would murder his father, commit incest with his mother, and sell his God. See *Explicator* 39, no. 3 (Spring 1981): 2–3.

13. Bettelheim, *Freud and Man's Soul,* 30.

Chapter 2. How We Danced: Fathers and Daughters

1. Critics who have identified this shift from personal to transpersonal, cultural, or mythic in Sexton's work include Alicia Ostriker and Estella Lauter; for full citations, see below.

2.   Karen Horney was the first to reenvision the father-daughter relationship from within psychoanalysis. See *Feminine Psychology* (New York: W. W. Norton, 1967), Horney's collected essays on patriarchal psychoanalytic theory.

3.   Phyllis Chesler, *Women and Madness* (New York: Avon Books, 1972), 20.

4.   Harold Feldman, "Children of the Desert," *Psychoanalysis and Psychoanalytic Review* (Fall 1958), cited in *To Bedlam and Part Way Back.*

5.   Chesler, *Women and Madness,* 111.

6.   Ibid, 20.

7.   Maxine Kumin, "How It Was: Maxine Kumin on Anne Sexton," in Anne Sexton, *The Complete Poems* (Boston: Houghton Mifflin Co., 1981), xxiii.

8.   Alicia Ostriker, "That Story: The Changes of Anne Sexton," in Ostriker, *Writing Like a Woman* (Ann Arbor: University of Michigan Press, 1983), 78; "That Story" also appears in *American Poetry Review* 11, no. 4 (July/Aug. 1982): 11–16.

9.   Estella Lauter, "Anne Sexton's 'Radical Discontent with the Awful Order of Things,'" *Spring: An Annual of Archetypal Psychology and Jungian Thought* (1979): 82.

10.   Editors' note, *Anne Sexton: A Self-Portrait in Letters,* ed. Linda Gray Sexton and Lois Ames (Boston: Houghton Mifflin Co., 1977), 4.

11.   Kumin, "How It Was," xxiii.

12.   Editors' note, *Anne Sexton: A Self-Portrait in Letters,* 4.

Chapter 3. The Zeal of Her House

1.   Barbara Kevles, "The Art of Poetry XV: Anne Sexton," *Paris Review* [13,] no. 52 (Summer 1971): 190.

2.   Ibid.

3.   Anne Sexton, *Anne Sexton: A Self-Portrait in Letters,* ed. Linda Gray Sexton and Lois Ames (Boston: Houghton Mifflin Co., 1977), 228.

4.   Dorothy Dinnerstein, *The Mermaid and the Minotaur: Sexual Arrangements and Human Malaise* (New York: Harper and Row, 1976), 64. See chaps. 3 ("The Rocking of the Cradle") and 4 ("Higamous-Hogamous"). Dinnerstein does not attempt to claim that "women have it harder than men," but rather that the tasks involved in developmental object relations are different for men and women. It is the female's tasks that concern me here.

5.   This attempt is not always successful, and I am aware that several mother-daughter poems urge a strong qualification to the generalization. Nevertheless, I think the basic pattern is clear. For a more detailed discussion of the mother-daughter configurations in Sexton, see Margaret Honton, "The Double Image and the Division of Parts: A Study of Mother/Daughter Relationships in the Poetry of Anne Sexton," *Journal of Women's Studies in Literature* 1, no. 1 (Winter 1979): 33–50.

6.   A few examples: "With Mercy for the Greedy," *All My Pretty Ones;* "Rats Live on No Evil Star," *The Death Notebooks;* and "Rowing," *The Awful Rowing.* For an illuminating discussion of Sexton's identification with the rat,

see Suzanne Juhasz, "Seeking the Exit or the Home: Poetry and Salvation in the Career of Anne Sexton," in *Shakespeare's Sisters: Feminist Essays on Women Poets,* ed. Sandra M. Gilbert and Susan Gubar (Bloomington: Indiana University Press, 1979), 261–68. Juhasz's study identifies the rat with what I am here calling the voice of the suicide, but she also connects the rat with what I call the maker. In a discussion of "Demon" (*45 Mercy Street*), Juhasz explains that the demon "cannot be covered, smothered, or denied speech: because the demon, exposed, is at the center of her poetry" (p. 266). The rat is the demon but, at the same time, "the source of her art. Its anxious visions needed to be nurtured so that she might be a poet" (p. 267).

    7. *Anne Sexton: A Self-Portrait in Letters,* 239.

    8. Some critics, however, choose to see related problems in Sexton's poetry as unfortunate failures of both nerve and imagination. See, for instance, Beverly Tanenhaus, "Politics of Suicide and Survival: The Poetry of Anne Sexton and Adrienne Rich," *Bucknell Review* 24 (1978): 106–18. Tanenhaus contrasts Sexton's politically impotent poetic stance with Adrienne Rich's developmentally political poetry, which finally empowers women to "surface as respected equals who reject their historical isolation as a destructive separation from the pooled female energy and wisdom that can change their lives" (p. 117). Sexton's "emotional desperation and her failure to understand her life in political terms," on the other hand, "undermine her ability to negotiate or to make moral choices" (p. 114). Tanenhaus may be correct about the politics of both poets, although I suspect she does not credit Sexton with enough knowledge of political structures. (Knowledge is not always power, even if we like to think it is.) We could not do without the vision of Adrienne Rich, without that potent voice of the woman poet whose words invite and inspire us to search out our own sources of strength. But, although I am sympathetic to Tanenhaus's intentions here, I am also somewhat weary of and distressed by discussions of Sexton that invite me to see her work as deficient *because* it is insufficiently feminist in vision. Such discussions (and Tanenhaus's is the best I have encountered) tend to overlook the full import of Sexton's joyous poems of celebration; but more important, they overlook the range of possible functions and meanings for poetry. A poetics that disallows dirge and mourning and the elegiac impulse, or that finds these insufficiently "political," is itself intellectually and spiritually "insufficient." For a gentler and more accurate reading of these issues, see Estella Lauter, "Anne Sexton's 'Radical Discontent with the Awful Order of Things,' " *Spring: An Annual of Archetypal Psychology and Jungian Thought* (1979): 77–92.

    9. Neo-Freudian studies such as Norman Brown's *Life against Death: The Psychoanalytical Meaning of History* (Middletown, Conn.: Wesleyan University Press, 1970) amply document this tendency; for the standard work in the field, see Philippe Ariès, *Western Attitudes toward Death: From the Middle Ages to the Present,* trans. Patricia Ranum (Baltimore: Johns Hopkins University Press, 1974). Readers familiar with Norman Brown's *Love's Body* (New York: Vintage Books, 1966) and *Life against Death* will note strong parallels between Brown's theses and Sexton's poetic plea for living in the body in such poems as "From the Garden" (*All My Pretty Ones*). On the other hand, poems that

dramatize the dualistic dilemma reinforce Brown's points about the depths of our self-betrayals.

Chapter 4. Is It True? Feeding, Feces, and Creativity

1. See Suzanne Juhasz, *Naked and Fiery Forms: Modern American Poetry by Women, a New Tradition* (New York: Harper and Row, 1976); Alicia Ostriker, *Writing Like a Woman* (Ann Arbor: University of Michigan Press, 1983); Estella Lauter, "Anne Sexton's 'Radical Discontent with the Awful Order of Things,'" *Spring: An Annual of Archetypal Psychology and Jungian Thought* (1979): 77–92; Diane Wood Middlebrook, "Poet of Weird Abundance," review of Anne Sexton, *The Complete Poems,* forthcoming; and idem, "Housewife into Poet: The Apprenticeship of Anne Sexton," *New England Quarterly* 56, no. 4 (Dec. 1983): 483–503. I am grateful to Diane Middlebrook for allowing me to see her review prior to its publication.

2. Alicia Ostriker, "That Story: The Changes of Anne Sexton," in Ostriker, *Writing Like a Woman,* 59.

3. Middlebrook, "Poet of Weird Abundance," typescript, 2, 6.

4. Middlebrook, "Housewife," 493.

5. James Dickey, review of Sexton's *To Bedlam and Part Way Back,* in "Five First Books," *Poetry* 97 (Feb. 1961): 318–19; reprinted in *Anne Sexton: The Artist and Her Critics,* ed. J. D. McClatchy (Bloomington: Indiana University Press, 1978), 117–18.

6. Rosemary Johnson, "The Woman of Private (but Published) Hungers," *Parnassus: Poetry in Review* 8, no. 1 (Fall/Winter 1979): 92.

7. Mary Douglas, *Purity and Danger* (London: Routledge and Kegan, 1978).

8. Middlebrook, "Poet of Weird Abundance," 20.

9. Ibid., 21.

10. Sigmund Freud, "On the Transformation of Instincts with Special Reference to Anal Erotism," trans. Edward Glover, in vol. 17 of *The Standard Edition of the Complete Psychological Works of Sigmund Freud* (London: Hogarth Press; Institute of Psycho-Analysis, 1955), 125–34; my citations, 127–30. Stephanie Demetrakopoulos, "The Nursing Mother and Feminine Metaphysics: An Essay on Embodiment," *Soundings* 65, no. 4 (Winter 1982): 430–43; my citations, 434–35.

Chapter 5. Sexton's Speakers: Many Kinds of "I"

1. Louis Simpson, cited in Barbara Kevles, "The Art of Poetry XV: Anne Sexton," *Paris Review* [13,] no. 52 (Summer 1971): 190.

2. See Sandra M. Gilbert and Susan Gubar, *The Madwoman in the Attic: The Woman Writer and the Nineteenth-Century Literary Imagination* (New Haven: Yale University Press, 1979); Alicia Ostriker, *Writing Like a Woman* (Ann Arbor: University of Michigan Press, 1983); idem, *Stealing the Language: The Emergence of Women's Poetry in America* (Boston: Beacon Press, 1986); Suzanne Juhasz, *Naked and Fiery Forms: Modern American Poetry by Women, a New Tradition* (New York: Harper and Row, 1976); Ellen Moers, *Literary*

Women (Garden City, N.Y.: Doubleday and Co., 1976); Elaine Showalter, *A Literature of Their Own: British Women Novelists from Bronte to Lessing* (Princeton, N.J.: Princeton University Press, 1977); and Patricia Meyer Spacks, *The Female Imagination* (New York: Alfred A. Knopf, 1975). Seminal to all the issues discussed in these works is Annette Kolodny's "A Map for Rereading: Gender and the Interpretation of Literary Texts," in *The New Feminist Criticism,* ed. Elaine Showalter (New York: Pantheon Books, 1985).

3. Marilyn R. Farwell, "Feminist Criticism and the Concept of the Poetic Persona," *Bucknell Review* 24 (1978): 149.

4. William Heyen with Al Poulin, "From 1928 to Whenever: A Conversation with Anne Sexton," in *American Poets in 1976,* ed. William Heyen (Indianapolis: Bobbs-Merrill Co., 1976), 310.

5. Kevles, "The Art of Poetry XV: Anne Sexton," 190.

6. "Worksheets," for Anne Sexton's "Suicide Note," *New York Quarterly,* no. 4 (Fall 1970): 81–94.

7. Patricia Marx, "Interview with Anne Sexton," *Hudson Review* 18 (Winter 1965–66): 563.

8. Maxine Kumin, "Four Kinds of I," in Kumin, *To Make a Prairie: Essays on Poets, Poetry, and Country Living* (Ann Arbor: University of Michigan Press, 1979), 147–56.

9. Ibid., 150–51.

10. Ibid., 154.

11. William Blake, from "Annotations" to Watson's *An Apology for the Bible,* in *The Poetry and Prose of William Blake,* ed. David V. Erdman (Garden City, N.Y.: Doubleday and Co., 1965), 606–7.

12. Galway Kinnell, *Walking Down the Stairs: Selections from Interviews* (Ann Arbor: University of Michigan Press, 1978), 5.

13. Ostriker, *Writing Like a Woman,* 65.

Chapter 6. Innocence and Experience: The Girl-Child and the Middle-Aged Witch

1. Kenneth Koch, *I Never Told Anybody: Teaching Poetry Writing in a Nursing Home* (New York: Random House, 1977).

2. Ibid., 242.

3. Ibid., 155.

Chapter 7. "The Violent against Themselves"

1. Dante, *The Inferno,* trans. John Ciardi (New York: New American Library, 1954), canto 13, lines 11, 103–8.

2. Allen Alvarez, *The Savage God: A Study of Suicide* (New York: Bantam Books, 1973), 119.

3. Ibid.

4. Kim Carpenter discusses "Wanting to Die" from a similar standpoint in "Four Positions on Suicide," *Journal of Popular Culture* 14, no. 4 (Spring 1981): 732–39. The "Indepth Section" of *Journal of Popular Culture* 14, no. 4, on

"American Attitudes toward Death," was coedited by me and by Malcolm Nelson; Ms. Carpenter's reading of "Wanting to Die" was the result of extended conversations among the three of us, and in that respect the current reading is an extension of Carpenter's work with us.

Chapter 8. *Leaves That Talk and Green Girls*

1. Linda Gray Sexton, "Editor's Note" for Anne Sexton, *Words for Dr. Y.* (Boston: Houghton Mifflin Co., 1978), vi.
2. Barbara Kevles, "The Art of Poetry XV: Anne Sexton," *Paris Review* [13,] no. 52 (Summer 1971): 184–85.
3. *Anne Sexton: A Self-Portrait in Letters,* ed. Linda Gray Sexton and Lois Ames (Boston: Houghton Mifflin Co., 1977), 231.
4. Juliet Mitchell, *Psychoanalysis and Feminism* (New York: Random House, 1974); see especially pp. 61–73, 174–81, 377–81.
5. Jane Gallop, *The Daughter's Seduction: Feminism and Psychoanalysis* (Ithaca, N.Y.: Cornell University Press, 1982), 115.
6. Phyllis Chesler, *Women and Madness* (New York: Avon Books, 1972), 49.
7. *Anne Sexton: A Self-Portrait in Letters,* 368.
8. Ernest Becker, *The Denial of Death* (New York: Free Press, 1973), 20.
9. Ibid., 50.
10. Erica Jong, "Remembering Anne Sexton," *New York Times Book Review,* Oct. 27, 1974, 63: "Anne Sexton sometimes seemed like a woman without skin." Jong also writes that "she had no numbness at all," so that "all the little denials, all the stratagems of non-feeling by which most of us endure from minute to minute were unavailable to her."
11. *Anne Sexton: A Self-Portrait in Letters,* 298.
12. Denise Levertov, "Anne Sexton: Light Up the Cave," *Ramparts* 13, no. 5 (Dec. 1974–Jan. 1975): 61.
13. Ibid., 61, 62.
14. Ibid., 63.
15. Becker, *Denial of Death,* 283.
16. The impetus for parts of this and other chapters in the "Wanting to Die" section of this book was a long-standing disagreement with my friend Richard Lehnert about the purposes and province of modern American poetry. Shortly after the publication of Sexton's *Words for Dr. Y.,* Richard wrote me a letter that expressed in personal terms many of the same concerns voiced by Denise Levertov in "Anne Sexton: Light Up the Cave." In its final form this chapter addresses Levertov rather than Lehnert because the terms of her essay are those of the institutional literary community that constitutes my primary audience. But because Richard (himself a writer now based in Santa Fe) deeply influenced my work, and because he represents a point of view about suicidal poets that I believe is common both within and outside of the literary critical community, the following excerpt from his letter will interest many readers. I thank Richard Lehnert for permission to quote from his personal correspondence to me, and I happily record that he has made it clear to me that in 1986 he would not agree with everything he wrote in 1978.

Dear Diana,

I read *Words for Dr. Y.* It's an attempt at consensus-by-imprimature, an affirmation of the reality of one's personal cosmos, no matter how bleak. It's not hard to find consensus for defeat and despair. . . . Look at the first halves of the opening two "Dr. Y." letters. This person recognized long ago that pain is a signal, that it bears important messages. But she seems to have put to death all other couriers. It is important to remember that she chose to limit her information, her options on a reality that is, admittedly, terrifyingly open-ended. I acknowledge her decision (literally, to "kill the alternative"), but I do not respect it. . . .

I know Sexton's state of mind intimately. Though our genders are adjacent at best, a love of death transcends sexual coinage. I barely squeaked through my own gourmanding with my life. It no longer holds any romantic overtones for me. I know how lethal it is, and how empty, when death is a step taken out of fear and loathing. I left death behind by making some clear, sober choices. Those choices were also Sexton's, and every human's. In fact, they were Sexton's specific responsibility as poet. Poets exist to make the strongest, hardest choices. Sexton was terrified by her own freedom and responsibility. . . . Her entire existence was her own choice, and it could have been changed. I do not condemn her so much as I use her as a very graphic signpost pointing out the road not taken. . . .

These are strong words, especially from one who has never considered himself a survivor. Suicide is supreme egomania. It is the last way to maintain one's world view in the face of overwhelming contradiction by that world itself. . . . Most killers of self make this statement: "I cannot reconcile the apparent disparity between my expectations and my experience." A few, with a bit more insight, say, "I *will* not reconcile it." The first is a failure of the will; the second, of the imagination. Both are insults to possibility. . . . End of sermon.

Love,
Richard

Chapter 9. Beyond the Pleasure Principle: The Death Baby

1. Sigmund Freud, "Analysis Terminable and Interminable," trans. Joan Riviere, in vol. 23 of *The Standard Edition of the Complete Psychological Works of Sigmund Freud* (London: Hogarth Press; Institute of Psycho-Analysis, 1955), 242.

2. Sigmund Freud, *Beyond the Pleasure Principle*, trans. James Strachey, vol. 18 of *The Standard Edition of the Complete Psychological Works of Sigmund Freud*, 57.

3. Ibid., 40–41.

4. Ernest Becker, *The Denial of Death* (New York: Free Press, 1973), 96.

5. Ibid., 98–99.

6.   Gregory Zilboorg, introduction to Freud, *Beyond the Pleasure Principle,* trans. James Strachey (New York: Bantam Books, 1972), 1.

7.   Becker, *Denial of Death,* 99.

8.   Ibid., 26.

9.   Ibid., 27, 178.

10.   Ibid., 19, 29.

11.   The resonance of the fear of consumption may well be inevitable in a carnivorous culture. For many years I was frequently visited near sleep by a scene from a Porky Pig cartoon I saw as a young child. Porky fell asleep while fishing in a boat. In his dream he was the "fish" and the fish were his predators. The father fish caught Porky on the hook and took him home to the mother fish, who bustled about the kitchen in a parody of middle-class human cookery, cleaning Porky and preparing to bake him. I remember distinctly that the mother fish, clad in apron and dress, placed Porky on a platter, lovingly plumping him about into aesthetically appetizing position. As she was about to put him in the oven, Porky woke up in his boat and rowed to shore double-speed. It must have been thirty years ago that I saw this cartoon, but I remember it vividly—and the moment I remember best is the placement on a platter, which produced in me feelings of horror and, although I could not have named it at the time, of sexuality. A hideously erotic component was attendant upon the presentation of live Porky for food, a component completely lacking in, say, Sylvester's near-gobble of Tweetie. I wonder how many children were both mesmerized and repulsed by that cartoon, especially at a time when the cartoon genre had taken on some of the functions of the fairy tale.

12.   Freud, *Beyond the Pleasure Principle,* 32.

13.   Ibid., 21.

14.   Ibid., 22.

15.   Ibid., 35.

16.   Ibid.

17.   The only critic who has noted the mythic qualities of Sexton's "The Death Baby" is Estella Lauter, who calls the death baby an image "stunning in the context of Western iconography where death is often figured as an adult skeleton posing as lover or monk." "Sexton's image is an externalization of an ever-present, all-seeing eye within all human lives—an entity that is at once the most private aspect of one's life (one's smell), and the most universal aspect (primordial eye). It is an aspect of self and world within the person that never grows and can elicit tenderness in moments of despair, presented here as maternal self-sacrifice." ("Anne Sexton's 'Radical Discontent with the Awful Order of Things,'" *Spring: An Annual of Archetypal Psychology and Jungian Thought* [1979]: 77–92.) To Lauter's assessment, with which I agree, I would add that Sexton envisioned and re-visioned death in many mythic guises throughout her poetic career, and that the death baby is only the most original and successful of these reimaginings. She also sees death as God, as an elegant lover and then a beer-bellied Lothario, as her father and mother, and as a series of "green girls," seductive young women superficially similar to the sirens of mythology. But whereas in all the other guises of death she is calling upon a minor historical tradition for the portrayal of death, the death baby is her own

creation and corresponds to no other poetic or artistic rendering of which I am aware.

18. Freud, *Beyond the Pleasure Principle,* 38.

19. Ibid.

20. Ibid., 57.

21. Ibid., 39.

22. One reader of this manuscript, Kim Krynock, writes to me about her way of understanding death as a man and the relationship between wish and fear that Anne Sexton's suicide and death poetry embodies. Both Sexton's poetry and my arguments in these chapters "meet with great resistance in me," writes Ms. Krynock. But "one of the most impressive things about Sexton, and probably the most difficult to ignore, is her ability to give me common ground, a place to meet her. . . . I do identify with her, I do feel for her. The past two weeks, I've been sleeping alone in an apartment for the first time in my life. I've been staying up late, sleeping with the radio on, or a light, frightened and conscious of the person who is not behind the door, the demons in my bed. I've noticed that it gets past fear to a wish that my intruder-man would get it over with, break through the damn window, already. It has to do with a special dual fear that comes from being very female and very mortal—any finality seems better than this vulnerable not knowing. I think of Sexton feeling like this all of the time, or most of the time—that, ultimately, is how I understand her."

Selected Bibliography

Poetry by Anne Sexton

To Bedlam and Part Way Back. Boston: Houghton Mifflin Co., 1960. Poems.

All My Pretty Ones. Boston: Houghton Mifflin Co., 1962. Poems.

Selected Poems. London: Oxford University Press, 1964. Poems.

Live or Die. Boston: Houghton Mifflin Co., 1966; London: Oxford University Press, 1967. Poems.

Poems (with Thomas Kinsella and Douglas Livingstone). London: Oxford University Press, 1968. Poems.

Love Poems. Boston: Houghton Mifflin Co., 1969; London: Oxford University Press, 1969. Poems.

Transformations. Boston: Houghton Mifflin Co., 1971; London: Oxford University Press, 1972. Poems.

The Book of Folly. Boston: Houghton Mifflin Co., 1972; London: Chatto and Windus, 1974. Poems, stories.

The Death Notebooks. Boston: Houghton Mifflin Co., 1974; London: Chatto and Windus, 1975. Poems.

The Awful Rowing toward God. Boston: Houghton Mifflin Co., 1975; London: Chatto and Windus, 1977. Poems.

45 Mercy Street. Edited by Linda Gray Sexton. Boston: Houghton Mifflin Co., 1976; London: Martin Secker and Warburg, 1977. Poems.

Words for Dr. Y: Uncollected Poems with Three Stories. Edited by Linda Gray Sexton. Boston: Houghton Mifflin Co., 1978. Poems, three stories.

The Complete Poems. Boston: Houghton Mifflin Co., 1981.

Children's Books

Coauthored with Maxine Kumin:

Eggs of Things. New York: Putnam, 1963.

More Eggs of Things. New York: Putnam, 1964.

Joey and the Birthday Present. New York: McGraw-Hill, 1971.

The Wizard's Tears. New York: McGraw-Hill, 1975.

Letters, Essays

Anne Sexton: A Self-Portrait in Letters. Edited by Linda Gray Sexton and Lois Ames. Boston: Houghton Mifflin Co., 1977.

No Evil Star: Selected Essays, Interviews and Prose. Edited by Stephen E. Colburn. Ann Arbor: University of Michigan Press, 1985.

Bibliographies

Northouse, Cameron, and Thomas P. Walsh. *Sylvia Plath and Anne Sexton: A Reference Guide.* Boston: G. K. Hall, 1974. Primary and secondary.

McClatchy, J. D. "Selected Bibliography." In *Anne Sexton: The Artist and Her Critics,* edited by J. D. McClatchy, 291–94. Bloomington: Indiana University Press, 1978. Primary and secondary.

Biographies

Middlebrook, Diane Wood. *Anne Sexton: A Biography.* Forthcoming.

Significant Interviews

Ames, Lois. "Anne Sexton: From 'Bedlam' to Broadway." *Boston Sunday Herald Traveler Book Guide,* Oct. 12, 1969, 1–2, 16.

"Anne Sexton." In *Talks with Authors,* edited by Charles F. Madden, 151–79. Carbondale: Southern Illinois University Press, 1968.

Balliro, Charles. "Interview with Anne Sexton." *Fiction* 1, no. 6 (1974): 12–13, 15.

Berg, Beatrice. " 'Oh, I Was Very Sick.' " *New York Times,* Nov. 9, 1969, sec. D, 1, 7.

Gerald, Gregory Fitz. "The Choir from the Soul: A Conversation with Anne Sexton." *Massachusetts Review* 19 (Spring 1978): 69–88.

Green, Carol. "A Writer Is Essentially a Spy." *Boston Review of the Arts* 2, no. 5 (Aug. 1972): 30–37.

Heyen, William, and Al Poulin. "From 1928 to Whenever: A Conversation with Anne Sexton." In *American Poets in 1976,* edited by William Heyen, 304–28. Indianapolis: Bobbs-Merrill Co., 1976.

Kevles, Barbara. "The Art of Poetry XV: Anne Sexton." *Paris Review* [13,], no. 52 (Summer 1971): 159–91.

Marx, Patricia. "Interview with Anne Sexton." *Hudson Review* 18 (Winter 1965–66): 560–70.

Packard, William. "Craft Interview with Anne Sexton." *The Craft of Poetry,* edited by William Packard, 19–23. New York: Doubleday, 1974.

Showalter, Elaine, and Carol Smith. "A Nurturing Relationship: A Conversation with Anne Sexton and Maxine Kumin, April 15, 1974." *Women's Studies* 4, no. 1 (1976): 115–36.

Weeks, Brigitte. "The Excitable Gift: The Art of Anne Sexton." *Boston,* Aug. 1968, 30–32.

Critical Studies

Collections of Essays:

McClatchy, J. D., ed. *Anne Sexton: The Artist and Her Critics.* Bloomington: Indiana University Press, 1978.

Special Issue:

Notes on Modern American Literature 3, no. 3 (Summer 1979). Robert Lowell and Anne Sexton number.

Major Articles and Book Sections; Reviews:

Ames, Lois. "Remembering Anne." In *Anne Sexton: The Artist and Her Critics,* ed. McClatchy, 111–14.

Axelrod, Rise B. "The Transforming Art of Anne Sexton." *Concerning Poetry* 7, no. 1 (Spring 1974): 6–13.

Bagg, Robert. "A Regime of Revelation." *Audience* 7, no. 3 (Summer 1960): 121–25.

Blackburn, Thomas. "Three American Poets." *Poetry Review* 58 (Autumn 1967): 255.

Bogan, Louise. "Verse." *New Yorker* 39 (Apr. 27, 1963): 175–76.

Boyers, Robert. "*Live or Die:* The Achievement of Anne Sexton." *Salmagundi* 2, no. 1 (Spring 1967): 61–71. Reprinted in *Anne Sexton: The Artist and Her Critics,* ed. McClatchy, 204–15.

Carruth, Hayden. From "In Spite of Artifice." *Hudson Review* 19 (Winter 1966–67): 698. Reprinted in *Anne Sexton: The Artist and Her Critics,* ed. McClatchy, 130–32.

Conarroe, Joel O. "Five Poets." *Shenandoah* 18 (Summer 1967): 84–91.

Demetrakopoulos, Stephanie. "The Nursing Mother and Feminine Metaphysics: An Essay on Embodiment." *Soundings* 65, no. 4 (Winter 1982): 430–43.

Dickey, James. "Five First Books." *Poetry* 97 (Feb. 1961): 318–19.

Dickey, William. "A Place in the Country." *Hudson Review* 22 (Summer 1969): 347–49.

Fein, Richard J. "The Demon of Anne Sexton." *English Record* 18, no. 1 (Oct. 1967): 16–21.

Fields, Beverly. "The Poetry of Anne Sexton." In *Poets in Progress,* edited by Edward Hungerford, 251–85. Evanston: Northwestern University Press, 1967.

Fraser, G. S. "New Poetry." *Partisan Review* 37 (1970): 299–300.

Gallagher, Brian. "The Expanded Use of Simile in Anne Sexton's *Transformations.*" *Notes on Modern American Literature* 3, no. 3 (Summer 1979), no. 20.

George, Diana Hume. "Anne Sexton and The Awful Rowing." *Women's Voices* 4, no. 2 (Winter 1976): 12–13.

———. "Beyond the Pleasure Principle: Anne Sexton's 'The Death Baby.' " *University of Hartford Studies in Literature* 15, no. 2 (1983): 75–92.

———. "Anne Sexton's Suicide Poems." *Journal of Popular Culture* 18, no. 2 (Fall 1984): 17–32.

———. "How We Danced: Anne Sexton on Fathers and Daughters." *Women's Studies* 12 (1985): 179–202.

———. "Kumin on Kumin and Sexton." *Poesis: A Journal of Criticism* 6, no. 2 (1985): 1–18.

———. "Oedipus Iscariot: Anne Sexton's Judas." Forthcoming.

Gilbert, Sandra M. "Jubilate Anne." *Nation* 219, no. 7 (Sept. 14, 1974): 214–16. Reprinted in *Anne Sexton: The Artist and Her Critics,* ed. McClatchy, 162–67.

Gullans, Charles. "Poetry and Subject Matter: From Hart Crane to Turner Cassity." *Southern Review* 6 (Spring 1970): 497–98.

Gunn, Thom. "Poems and Books of Poems." *Yale Review* 53 (Autumn 1963): 140–41.

Hartman, Geoffrey H. "Les Belles Dames sans merci." *Kenyon Review* 22 (Autumn 1960): 696–99.

Hoffman, Nancy Jo. "Reading Women's Poetry: The Meaning and Our Lives." *College English* 34, no. 1 (Oct. 1972): 48–62.

Hoffman, Nancy Yanes. "A Special Language." *Southwest Review* 64 (Summer 1979): 209–14.

Honton, Margaret. "The Double Image and the Division of Parts: A Study of Mother/Daughter Relationships in the Poetry of Anne Sexton." *Journal of Women's Studies in Literature* 1, no. 1 (Winter 1979): 33–50.

Howard, Richard. "Five Poets." *Poetry* 101 (Mar. 1963): 413–14.

———. "Anne Sexton: 'Some Tribal Female Who Is Known but Forbidden.' " In Howard, *Alone with America: Essays on the Art of Poetry in the United States since 1950*, 442–50. New York: Atheneum, 1971. Reprinted in *Anne Sexton: The Artist and Her Critics*, ed. McClatchy, 193–203.

Johnson, Greg. "The Achievement of Anne Sexton." *Hollins Critic* 21, no. 3 (June 1984): 1–13.

Johnson, Rosemary. "The Woman of Private (but Published) Hungers." *Parnassus: Poetry in Review* 8, no. 1 (Fall/Winter 1979): 92–107.

Jones, A. R. "Necessity and Freedom: The Poetry of Robert Lowell, Sylvia Plath and Anne Sexton." *Critical Quarterly* 7, no. 1 (Spring 1965): 11–30.

Jong, Erica. "Remembering Anne Sexton." *New York Times Book Review*, Oct. 27, 1974, 63.

Juhasz, Suzanne. " 'The Excitable Gift': The Poetry of Anne Sexton." Chap. 6 in Juhasz, *Naked and Fiery Forms: Modern American Poetry by Women, a New Tradition*. New York: Harper and Row, 1976.

———. "Seeking the Exit or the Home: Poetry and Salvation in the Career of Anne Sexton." In *Shakespeare's Sisters: Feminist Essays on Women Poets*, edited by Sandra M. Gilbert and Susan Gubar, 261–68. Bloomington: Indiana University Press, 1979.

Kammer, Jeanne H. "The Witch's Life: Confession and Control in the Early Poetry of Anne Sexton." *Language and Style* 13, no. 4 (Fall 1980): 29–35.

Kumin, Maxine. "Reminiscence Delivered at Memorial Service for Anne Sexton in Marsh Chapel, Boston University, October 15, 1974." In Kumin, *To Make a Prairie: Essays on Poets, Poetry, and Country Living*, 78–80. Ann Arbor: University of Michigan Press, 1979.

———. "Sexton's *The Awful Rowing toward God*." In Kumin, *To Make a Prairie*, 81–82.

———. "A Friendship Remembered." In *Anne Sexton: The Artist and Her Critics*, ed. McClatchy, 103–10. Reprinted in Kumin, *To Make a Prairie*, 83–92.

———. "How It Was: Maxine Kumin on Anne Sexton." In Anne Sexton, *The Complete Poems*, xix–xxxiv. Boston: Houghton Mifflin Co., 1981.

Lacey, Paul A. "The Sacrament of Confession." In Lacey, *The Inner War*, 8–31. Philadelphia: Fortress Press, 1972.

Lant, Jeffrey L. "Another Entry in the Death Notebooks." *Southwest Review* 64 (Summer 1979): 215–19.

Lauter, Estella. "Anne Sexton's 'Radical Discontent with the Awful Order of Things.'" *Spring: An Annual of Archetypal Psychology and Jungian Thought* (1979): 77–92.

Legler, Philip. "O Yellow Eye." *Poetry* 110 (May 1967): 125–27.

———. Review of *Live or Die*, by Anne Sexton. *New Mexico Quarterly* 37 (Spring 1967): 89–92.

Levertov, Denise. "Anne Sexton: Light Up the Cave." *Ramparts* 13, no. 5 (Dec. 1974–Jan. 1975): 61–63.

Lowell, Robert. "Anne Sexton." In *Anne Sexton: The Artist and Her Critics*, ed. McClatchy, 71–73.

McCabe, Jane. "A Woman Who Writes: A Feminist Approach to the Early Poetry of Anne Sexton." In *Anne Sexton: The Artist and Her Critics*, ed. McClatchy, 216–43.

McClatchy, J. D. "Anne Sexton: Somehow to Endure." In *Anne Sexton: The Artist and Her Critics*, ed. McClatchy, 244–90. Shorter version in *Centennial Review* 19, no. 2 (Spring 1975): 1–36.

McDonnell, Thomas P. "Light in a Dark Journey." *America* 116 (May 13, 1967): 729–31.

McGill, William J. "Anne Sexton and God." *Commonweal*, May 13, 1977, 304–6.

Marras, Emma. "After a Conversation with Linda and Joy Sexton." *Paintbrush* 6, no. 11 (Spring 1979): 34–38.

Maryan, Charles. "The Poet On Stage." In *Anne Sexton: The Artist and Her Critics*, ed. McClatchy, 89–95.

Mazzocco, Robert. "Matters of Life and Death." *New York Review of Books*, Apr. 3, 1975, 22–23.

Middlebrook, Diane Wood. "Three Mirrors Reflecting Women: Poetry of Sylvia Plath, Anne Sexton, and Adrienne Rich." *Worlds into Words: Understanding Modern Poems*, 65–96. New York: W. W. Norton, 1978.

———. "Housewife into Poet: The Apprenticeship of Anne Sexton." *New England Quarterly* 56, no. 4 (Dec. 1983): 483–503.

———. "Becoming Anne Sexton." *Denver Quarterly* 18, no. 4 (Winter 1984): 23–34.

———. "Poet of Weird Abundance." Review of Anne Sexton, *The Complete Poems*. Forthcoming.

Mills, Ralph J., Jr. "Four Voices in Recent American Poetry." *Christian Scholar* 46 (Winter 1963): 327–32.

———. "Anne Sexton." In Mills, *Contemporary American Poetry*, 218–34. New York: Random House, 1965.

Mood, John J. "'A Bird Full of Bones': Anne Sexton—a Visit and a Reading." *Chicago Review* 23, no. 4/24, no. 1 (1972): 107–23.

Morse, S. F. "Poetry 1966." *Contemporary Literature* 9 (Winter 1968): 122–23.

Myers, Neil. "The Hungry Sheep Look Up." *Minnesota Review* 1 (Oct. 1960): 99–104.

Nichols, Kathleen L. "The Hungry Beast Rowing toward God: Anne Sexton's

Later Religious Poetry." *Notes on Modern American Literature* 3, no. 3 (Summer 1979), no. 21.

Oates, Joyce Carol. "Singing the Pathologies of Our Time: *The Awful Rowing toward God.*" *New York Times Book Review,* Mar. 23, 1975, 3–4.

———. "The Rise and Fall of a Poet: *The Complete Poems* of Anne Sexton." *New York Times Book Review,* Oct. 18, 1981, 3, 37.

Ostriker, Alicia. "That Story: Anne Sexton and Her Transformations." *American Poetry Review* 11, no. 4 (July/Aug. 1982): 11–16. Reprinted as "That Story: The Changes of Anne Sexton," in Ostriker, *Writing Like a Woman,* 59–85. Ann Arbor: University of Michigan Press, 1983.

———. *Stealing the Language: The Emergence of Women's Poetry in America.* Boston: Beacon Press, 1986.

Phillips, Robert. "Anne Sexton: The Blooming Mouth and the Bleeding Rose." In Phillips, *The Confessional Poets,* 73–91. Carbondale: Southern Illinois University Press, 1973.

Pritchard, William H. "The Anne Sexton Show." *Hudson Review* 31 (Summer 1978): 387–92.

Rosenthal, M. L. "Seven Voices." *Reporter* 28 (Jan. 3, 1963): 47–48.

———. "Other Confessional Poets." In Rosenthal, *The New Poets: American and British Poetry since World War II,* 131–38. London: Oxford University Press, 1967.

Rukeyser, Muriel. "Glitter and Wounds, Several Wildnesses." *Parnassus: Poetry in Review* 2, no. 1 (Fall/Winter 1973): 215–21. Reprinted in *Anne Sexton: The Artist and Her Critics,* ed. McClatchy, 154–61.

Shurr, William H. "Anne Sexton's *Love Poems:* The Genre and the Differences." *Modern Poetry Studies* 10 (1980): 58–68.

———. "Sexton's 'The Legend of the One-Eyed Man.'" *Explicator* 39, no. 3 (Spring 1981): 2–3.

Simpson, Louis. "New Books of Poems." *Harper's* 235 (Aug. 1967): 90–91.

Smith, Hal. Review of *To Bedlam and Part Way Back,* by Anne Sexton. *Epoch* 10 (Fall 1960): 253–55.

———. Review of *All My Pretty Ones,* by Anne Sexton. *Epoch* 12 (Fall 1962): 124–26.

Spacks, Patricia Meyer. "45 Mercy Street." *New York Times Book Review,* May 30, 1976, 6. Reprinted in *Anne Sexton: The Artist and Her Critics,* ed. McClatchy, 186–89.

Spivak, Kathleen. "Sharers of the Heart: A Friend Remembers Anne Sexton." *Boston Globe Magazine,* Aug. 9, 1981, 10–13, 35–42.

Swan, Barbara. "A Reminiscence." In *Anne Sexton: The Artist and Her Critics,* ed. McClatchy, 81–88.

Swenson, May. "Poetry of Three Women." *Nation* 196 (Feb. 23, 1963): 164–66. Reprinted in *Anne Sexton: The Artist and Her Critics,* ed. McClatchy, 122–24.

Tanenhaus, Beverly. "Politics of Suicide and Survival: The Poetry of Anne Sexton and Adrienne Rich." *Bucknell Review* 24 (1978): 106–18.

Tillinghast, Richard. "Five Poets." *Sewanee Review* 71 (Summer 1963): 510–13.

Wagner, Linda W. "45 Mercy Street and Other Vacant Houses." In *American*

Literature: The New England Heritage, edited by James Nagel and Richard Astro, 145–65. New York: Garland Publishing, 1981.

White, William. "Lyrics Back to Sanity and Love." *Prairie Schooner* 35 (Spring 1961): 3–4.

Williams, Polly C. "Sexton in the Classroom." In *Anne Sexton: The Artist and Her Critics,* ed. McClatchy, 96–101.

Zweig, Paul. "Making and Unmaking." *Partisan Review* 40 (1973): 277–79.

Index

A Note on the Author

Diana Hume George is a professor of English at The Pennsylvania State University, Behrend College, where she teaches poetry and creative writing. She writes about psychoanalytic theory, feminist criticism, and American attitudes toward death and dying, and has published articles on these subjects in many journals and anthologies of essays. Her books include *Blake and Freud* (1980) and *Epitaph and Icon* (1983; with Malcolm A. Nelson). She is working on two books: a study of the professional and personal relationship between Maxine Kumin and Anne Sexton, and a guide to the early American burying grounds and gravestones of Boston.